HOLY CONVERSATION

SPIRITUALITY FOR WORSHIP

Jonathan Linman

To Hans & Christa:
With best wishes in Christ,
thanks to God for the ways in which
our paths have crossed from
Holden to India, and with the
prayer that this work may serve
to still deepen your worshipful
holy conversation.

Fortress Press

Minneapolis

In blessed and loving memory of
Walter Bouman and Faith Mikita

HOLY CONVERSATION
Spirituality for Worship

Cover image: © Wolfgang Kaiser/iStock
Cover design: Laurie Ingram
Book design: PerfecType, Nashville, Tenn.

Library of Congress Cataloging-in-Publication Data
Linman, Jonathan, 1961-
Holy conversation : spirituality for worship / Jonathan Linman.
p. cm.
Includes bibliographical references (p. 182) and index.
ISBN 978-0-8006-2130-8 (alk. paper)
1. Worship. 2. Spirituality. 3. Bible—Liturgical use. 4. Bible—Devotional use. 5. Pentecost Festival—Liturgy—Texts. 6. Pentecost Festival—Liturgy—Texts—History and criticism. I. Title.
BV15.L56 2010
263'.94--dc22
2009040033

Manufactured in the U.S.A.

14 13 12 11 10 1 2 3 4 5 6 7 8 9 10

CONTENTS

PART TWO: MEDITATIONS ON THE MASS

ACKNOWLEDGMENTS

The passion to write this book emerged in the context of my first academic sabbatical during the autumn of 2004 when varied circumstances in my life coincided: the leisure to write; accumulated years of liturgical leadership in a congregation and extensive reflection on worship practices; my first years of teaching courses in spirituality at a theological seminary and leading educational/formational events for the wider church; the opportunity to lead liturgy in varied settings as a guest pastor; and, quite significantly, ample opportunities during these years to worship apart from leading at the ambo or at the table. I also have been increasingly aware in recent years of a strong desire to explore implications of *lectio divina*—sacred reading, an ancient way of praying with the Scriptures, the subject of my doctoral dissertation, and a centerpiece of my spiritual life—for participation in liturgy as a means of providing insights and resources for the renewal of the church's worship life. Many have written good books on the practice of *lectio divina*. Numerous are the books on and resources for worship renewal. Now I claim the opportunity to put these pieces together and offer years of liturgical leadership and practice, research, reflection, and teaching to a wider public via this book.

Spiritual and liturgical formation is the fruit of the Spirit's work in Christian community. So I offer my deep, abiding, and loving appreciation and thanks to the people of Bethlehem Lutheran Church in Pittsburgh, Pennsylvania, where I served for twelve years as pastor, for their innumerable contributions to my pastoral and faith formation. Likewise, I offer thanks to the people of St. Peter's and Holy Trinity Lutheran Churches in New York City, where I am a member (at the former), where I have served as a pastoral associate (the latter), and where in both settings I have benefited from a compelling and beautiful liturgical life. Beyond these congregational settings, I am grateful to the varied constituencies of the Southwestern Pennsylvania and Metropolitan New York Synods of the Evangelical Lutheran Church in America (ELCA), the leaders of which have given me many opportunities to try out my ideas in teaching and devotional settings and also have contributed greatly to my vocational formation and to my experience of the bonds of affection in the church.

I am especially indebted to the General Theological Seminary of the Episcopal Church where until recently I had served as the director of the Center for Christian Spirituality and a professor of ascetical theology. It is this seminary's generous sabbatical policy, wonderfully thoughtful students, and collegially supportive faculty and administration that have made possible the particular adventure of writing a book. Three students in particular at General have assisted me over the years with this project from its conceptual and research stages to the editing process. So my thanks to Stephen Shaver, Steven Paulikas, and Kelly Ayer for their valuable assistance, respectively, in helping with initial research, reading and evaluating first drafts, and helping to edit the bibliography.

I am likewise indebted to friend and mentor Philip Pfatteicher who first introduced me to the connections between spirituality and liturgy and whose *Commentary on the Lutheran Book of Worship*—and my rereading of this work when writing my meditations on a *Mass for the Day of Pentecost*, a focus of the second half of this book—provides much of the general knowledge content of my comments on the biblical sources for and historical background of features of the liturgy.

Several people read first drafts of this work and offered enormously helpful comments, suggestions, and insights that have been incorporated into the final version. So I thank Lowell Almen, for his keen editorial eye, liturgical sensitivities, and faith in me as a writer; Eugene Brand, for his extensive historical and liturgical theological knowledge and decades of wisdom made personally available to me in many conversations; Lisa Dahill, whose work *Truly Present: Practicing Prayer in the Liturgy* is closely allied with mine; Gigi Kovac, for her particularly helpful insights and sensitivities as a congregational practitioner, organist, and choir director; and Robert Rimbo, whose passion for the renewal of worship life and collegial support have inspired me to complete this work. David Lott, my editor at Fortress Press, has been a profound gift in patiently shepherding me through a process wholly new to me, that of writing and publishing a book.

I want to especially thank my wife, Jennifer, and my son, Nathan, who at the time of this writing is a mere seven months old. Jennifer has been enormously supportive, generous with time as we negotiate the rigors of our vocations, and patient with me—always in our marriage, but particularly during the times when the burdens of publishing a book have weighed on me. Her keen attention to detail also made this book's index possible. Nathan has been a constant source of grounding, centering, and spiritual nourishment to me—I realized quickly as a new father that he has become my chief spiritual mentor—and has provided me with new experiences of the church's worship life, as when a father holds an infant son in his arms during the liturgy (perhaps wisdom from this experience can be the focus of another writing project!).

Finally, in the spirit of my theological heritage and with thanks to God for sacred and formative guidance in the practice and experience of liturgical worship: *Soli Deo gloria.*

INTRODUCTION

However it is variously named—Mass, Holy Communion, Holy Eucharist, Service of Word and Table, Divine Liturgy, Service for the Lord's Day—the event occurring when Christians gather to hear and respond to the Word, to pray and share in the sacramental meal, and to be sent into the world for mission is a source of awe, wonder, joy, and even holy fear. Through my years of worshiping, leading liturgy, and studying liturgical experience, I have marveled more and more at the richness of liturgical worship as a divine-human phenomenon. Think of it: In the space of what typically occurs in an hour or so, there is so much to hear, say, see, touch, taste, and perhaps even smell. There is so much to think about, reflect on, remember, feel, and experience directly. There is so much to do. The full range of human experience is present. Think of all the words, the stories, and the narrative shape of what we do—the liturgy consists of language, of speech, of texts and symbols from beginning to end. We are encountered by the Word of God contained in and emanating from the Scriptures. We are grasped by the Word of God visibly, tangibly, in the sacraments as nontextual signs.

At the same time, what we do in liturgy is so ordinary and can be quite routine—so much so that we often take for granted our experiences of worship, commonly following, as it were, the script, seeing and experiencing only the tip of the iceberg of this profound event. Yet liturgical worship is about the extraordinary breaking into the ordinary, for through these means the power

1

of God in the Spirit forms us in faith, conforms us to the will of God and the mind of Christ, reforms us when we forget and go astray, and ultimately transforms us as new creations in Christ. It can seem like too much to take in.

How do we relate to and participate in this profound event, attending to it more deeply, going beyond the mechanics of "doing the liturgy"? How do we meaningfully contribute to the encounter, the dialogue, the holy conversation that is a constituent feature of liturgical participation, that we may know life-changing experiences? The answers to these questions have to do with addressing the spirituality of the liturgical experience. This is a book that links spirituality and worship, more particularly, that nurtures understandings of spirituality *for* worship, that our practices may evoke our sense of awe, peace, joy, and holy fear at being in the presence of God, aware of what the Spirit accomplishes through the means of grace.

In particular, my focus in this book is the spiritual power of language—the Spirit active in the words, stories, and shape of the liturgical drama—and how we can be more present to the Spirit's work in the movements of the liturgy, thus contributing to the breadth and depth of our experiences, making the most of our engaging in holy conversation, sharing, too, in the Spirit's work of formation. I offer a new approach to viewing and understanding the conversational trajectory of what we ordinarily do in Christian assembly, but an approach rooted in centuries-old spiritual practice. *Lectio divina*, often translated sacred or divine reading, is a simple and straightforward spiritual discipline that nurtures varied ways of being present to the Word of God according to basic movements of Christian spiritual life: reading, meditation, prayer, and contemplation. While *lectio divina* emerged as a practice in monastic communities, it is not just a private discipline for monks, but has wide-ranging applicability in the Christian life, including liturgical participation.

Current liturgical scholarship and practice make much of the basic pattern for and shape of worship on the Lord's Day, the *ordo* that has been handed down to us through the generations. In a simple and straightforward way of conceiving it, this pattern focuses on four segments:

- Gathering—"The Holy Spirit calls us together as the people of God."
- Word—"God speaks to us in Scripture reading, preaching, and song."
- Meal—"God feeds us with the presence of Jesus Christ."
- Sending—"God blesses us and sends us in mission to the world."[1]

In order to enrich the understandings of the meanings and logic of this basic shape of liturgical worship, I offer the movements related to *lectio divina* as a new overlay, a complementary way of conceiving the *ordo*, with the humble awareness that no single approach can begin to exhaust our comprehension of what occurs in the liturgy and what liturgy means. Mine is a contribution among many, but an important one in terms of nurturing deeper spiritual practice for worship, giving worshipers tools, both practical and perspectival, through which to engage in holy conversation as a feature of liturgical partici- pation, thus deepening awareness of the Spirit's work in the means of grace and enriching and renewing the experience of worship.

Using *lectio divina* as an overlay to demarcate the rhythms of the liturgy, there are six movements:

- *praeparatio* or preparation—the Spirit calls us together and we prepare for holy encounter;
- *lectio* or reading—God speaks the Word as we hear and participate in the public reading of Scripture;
- *meditatio* or meditation—the Spirit leads us more deeply into under- standing as we reflect on and discern meanings of the living Word for us in our day;
- *oratio* or prayer—the Spirit moves us to intercede for the world and to offer ourselves to each other and in service of the world's need;
- *contemplatio* or contemplation—Christ dwells with us bodily in the meal as we eat and drink the visible Word;
- *missio* or sending—the Spirit propels us into the world for the mission that we have discerned is ours to do in God's name.

This approach to understanding the *ordo* inspired by the movements of *lectio divina* takes seriously the role of each worshiper as a participant in the work of the Holy Spirit, deeply aware of the Spirit's activity in us. *Liturgy* is commonly understood as "the work of the people." A Christian understand- ing of vocation affirms that each baptized member of the body of Christ shares in ministry, in the people's work. A principal focus for the work of liturgy to which we are all called is holy conversation, to respond to the Spirit's voice heard and active in the means of grace, to be present to God, well prepared for the holy encounter, obediently attending to the readings, actively engaged in meditation in response to the readings, prayerfully present, open to the contemplative encounter in the meal, and poised to leave the assembly with a specific sense of the missional work that we will do in the time following the sacred hour until we meet again.

Full participation enabled by applying the movements of *lectio divina* to liturgical worship is an antidote to the common lament about boredom in liturgical services. When liturgy is not reduced to a spectator sport, when worshipers are given the tools through which to do the work of holy conversation in liturgy, when each worshiper is a liturgical minister, a sense of boredom, the fruit of passive disengagement, can dissipate. When people are engaged, time flies. Or, better, when the people of God are spiritually engaged, God's time breaks in upon us, the Spirit active in our responsive participation and speaking a living word to us.

People long for rich and deep spiritual experiences. Sadly, many seek those experiences apart from the principal gathering of Christians on the Lord's Day. Applying the sensibilities of *lectio divina* to our worship can make for greater depth and enthusiasm in Christian assembly—but enthusiasm not in terms of excitement, the default mode of our entertainment-oriented culture, nor in terms of vainglorious religious fervor. Rather, I speak of enthusiasm in terms of the Greek origins of the word: *entheos*, "inspired," and *en theos*, "being in God." Of course, our efforts cannot confect a greater quantity of spiritual presence and activity. God in Christ through the power of the Holy Spirit is already fully present in Word and sacraments. We can, however, nurture a deeper awareness of divine presence in our midst, seeing below the tip of the iceberg, catching glimpses of the deeper things of God in, with, and under the means of grace operative in the liturgy as those gifts of grace embrace our lives. Liturgical participation that is of holy conversation in the spirit of *lectio divina* can nurture this awareness that the liturgy is already *enthused*, full of God's presence.

Worshiping in the manner and spirit of *lectio divina* can also enable us to become more present to ourselves, aware of what we bring to the encounter, what is on our minds and hearts, what is in our memories, what we hope for and desire. As Christ offers real presence to us in the meal, we are called to offer an authentic presence to God in our worship. When the real presence of Christ meets us in our authentic, open, nondefensive presence, transformative things can begin to happen as the story of God's salvation addresses us in the particularities of our stories and we cry out for that salvation, salve, spiritual balm touching us to heal us and make us whole. Holy conversation inspires us to offer all that we are to God throughout the movements of the liturgy, a living sacrifice of praise and thanksgiving, that God in Christ through the Spirit may claim us in the deep places and transform us into new creations.

Worship informed by *lectio divina* gives us a new relationship to language, fuller ways of being present to God's Word when we might otherwise feel overwhelmed by that Word. We live in a time when language is much abused—"talk is cheap"—and is too often abusive and manipulative. Through many and various technologies we are awash in words. "Too much information!"

is a cry of our age. Liturgical *lectio divina* invites us to slow down, to create open spaces to let the Word soak in, that we may dwell with it and really chew on its meanings for us, praying fervently in response to it, eating it and drinking it, and finally becoming that Word to be enacted in our mission in the world. This way of worshiping, of being with the Word, is admittedly inspired by and resonant with monastic routines unfamiliar to many. Yet in our busy, noisy, overstimulating mission field of the world, it is one of the church's high callings to give the gift of silence, of greater spaciousness to make room for contemplative encounters with the means of grace, so that the Spirit may most freely do the works of salvation to form us in faith.

Liturgical worship inspired by the movements of *lectio divina*, furthermore, holds promise to renew the worship life of the church and thus to renew the church for mission. Few topics are more important to the health, vitality, maturity, and faithfulness of the church and its mission than worship and its renewal. The Sunday assembly is the principal gathering of Christians, the main point of contact the baptized have with the church, the very embodiment of Christian community. Moreover, this weekly gathering is inevitably the focus for Christian formation in discipleship. Above all, it is the time when God in Christ is most intimately present to us, creating and nurturing faith through the Holy Spirit as that Spirit speaks to us through Word and sacraments. In short, the liturgical assembly carries enormous weight as it serves as the vessel for such profound gifts and opportunities. It is our high calling and privilege as the people of God to take seriously our stewardship of God's mysteries (1 Cor. 4:1) in the assembly, that our worship may ever be renewed, that we may be formed, conformed to Christ, reformed, and transformed for the work God would have us do in the world.

The church has indeed seen significant worship renewal in the past generation. Liturgical-renewal movements in recent decades have in great measure returned the liturgy to the people, offering worship in the language of the people and encouraging their full participation. The reforms of Vatican II, influential well beyond the Roman Catholic Church, suggest a principal goal of liturgical reform, that the people of God would share in worship knowingly, actively, and fruitfully, and that worship should involve "full, conscious, and active participation."[2]

Recent years have seen the publication of a number of new worship books and hymnals in several Christian traditions. In addition to accommodating the recovery of such things as the centrality of baptism and weekly celebration of the Eucharist in the life of the church, the worship renewal of the past generation gave significantly more voice to the people of God, to worship leaders beyond the ordained presiding minister, most notably in the persons of lay readers and assisting ministers and in the addition of various congregational responses, spoken and sung, in the liturgy. Congregations have done well in implementing these reforms. It is typical to hear many voices beyond that of the pastor or priest in congregations on Sunday mornings across the country today. But "doing the liturgy," giving more people voice in worship services, is but one step, albeit a crucial one, along the way to fuller expressions of worship renewal. This book will explore the dynamics of such fuller dimensions of renewal, focusing not only on what we do in the liturgy, but on how, in what manner and spirit, we engage what we do in our liturgical assemblies toward nurturing full, conscious, active participation.

Viewing the shape of liturgical worship—the gathering, Word, meal, and sending—in the light of *lectio divina* involving preparatory activity, reading, meditation, prayer, contemplation, and the incarnation of this divine encounter for our mission will aid us greatly in making thoughtful response to various challenging questions concerning worship today:

- How do we best gather in preparation for literally meeting Christ in Word and sacraments?
- How do we make the most of listening to and fully engaging the various scriptural readings for the day?
- What is the hearer's active role in listening to a sermon and other forms of proclamation?
- How can singing hymns and hearing music offered by others become a spiritual exercise, giving expression to a saying popularly associated with St. Augustine that "the one who sings prays twice"?
- How can we encourage people to pray the creed as praise and not just recite it?
- How do we, during the prayers of the people, pray closely to the Scriptures after they are read and meditated upon and as the Word gives focus and content to our prayers during the liturgy?
- What is going on in the minds, hearts, and experiences of worshipers as they encounter Christ's real presence in the Holy Communion?
- What devotional or contemplative practices might we employ in the liturgy to nurture a deeper appreciation of Christ made known to us in the breaking of bread?
- How can we make more of the sending rites to give expression to the specific agendas for mission set by the particular liturgical and scriptural themes of the day?

- And through all of this, how can we instill in worshipers a sense that God's Word in Scripture and visibly expressed in the sacraments is "living and active, sharper than any two-edged sword, piercing until it divides soul from spirit, joints from marrow," that "it is able to judge the thoughts and intentions of the heart" (Heb. 4:12)?

These are the kinds of questions I will endeavor to address in this exploration of spirituality for worship and in applying *lectio divina* to liturgical participation.

This book is *about* holy conversation, and quite importantly it is *itself* holy conversation, meditations on the principal gathering of Christians around Word and sacraments that will also evoke your own reflections about experiences of worship in the places where you worship. The story of this book is carried first as commentary on the event of Pentecost recorded in the book of Acts (part 1). This commentary gives occasion for me to offer understandings of spirituality for worship, centering on the dynamics of holy conversation and *lectio divina* as a way of organizing and giving trajectory to that conversation. The story continues (part 2) as meditations on a *Mass for the Day of Pentecost*, a specific liturgy encompassing all of the segments of a typical Lord's Day liturgy, illustrating how the movements of *lectio divina* make sense of the particulars and of the whole of what we do when we worship. Liturgy does not exist in the abstract, but is always particular and contextualized—hence my inclusion of a particular order of service. Yet the meditations on the liturgy— giving expression to the kinds of reflections that make for holy conversation— will also serve to illustrate general principles of applying the sensibilities of *lectio divina* to liturgical participation.

Some further word about my method in reflecting on liturgy as holy conversation. *Lectio divina*—sacred *reading*—is primarily a text-oriented spiritual discipline, so my principal focus is on the texts, words, and narrative structure of the liturgy. That is to say, I give some attention to the nontextual aspects of liturgical worship, for example, the role of music and ceremonial movement and signs and symbols, but these explorations are in the service of the main focus on texts. Liturgical experience is a phenomenon that is just too rich and complex to be treated comprehensively in this volume of modest length. Consideration of the extratextual dimensions of liturgical practice and experience warrants the studied attention of additional volumes—perhaps a volume on *audio divina* (sacred listening in relation to music) and another on *video divina* (sacred viewing in relation to signs and symbols). Also, specific consideration in this volume is limited to the service on the Lord's Day. It is important to say that the general principles of holy conversation following the movements of *lectio divina* are applicable to other forms of worship such as daily prayer and other services of the Word.

In terms of my approach to meditative explorations of the features of liturgical worship, at times I call attention to the historical origins of aspects of the liturgy, revealing how our liturgical holy conversation echoes with that which has occurred through the centuries in the communion of the saints. I also on occasion explore word origins, striving to break through connotations and the humdrum of conventional meanings, reclaiming words for fresh meaning in our day, a living voice contributing to our spiritual and faith formation. I make extensive use of biblical material, including that voice in my holy conversation, illustrating the kind of biblical reminiscence—making connections among stories in the Bible—that is characteristic of meditation in *lectio divina*. Quite significantly, my meditations center on the meaning of segments of the liturgy in light of the movements of *lectio divina*—really the heart of this project in exploring spirituality for worship. Finally, my commentary is interspersed with personal anecdotes and some practical suggestions for how to do liturgy in ways that nurture deeper holy conversation.

I address my thoughts to you who have responsibilities for undertaking liturgical worship. You may be pastors, priests, and other ministers called to exercise public liturgical leadership. You may be musicians and other worship planners and leaders. You may be students of liturgy. But above all, I write to all worshipers who seek deep, profound, and authentic spiritual experiences when you worship. Whoever you are in relation to liturgy, I offer this book to you, that in the power of the Spirit, the dialogue that results from your reading of this work may contribute both to the renewal of your experiences of worship and to your formation in Christ—ultimately, that this offering may be in service of the Spirit's work in building up the body of Christ for its mission in the world.

This whole work and its approach imply a conversation with you. As you read my meditations, I encourage your own reflections as you read. Let my musings provoke and evoke your spiritual, liturgical, worshipful imaginations. Take your time as you read. Approach this work perhaps in sections as a devotional exercise over a period of weeks, for I seek to examine the linguistic fullness of liturgical worship as a divine-human phenomenon—reflection on the depth, breadth, and extent of this holy encounter calls for extended engagement lest you become overwhelmed by the sacred weight of the gifts known to us in the means of grace.

As a worshiper myself and as a leader of liturgy, I have often looked around during the sacred time of assembly, wondering about your experiences of worship. What in fact are your experiences? How are you being affected by the liturgy? Are you being changed? Are you experiencing the power of God in your life as you worship? I see you singing and praying and otherwise following along. These externals are visible to me. But what is happening at deeper levels in your mind as you engage the public expressions of liturgy? With such questions in mind, let our holy conversation begin. 1/22/12

Part One

SPIRITUALITY, WORSHIP, AND
LECTIO DIVINA

The first part of this book is an exploration of the general terms *spirituality* and *worship* toward understanding spirituality *for* worship. Meditations on the day of Pentecost recorded in the book of Acts serve to carry this segment of our holy conversation. It is compelling how much light the biblical narrative sheds on understandings of spirituality and Christian practices such as worship that will lay the foundations for the further explorations of this book. In short, a major gift of the Spirit at Pentecost is speech—Peter's tongue is released in proclamation of Jesus as resurrected from the dead. This gift of speech in proclamation sets the stage for understanding liturgical participation in large measure as holy conversation, a divine-human dialogical encounter.

What is it to be a good holy conversationalist? I will also take up that question, exploring the dynamics of conversation as an offering of our whole selves to the task of profound communication that can result ultimately in our transformation by the Spirit as new creations in Christ. *Lectio divina*, or sacred reading, and its movements—preparation, reading, meditation, prayer, contemplation, and incarnation of the Word in mission—serve to guide liturgical holy conversation on a trajectory that leads to intimate communion with Christ. Each movement represents a qualitatively different way of being present to each other and to God in liturgy, each being a mode of holy conversation. What is revealed in the application of *lectio divina* to the pattern for liturgical worship on the Lord's Day is a new way of engaging and being engaged by the language of liturgy for our growth in faith, hope, and love—and courage to be witnesses to God's reign evident in the Word which is Christ.

1/23

Applying... reveals (or will reveal) my

Chapter 1

UNDERSTANDING SPIRITUALITY
FOR WORSHIP

K arl Rahner, a prominent twentieth-century Roman Catholic theologian, summed up well the spirit of our age when he suggested that "the Christian of the future will be a mystic or he or she will not exist at all."[1] Rahner's observation suggests a recognition of people's yearnings for direct experience of God, aspirations that go hand in hand with the current interest in spirituality. Walk through bookstores, browse through book catalogs, witness popular discourse, both sacred and secular, and you will see evidence of the explosion of interest in spirituality. Spirituality has largely replaced religion as the category of choice to speak of themes of transcendence or religiosity, as captured by the popular phrase "I am spiritual, but I am not religious." Furthermore, given the explosive growth of Pentecostal Christianity through the twentieth century and throughout the world, one might conclude that ours is the era of the third person of the Trinity, the Holy Spirit. But what on earth is spirituality, and what is the role of the Holy Spirit in our lives? There are perhaps as many definitions and viewpoints as people and schools of thought employing the term and invoking the Spirit.

There is also great current interest in worship, indicated, for example, by exponential growth in the publication of worship books, hymnals, and various resources supporting liturgical life in a number of Christian traditions. But what exactly is worship? In a similar vein to the use of the term *spirituality*, there are perhaps as many approaches to understanding and defining worship as there are worship styles and traditions. The explorations that follow offer insights that will enrich understandings of both terms, *spirituality* and *worship*. These insights will also serve to link the two categories, because I believe that current societal fascination with these two phenomena is likewise intimately related. Interest in spirituality gives birth to interest in worship and vice versa.

Exploring the connection between spirituality and worship enriches and reinforces the understanding and experience of each. Linking spirituality with corporate worship keeps the notion of spirituality grounded, tethered to worshiping communities. Otherwise, spirituality might be reduced to individualistic practice and idiosyncratic experience. Likewise, linking spirituality and worship serves to deepen our understanding and experience of worship, keeping worship lively, vital, passionate, and attentive to the Spirit's transformative power working in our assemblies.

I will not attempt to explore here comprehensive views of either spirituality or worship. To do so would go far beyond the scope and needs of this work. Rather, I wish to take up understandings of spirituality *for* worship, focusing particularly on aspects of spiritual experience that will help us engage the language of liturgy for deeper spiritual experience, for more transformative encounters with and experiences of the Spirit in worship.   1/23

Spirituality and the Holy Spirit

The word that may be translated "spirituality" does not as such appear in the Bible. However, the word translated "spiritual" (*pneumatikos*) does appear, for example, in the Pauline letters. In such Pauline passages, the referent concerning that which is spiritual is specifically the Holy Spirit, and life in and according to that Spirit. For example, in Paul's discourse in the first chapters of 1 Corinthians, he explores the wisdom of God that contrasts with the wisdom of the world, and employs the category *spiritual* to speak of that which in fact comes from God through the Spirit: "Now we have received not the spirit of the world, but the Spirit that is from God, so that we may understand the gifts bestowed on us by God. And we speak of these things in words not taught by human wisdom but taught by the Spirit, interpreting spiritual things to those who are spiritual" (1 Cor. 2:12-13).

In this way, the word *spiritual* as used here does not refer to innate human capacity as much as it makes clear reference to the Holy Spirit as a focus for understanding what is spiritual. In other words, the content of the word *spiritual* is the Holy Spirit. This is a crucial feature of a specifically Christian understanding of spirituality. "Spiritual" comes to be connected with "spirituality," and all of this has to do with the Holy Spirit.

An early appearance of the word translated "spirituality" (from the Latin, *spiritualitas*) occurred in the fifth century in Epistle 7 of Pseudo-Jerome, which reads, "So act as to advance in spirituality." Pseudo-Jerome uses this term in a Pauline sense with reference to life in and according to the Holy Spirit of God.[2] This fragment from an ancient letter reveals significant aspects of an understanding of Christian spirituality. One such aspect is that Christian spirituality involves activity, practice, deeds, behavior—"so *act*" as the text from Pseudo-Jerome suggests. Additionally, Christian spirituality has to do with processes of change, growth, progress, maturation—"so act as to *advance* in spirituality." Such activity and growth happen via the guidance and in the power of the Holy Spirit in terms of the Pauline theology that informed Pseudo-Jerome.

SPIRITUALITY AND THE DAY OF PENTECOST

Any attempt to understand further Christian spirituality naturally involves considerations of the day of Pentecost, when the Holy Spirit, the very power of God, descended upon the apostles gathered in Jerusalem: "When the day of Pentecost had come, they were all together in one place. And suddenly from heaven there came a sound like the rush of a violent wind, and it filled the entire house where they were sitting. Divided tongues, as of fire, appeared among them, and a tongue rested on each of them. All of them were filled with the Holy Spirit and began to speak in other languages, as the Spirit gave them ability" (Acts 2:1-4).

This brief passage from Acts throws a window wide open for revealing numerous aspects of Christian spirituality that are pertinent to understanding its relationship to worship. First of all, spirituality, the power of God known in the Spirit, joins heaven and earth, things human with things divine—the rush of wind comes from heaven, the realm of God, after all. Spirituality and worship involve human encounter with the divine.

Next, the sound, the wind, the Spirit "filled the entire house." That is to say, the Spirit did not find a particular or secluded niche in which to roost. The Spirit of God infuses all of our surroundings and gets into everything where it would go. Spirituality, then, involves the whole of human life. It cannot be reduced to practices and experiences that are compartmentalized or segmented away from our ordinary routines and from what we commonly experience. Spirituality does not require a separate or distinct form of consciousness. Rather, it is part and parcel of our everyday sensate experience. Likewise, Christian worship that is spiritually oriented focuses on what we commonly do in assembly as we gather to hear the Word, share the meal, and be sent into the world to do God's work. Worship can be quite routine, even as it can also result in extraordinary experiences, as suggested by the events of the day of Pentecost itself.

Even so, and this may seem paradoxical in light of the Spirit's sharing in ordinary things, the Spirit interrupts business as usual and comes from without. The sound of the violent wind was sudden. The Spirit descended upon and filled the apostles. It did not well up within them. Christian spirituality, informed by reflections on the day of Pentecost, has to do with God coming to us *extra nos*—from outside of ourselves, even as the Spirit works through ordinary means and also dwells within us. Worship is an occasion when God breaks into our lives to address us and to bring about change.

"[The apostles] were all together in one place." The apostles had assembled. Pentecost was a communal event. Likewise, Christian spirituality has primarily a communal orientation in assembly, though popular understandings of spirituality can reduce it to individual and interior experiences. Moreover, reinforcing the communal dimension of the experience of the Spirit, when the Spirit comes, other people begin to arrive as well. "At this sound the crowd gathered" (Acts 2:6). So it is that we assemble for worship as the Spirit gathers us, and others also find their way to our assemblies to see what is going on.

Even though the context is communal, the experience of the Spirit is individual and particular. "Divided tongues, as of fire, appeared among them, and a tongue rested on each of them." Christian spirituality touches our unique identities as children of God. As the apostle Paul writes, "Now concerning spiritual gifts, brothers and sisters, I do not want you to be uninformed. . . . Now there are varieties of gifts, but the same Spirit; and there are varieties of services, but the same Lord; and there are varieties of activities, but it is the same God who activates all of them in everyone. To each is given the manifestation of the Spirit for the common good" (1 Cor. 12:1, 4-7). We worship God in community, but according to the particular gifts given to us by the Spirit.

"All of them were filled with the Holy Spirit and began to speak in other languages, as the Spirit gave them ability." The coming of the Spirit, symbolized by tongues as of fire, unleashes tongues, *glossa* in the Greek, meaning the tongue as physical organ, but also language and speech. The Spirit's power gives birth to discourse, to proclamation, the telling of stories made intelligible and understandable by the same Spirit. In short, the Spirit makes possible effective communication. Prior to the day of Pentecost, Jesus' followers remained in Jerusalem and were silent, speechless at least in terms of their public witness. God's sending of the Holy Spirit released the apostles' own tongues to give forth the public proclamation of the gospel. Visitors attracted by this commotion heard and understood in their own native tongues speech about "God's deeds of power" (Acts 2:11b). Peter was moved in the power of the Spirit to give an address that drew this conclusion: "This Jesus God raised up, and of that all of us are witnesses. Being therefore exalted at the right hand of God, and having received from the Father the promise of the Holy Spirit, he has poured out this that you both see and hear" (Acts 2:32-33). Peter's en-Spirited proclamation is about Jesus Christ, whom God, the One both Jesus and we know as Father, raised from the dead. An understanding of Christian spirituality rooted firmly in the proclamation of the gospel has particular content—namely, the saving work of the God whom we confess as Trinity: Father, Son, and Holy Spirit. The language of worship centers on this proclamation, rehearsing again God's deeds of power throughout history.

To be human is to be a creature of language, speech, and narrative, which is arguably a distinguishing characteristic of Christian theological and spiritual anthropology, an expression of *imago Dei*, that we are created in God's image. We confess that as God seeks to relate to human beings, God speaks, reveals Godself via narrative. God speaks order into the formless void at the beginning of creation. God establishes covenant and law in the language of the commandments. God's voice and will are known in prophetic discourse. God's very Word (*logos*) is offered to us in the flesh for our salvation. Jesus whom we confess as Christ is the fullest revelation of God, and that revelation is known now through the language and stories of Holy Scripture, a centerpiece of Christian worship. God's Holy Spirit at Pentecost gives birth to apostolic proclamation of the gospel. So from beginning to end, God has chosen natural means, speech and story, to communicate with human beings, creatures who have voice and who likewise offer up narrative accounts of our experience. This is a crucial point in the context of this exploration of spirituality and worship. Both rely on the centrality of linguistic experience.

This language-oriented experience of the Spirit effects change. The ones formerly known as disciples, students of Jesus Christ, now become apostles, teachers if you will, the ones sent to proclaim the message of the gospel. The Spirit's activity in the apostles' proclamation makes the message intelligible to the hearers: "In our own languages we hear them speaking about God's deeds of power" (Acts 2:11). This Spirit-filled proclamation provokes reactions: "All were amazed and perplexed, saying to one another, 'What does this mean?' But others sneered and said, 'They are filled with new wine'" (Acts 2:12-13). Spirituality involving the Spirit's activity in speech about God's deeds of power provokes responses, positive or negative—amazement, perplexity, even sneering. In worship, a language-oriented experience from beginning to end, our thoughts, feelings, memories, and imaginations are likewise evoked and provoked by divine-human discourse. We respond and thus participate in the Spirit's activity in us.

Moreover, the Spirit's birthing of proclamation leads also to hearers' curious engagement with the message being proclaimed: "What does this mean?" the onlookers asked. Here the Spirit's work at Pentecost is significantly located in dialogical engagement, in discourse, that is, holy conversation. This dialogue also involves the interpretation of current sacred events in light of previous revelation in sacred writ, for example, in the words of prophets. Peter, in his address to the crowd, invoked well-known prophecy to make sense of the Pentecost event: "This is what was spoken through the prophet Joel: 'In the last days it will be, God declares, that I will pour out my Spirit upon all flesh, and your sons and your daughters shall prophesy, and your young men shall see visions, and your old men shall dream dreams'" (Acts 2:16-17). Christian spirituality and worship focus on holy conversation, dialogue between God and humans. Christian spirituality and worship make sense of this experience by further invoking and meditating on God's Word.

This Spirit-led conversational engagement with proclamation effects still more change in the lives of receptive hearers. "Now when they heard this, they were cut to the heart" (Acts 2:37a). The hearers were filled with compunction. They welcomed the message, repented, and were baptized, and they themselves, some three thousand persons, also received the gift of the Holy Spirit (Acts 2:37-41).

All of this is to say that God's Word in the power of the Spirit is effective. It accomplishes change in our lives, as suggested by the promises in Isaiah: "So shall my word be that goes out from my mouth; it shall not return to me empty, but it shall accomplish that which I purpose, and succeed in the thing for which I sent it" (Isa. 55:11). God's Word is thus performative. It forms us, conforms us to the will of God and to the mind of Christ, reforms us when we go astray, and ultimately transforms us, bringing to birth new creations in Christ. Liturgical worship is a primary school for this work of formation, conformation, reformation, and transformation. Liturgy as the locus for encounter with God's Word is the pedagogy, the method through which Christ the teacher teaches us, disciples us in the power of the Spirit, and sends us forth to share in apostolic proclamation. 1/25

SPIRITUALITY, CHRISTIAN PRACTICES, AND DISPOSITIONS

The Spirit's work is by no means finished on the day of Pentecost. The Spirit's outpouring that birthed proclamation and the reception of the gospel likewise issued forth in devotion to basic practices in community described in a passage following the Pentecost event: "They devoted themselves to the apostles' teaching and fellowship, to the breaking of bread and the prayers" (Acts 2:42). The Spirit's work also resulted in generous acts of communal self-giving: "All who believed were together and had all things in common; they would sell their possessions and goods and distribute the proceeds to all, as any had need" (Acts 2:44-45). In this brief passage the rudiments of the *ordo* of Christian life are revealed—the basics of the pattern of Christian life. Christian spirituality involves what would become our liturgy and the whole of Christian life. In these very revealing moments in Acts, we see the basic, foundational Christian spiritual practices: proclamation of the gospel, evangelization and making of disciples, baptism, study of apostolic teaching, the Lord's Supper, the practice of prayer, fellowship (*koinonia*) or participation in Christian community, the exercise of stewardship of possessions, and works of charity on behalf of those in need. These are practices that begin in and grow out of the power of the Holy Spirit working, for example, in liturgical assembly.

The Spirit's work also bears the fruit in us of attitudes and dispositions central to the understanding of Christian life in the Spirit. "Awe came upon everyone. . . . They broke bread at home and ate their food with glad and generous hearts, praising God and having the goodwill of all the people" (Acts 2:43a, 46b-47a). Awe, gladness, generosity, praise, and goodwill—all are characteristics of en-Spirited Christian life. Or, as the apostle Paul elaborated elsewhere: "The fruit of the Spirit is love, joy, peace, patience, kindness, generosity, faithfulness, gentleness, and self-control" (Gal. 5:22-23a).

All of this is the Spirit's work. This process happens daily over the course of a lifetime, or as Acts puts it, "day by day" as the followers engaged in the community's work. The activity is all quite ordinary. Christian spirituality, in this way, does not focus on the exotic and the extraordinary in terms of practice and experience. Rather, it is about awe and praise cultivated in the mundane but sacred routines we undertake in Christian community. Christian spirituality reclaims the commonplace, especially in terms of liturgy, the Ordinary of the Mass, the regular segments that comprise the pattern for liturgy, that is, the *ordo*, what we ordinarily do in assembly and how we do it; we come to see the extraordinary in what is common and routine.

Finally, the Spirit's work is directed outward, to the nations and peoples who would hear and respond to the proclamation of the gospel. The whole point of the Pentecost event recorded in Acts is the telling of God's deeds of power in raising Jesus from the dead in many different languages, the languages of varied nations and cultures. Christian spirituality thus also has an outward focus, embraces the gift of cultural diversity, and serves the church's mission in and for the sake of the world, to be the body of Christ broken for the world. It may well be that Christian spiritual practices enrich our inner lives, and that is well and good. But if spirituality ends in interiority, its true end is in fact missing altogether. Varied spiritual practices, including liturgical worship, build us up in the power of the Spirit for the sake of mission among the many diverse peoples of the world.

SPIRITUALITY AND DEEPER UNDERSTANDINGS OF LITURGY AND WORSHIP

The Spirit's work involves us in liturgy and worship, two words common in discourse about what Christians do when they assemble, often used interchangeably and sometimes with inadequate attention to precision about definitions and word origins. Liturgy is distinct from worship. Briefly, liturgy can be seen as the agenda of activities that may result in worship, worship having a more dispositional quality than liturgy. Liturgy is what we do. Worship is how we do it, in what manner or spirit. Liturgy results in worship and is best undertaken worshipfully. We can well speak of worshipful liturgy and also liturgical worship.

The word *liturgy*—from *leitourgia* in Greek—is derived from the word *latreuo*, meaning "to serve," or *latreia*, "service." *Latreuo* means "to work for reward" and then, by extension, "to serve." Literally, this has to do with physical service but also figuratively involves cherishing. In terms of New Testament usage, *latreuo* and related words imply service to God, sacrificial ministry, the ministry of prayer and praise, righteous behavior with interior and outward dimensions.[3]

In the New Testament, a common Greek word translated as "worship" is *proskynesis* as a noun and *proskyneo* as a verb, meaning "to bow down," or perhaps more graphically, "to stoop and to kiss the earth," either literally as an outward gesture or metaphorically as an inward impulse. It can more generally mean to love and to respect. In the New Testament literature itself, *proskynesis* is common in the Gospels, Acts, and Revelation. While it can refer to the worship of idols or false gods, *proskynesis* is often seen in reference, for example, to persons kneeling before Jesus, seeking his intervention in their circumstances, as in Matthew 15:25, where the Canaanite woman kneels before Jesus, pleading, "Lord, help me." Quite significantly, *proskynesis* is the response to signs and wonders performed by Jesus. In response to Jesus' walking on the waves and his rescue of Peter, the disciples "worshiped him, saying, 'Truly you are the Son of God'" (Matt. 14:33). It is instructive that this attitude of worship in bowing down is connected with a kind of creedal affirmation, "Truly you are the Son of God."

Worship is also the response to encountering the risen Lord. "Suddenly Jesus met [the women] and said, 'Greetings!' And they came to him, took hold of his feet, and worshiped him" (Matt. 28:9). Such worship can indeed include elements of holy fear, as suggested by Jesus' reply to their gesture, "Do not be afraid" (Matt. 28:10a). When Jesus meets the disciples on the mountain in Galilee as he instructed them, their response is also that of worship, of bowing down: "When they saw him, they worshiped him" (Matt. 28:17a). And it is curious that the response of worship also includes doubt: "but some doubted" (Matt. 28:17b)—how very true to human nature.

These explorations begin to capture the tone of what it means to worship in a spiritually qualitative sense. It is this attitude of awe, wonder, holy fear— of experience so dramatic that we fall down in praise and adoration—that we are called upon to cultivate in Christian assembly. Liturgical worship as everdeepening holy encounter evokes and provokes the experience of worship, of bowing before the Holy One and that One's gracious acts in the Word and in the sacraments in the power of the Spirit. Liturgy, again, is the agenda of activity that gives rise to worship even as the activity is done worshipfully. Liturgy is the activity we engage in, such as devotion to the apostles' teaching, fellowship, breaking of bread, and the prayers. Worship is the quality of experience that results from the activity, the awe and the glad and generous hearts. The deeper this liturgical encounter, the more profound the experience of worship.

How do we move from simply doing the liturgy to worshiping God? What happens between liturgy as activity and worship as disposition? What occurs between hearing the proclamation of the gospel and its effects in changing our lives, in prompting us to bow down in awe and holy fear? The answer to each question has to do with ever-deepening holy conversation, and it is to these dialogical dimensions of liturgical worship that we now turn.

Chapter 2

WORSHIP AND HOLY CONVERSATION

The understanding of liturgical worship as holy conversation is reinforced by a German word for worship, *Gottesdienst*, which can mean simultaneously God's service to human beings and human service in response to God. In the spirit of this dual exchange, Martin Luther understood worshipful liturgy as a kind of conversation with God. In a sermon for the dedication of the castle church at Torgau in 1544, Luther proclaimed that the church building is a place for worship, wherein "our dear Lord himself may speak to us through his holy Word and we respond to him through prayer and praise."[1] This quotation is commonly understood as Luther's brief definition of worship. German theologian Peter Brunner, in his classic volume *Worship in the Name of Jesus*, elaborates on these dialogical aspects of liturgy, stating that every occasion of worship is a service of God to the congregation and also the congregation's service before God. God's service to us involves various forms of proclamation—salutation or greetings, the reading of Scripture, the sermon, absolution, Holy Communion, and benediction—through which the Spirit evokes our remembrance of Christ and conveys to us salvation. The congregation's response, according to Brunner, involves prayer, confession, thanksgiving, and praise, dimensions of our liturgical participation I will later take up and add to in light of the movements of *lectio divina*.[2]

Holy Conversation and the Vocation of All the Baptized

Our liturgical worship involves the sacred conversation between God, speaking in the context of the church's liturgy, and worshipers, responding through active listening and prayerful self-offering. Holy conversation involves presenting our whole selves to God for sacred encounter in the liturgy. In this context, God addresses and claims us, and we respond in listening and thinking, speaking and praying, singing and praising, giving thanks, and so on. This is the holy conversation. This dialogical dynamic breathes renewed life into the theological category of the vocation of all the baptized, an understanding that sometimes can lack specific content. If liturgy is the work of the people, as commonly understood, then the people's work in liturgy is holy conversation, offering to God the fullness of who we are in dialogical and thankful response to the Word.

This view takes seriously the role of each person present for a worship service, not just those leading worship. Every worshiper has the weighty responsibility and joyful privilege of attending fully to the Word proclaimed, exploring what we bring to the encounter and discerning a word from God for us in our time. In this sense, there is no room for passive participation in liturgical contexts. Each member of the assembly is, in this sense, a liturgical minister. There can be no mere spectators or passive observers. We are the body of Christ together, and our intentional and active participation binds us together as one. It is not a matter of us and them, people in the pew in distinction from those who exercise public leadership of liturgy. That all in the assembly exercise priesthood, ministry, and service is one of the key insights that undergirds an understanding of the formative and transformative power of liturgical worship. \ / 27

Characteristics of Holy Conversation

To be a prayerful worshiper is to be a good conversationalist. Given this, it is helpful here to explore the nature and characteristics of good conversation. Conversation emphasizes relationship between conversation partners, as in the Latin origins of the word *conversari*, meaning "to keep company with," *com + panis*, "to share bread with." Conversation at its best involves effective communication. The word *communication* derives from the Latin words *communicare* and *communis*, meaning "to share in common." In this sense good conversation results in communion, a sharing between the parties doing the communicating, a sense of being connected. This communion is made possible in large measure by both speech and deep and attentive listening by those in conversation. In speaking and listening, the conversation partners are present to each other. Presence and attentive listening result in the significant human experience of feeling that one is heard, and this results in a sense of being attended to, seen, acknowledged, affirmed, and confirmed—in short, loved.

Good conversation involves reciprocity and a balance between speaking and listening. It requires caring enough about the other to offer appropriate challenge on occasion, holding the other accountable, not simply glossing over faults and shortcomings. It involves vulnerability and openness, authenticity and willingness to offer the fullness of who we are to the other.

Good conversation can result in long periods of comfortable silence, a kind of resting in deep, loving familiarity with each other, a state suggestive of contemplative presence. The divine-human relationship has parallels in human relationships, especially relationships between friends, significant others, and lovers. Christians believe in a personal God and affirm the incarnation. How, then, can we not relate to God in manners that parallel our loving relationships with each other? Many writings of the Christian mystics and other spiritual writers have the flavor of love stories and love letters. Bridal mysticism, focusing on the love relationship between God and humanity, is a major theme in much Christian devotional literature, as suggested in this stanza from a hymn on the Holy Eucharist by the hymnwriter Johann Franck:

> Hasten as a bride to meet him,
> eagerly and gladly greet him.
> There he stands already knocking;
> quickly, now, your gate unlocking,
> open wide the fast-closed portal,
> saying to the Lord immortal:
> "Come, and leave your loved one never;
> dwell within my heart forever."[3]

Holy conversation is intimate, familiar, as that between lovers in communion with each other.

Liturgical worship as holy conversation embodies the characteristics and dynamics of human communication described above. In the proclamation of the Word and in the celebration of the sacraments, God discloses the divine identity. In the worshipful encounter, communication and communion result, and God in Christ is present through the working of the Holy Spirit in Word and sacraments. Proclamation is dialogical. God speaks through these means, and we listen, also giving voice to our concerns in preaching, singing, and praying. We listen to God and to each other. As God in Christ comes to us in the fullness of Passiontide vulnerability, so, too, we offer the fullness of who we are in open and nondefensive ways.

Conversations have movements and trajectories. Friends gather and get caught up with each other. They move on to the main topics for conversation. They might share a meal. Then they say their good-byes and go on their way changed in some way by the exchange. This trajectory is not unlike that of liturgical worship. The people gather, hear and respond to the Word, share the meal, and then are sent to do the work God has called them to do.

Naming liturgical worship as holy conversation is apt in describing the phenomenon of worship, what actually occurs during the liturgical hour. Conversations happen throughout the time of Christian assembly, occurring at several different levels:

- between God and the whole assembly collectively;
- between God and individual members of the assembly particularly;
- among members of the assembly.

Some conversations are programmed and scripted, as in the liturgical agenda for the day. Others are spontaneous, unprogrammed, and unscripted. Members talk to one another before, sometimes during, and then also after the liturgy, sometimes in distraction and distinction from the main, intended holy conversation. We have conversations with ourselves in our own minds and imaginations. During the liturgy, we may otherwise be distracted by our thoughts of work and family situations, critiques of hymns chosen for the day, the style of the preacher, what other members of the assembly happen to be wearing, and so on. Such less-than-holy or sidebar conversations may occur consciously, preconsciously, or unconsciously. We may resist or struggle to pay attention to what in fact is happening as God through the Spirit addresses us in the Word.

The call of holy conversation is to pay attention at ever deeper levels, participating in liturgy with all of our heart, mind, soul, and strength. When our mind wanders, we call it back again. When we forget, we endeavor to remember. Much of the Christian life consists of the dynamic of forgetting and remembering. Liturgy is our primary source for remembrance of who and whose we are and what we are called to do.

Liturgical holy conversation has individual, interior dimensions as well as exterior and communal dimensions. That is to say, the conversation happens simultaneously within our individual selves and with others in the assembly.

Attending to these simultaneous and mutually-reinforcing dynamics in actual worship has the effect of building up the body of Christ as we engage a full range of human experience, accounting for both individual and communal dimensions of that experience. 2/8/12

Presenting Our Whole Selves in Holy Conversation

A brief passage from Paul's letter to the church at Rome is important for understanding the dynamics of the fullness of what we offer in holy conversation: "I appeal to you therefore, brothers and sisters, by the mercies of God, to present your bodies as a living sacrifice, holy and acceptable to God, which is your spiritual worship" (Rom. 12:1). The Greek *logiken latreian*, rendered here as "spiritual worship," is translated in other versions as "reasonable service." These legitimate alternatives in translation are suggestive for our purposes. Paul here is not talking specifically about liturgical worship. Rather, the living sacrifice involves the whole of the Christian life, especially its moral and ethical dimensions. But liturgical worship is central to the Christian life and as such is part of the living sacrifice. It is important to note also that this offering is not the domain of a singular priest. Rather, all of God's people share in the spiritual worship, the reasonable service. What we individually and collectively do in liturgy is both service and worship, recalling that *latreia* means service and is the source for "liturgy," *leitourgia*, and that liturgy leads to worship as a gesture of adoration. What we do in liturgy also is reasonable, rational, and spiritual. *Logiken* is a form of *logikos* (cf. logic), which itself is derived from the root word *lego*, meaning "to speak." This root also relates to the Greek *logos*, "word," used prominently in John's Gospel, for example, to refer to Jesus as God's Word made flesh.

The relationships among these words suggest that spiritual worship and reasonable service are related to the activity of speaking, of making words, creating and responding to stories with logical plotlines, and that all of this as spiritual worship happens in faith practices, including liturgical worship. These relationships thus reinforce the previous conclusions that Christian spirituality, according to Paul's language, has everything to do with the work of God's Spirit in generating proclamation of the Word, with the Spirit's activity in the celebration of the sacraments as visible Word, creating faith in us, and with our response to that Word. Reasonable service and spiritual worship thus complement each other as alternatives for translating *logiken latreian*. Holy conversation, involving the Spirit addressing us in proclamation and our response to that address, is a crucial feature of our spiritual worship, our reasonable service.

Liturgical worship understood as holy conversation invites us to offer ourselves, individually and collectively, as our spiritual worship. More particularly, in Romans 12:1, Paul exhorts us to present our *bodies* as living sacrifices. "Body," *soma* in the Greek, denotes our physical embodiment, but it cannot be reduced to physicality as a singular focus. Rather, *soma* also suggests the totality of ourselves, yes, contextualized in a physical body, but also involving the aspects of what we think and feel, our character, our uniqueness as persons, our experiences and our behaviors, all expressed in terms of being living bodies with souls and minds. In short, *soma* is all that we are. Furthermore, *soma* is the locus for our relationship with God and thus the focus for making the living sacrifice, our spiritual worship. Recall that elsewhere (1 Cor. 6:19) Paul refers to the body (*soma*) as the temple of the Holy Spirit. Liturgy as holy conversation is a presentation of our bodies; it is an offering, a living sacrifice of all that we are. This offering has liturgical focus, located in the rites of Christian community, even as it is also expressed in all of Christian ministry, or service, throughout our lives.

What is the fullness of our humanity in this somatic, holistic sense? What are the constituent aspects of the fullness of human experience that we bring to holy conversation?

Picture the Christian community where you typically worship. Have in mind the particular people who normally attend. Imagine the aspects of human experience occupying the attention and weighing on the hearts and minds of members of that Christian assembly during any given liturgy. Consider the range of your own human experiences. You and other worshipers bring to holy conversation a wide array of thoughts, feelings, memories, hopes and dreams and the content of your imagination. Our physical bodies are part of holy conversation, what we see, hear, touch, taste, and smell. We bring the joys and pains of our physical mortality to worship as holy conversation, as well as concerns related to where we are in our stages of life, ranging from infants to seniors and including all those in between. Consider the many personality types represented in Christian assembly, the introverts and extroverts, thinkers and feelers, and so on. Think of the many vocations represented in the assembly and the particular concerns of each in holy conversation.

Worshipers have in mind concerns about relationships, at home, work, and school and in local communities. In our increasingly "global village," relationships at national and international levels also occupy our attention, not to mention our relationship to the natural world. Concerns about our many and various relationships are present in holy conversation. Likewise, we bring to Christian assembly our historical, social, racial, ethnic, and cultural contexualization. In any Christian assembly numerous constellations of sub-cultures are present. The country of which you are a citizen, your cultural and ethnic heritage, your birthplace, and more, all contribute to how you understand yourself as a unique child of God.

All of these dimensions of human experience interact and are interdependent. They occur at all levels of human consciousness: our conscious awareness; our preconscious levels of awareness, memory, and experience that can easily come into mind; and unconscious levels that encompass reservoirs of experience that may never come to focal awareness, but nonetheless may influence our decisions, behavior, and experience. The deepest level of human consciousness may be that place where the very Spirit of God prays with "sighs too deep for words" (Rom. 8:26).

Because of these rich complexities of human experience, each worship service engages many paradoxical tensions of participation and experience, finding a place on continua, poles of human experience that include these dimensions and more:

- interior and exterior;
- individual and communal;
- occasions for speech and for silence;
- considerations of local and global circumstances;
- enactments that are contemporary and ancient;
- affectivity that makes room for a range of emotions ranging from lament to joy.

Each and every waking and even sleeping human moment via dreams is filled with the multivariate dimensions of human experience.

Through these many aspects of human experience, the *soma*, the temple of the Holy Spirit, is infused with divine presence and potential. The Spirit fills these temples with divine presence and indwelling as at Pentecost. The Spirit gives us gifts, charisms, that form our unique identities. These unique constellations of gifts emerge from and return to the soul, the seat of our unique identity, of being singularly created in the image of God. This is not to posit the existence of a separate religious consciousness. Religiosity and spirituality find expression in each dimension of human experience and in their interrelationships. It is a naïve impulse to compartmentalize spirituality, attempting to locate it apart from the ordinary aspects of human experience. An integrative approach to seeing sacrality in every facet of human phenomena is faithful to the incarnational and sacramental orientations of Christianity.

In sum, our holistic, somatic self-offering, which hands over our bodies as living sacrifices, our spiritual worship, includes the totality of the human experience. This complete package is indeed present, consciously, preconsciously, or unconsciously, in every worship service and in each holy conversation. We listen deeply to God's story as narrated in Word and sacraments. But we also are called upon to listen deeply to our own narratives, an aspect of liturgical participation not often given significant attention. Each part of being human that we bring to a liturgy is a component of our unique human narrative. Attentiveness to the fullness of our stories contained in the many dimensions of human experience is our spiritual worship, our reasonable service, our work in the liturgy.

This liturgical work can result in worship (*proskynesis*), the attitude of awe, praise, and adoration that characterizes worship spiritually understood. The deeper the converse, the deeper the worship, that is, the falling-down-on-your-face kind of awe at being in the very presence of God. It is at this point where we find our deepest identity in our relationship to God.

TRANSFORMATION THROUGH HOLY CONVERSATION

When God finds us in holy conversation where we most deeply are, then the Spirit working in that holy conversation has the chance to form us, to conform, reform, and transform us, again echoing the promise in Isaiah 55:10-11, that the Word of God will accomplish that for which it is purposed. Holy conversation forms us in faith and discipleship. Holy conversation conforms us to the mind of Christ and the will of God. Holy conversation reforms us when we forget who we are and whose we are. This is the work of remembrance, *anamnesis*, helping us to remember at deep levels that we are beloved children of God. Holy conversation likewise nurtures our transformation in the power of the Spirit, as we participate in the Spirit's work of turning us around, receiving the gift of *metanoia*, of repentance and conversion, the Spirit-led about-face, enabling us to change our minds and thus to share in the divine life, taking on the mind of Christ. When the holy conversation is deep in the community, then the whole body of Christ, not just individuals, is built up for the work it is called to do in the world.

To nurture worshipers' awareness of these many dimensions of human experience is a crucial feature of giving the people of God the tools with which to carry out our work, to engage in our liturgy, exercising our baptismal ministry, offering the living sacrifice of all that we are to holy conversation with

God in Christ known in Word and sacraments through the power of the Spirit.
How, then, do we convey practical insights that we may fully and deeply
engage in holy conversation, encouraging each other to ask of ourselves such
questions as these:

- What are we thinking, feeling, hoping for, remembering when we gather
  to be encountered by God in worship?
- How best do we listen attentively to God's Word?
- In light of this deep listening, how do we discern the meanings of God's
  Word for us when we worship?
- How are we drawn to pray, and for what and for whom shall we pray?
- How do we settle in to rest contemplatively in the presence of Christ
  known to us in the breaking of bread?
- To what ministry and mission do we discern that God is sending us?

To encourage people to respond to these kinds of questions is to encourage liturgical worship as holy conversation. To these more specific dimensions
of liturgical practice I now turn, namely, to suggest that an ancient monastic
practice, *lectio divina*, can be a compelling way to guide and make the most of
holy conversation.

Chapter 3

LECTIO DIVINA AND HOLY CONVERSATION

B oth explicit and implied rules aid and guide conversation. At an informal level, for example, conversationalists know the conventional rule of not interrupting when another is speaking. In formal legislative sessions, *Robert's Rules of Order* and other manuals on parliamentary procedure establish strict guidelines for discourse—what can and cannot be said and done, when and in what circumstances. Such dynamics are common in human conversational interactions. In terms of divine-human encounter in liturgy understood as holy conversation, the practice and principles of the ancient discipline of *lectio divina*, or sacred reading, provide structure, parameters, and trajectory for participating meaningfully in that holy converse. I offer the movements of *lectio divina* as a new overlay for understanding the logic of liturgical worship, particularly the common pattern of liturgical assembly when Christians gather around Word and sacrament, that is, the Mass as it is commonly known, the service typically held on the Lord's Day, Sunday. Before I explore the relevance of the dynamics of *lectio divina* for understanding and participating in liturgy, some general comments about sacred reading are in order.

Lectio Divina in Historical Perspective

Lectio divina has its ultimate origins in ancient practice. Reading sacred texts devotionally has been a key spiritual discipline of both Judaism and Christianity since ancient times. Indeed, any faith tradition centered on Scripture employs some form of discipline involving reading and hearing the Sacred Word. In the Hebrew tradition, the centrality of scriptural engagement is clear: "This book of the law shall not depart out of your mouth; you shall meditate on it day and night, so that you may be careful to act in accordance with all that is written in it" (Josh. 1:8). Such devotion also is echoed in the exclamation of the psalmist: "Oh, how I love your law! It is my meditation all day long. . . . How sweet are your words to my taste, sweeter than honey to my mouth! . . . Your word is a lamp to my feet and a light to my path" (Ps. 119:97, 103, 105).

In the early Christian community, the practice of attending to Scripture is evident in the instruction to Timothy: "Until I arrive, give attention to the public reading of scripture, to exhorting, to teaching" (1 Tim. 4:13). Scripture intends to nourish the spiritual life and connect to ultimate salvation, as suggested in the purpose behind John's Gospel: "Now Jesus did many other signs in the presence of his disciples, which are not written in this book. But these are written so that you may come to believe that Jesus is the Messiah, the Son of God, and that through believing you may have life in his name" (John 20:30-31). Engaging the Scriptures, then, can be viewed as a principal spiritual discipline within the Christian faith tradition.

Lectio divina has its specific origin in the sixth-century appearance of the term in the Rule of St. Benedict. In his chapter on manual labor, Benedict writes, "Idleness is the enemy of the soul. Therefore, the brethren should have specified periods for manual labor as well as for prayerful reading [*lectio divina*]."[1] Meditative and prayerful engagement with biblical texts and other sacred works was part of the fabric of monastic life, individually and communally. The noonday meal was taken in silence, other than the voice of a monk reading aloud from a work for the edification of the community. Monks would ruminate on passages heard in the daily prayer offices while working in the fields and elsewhere, thus memorizing sacred texts and also internalizing their meanings for the spiritual life. In the monastery, *lectio divina* was primarily an activity taken up by individual monks in their own private devotional lives. But *lectio divina* also came to represent the movements of the whole of monastic spirituality. It was a centerpiece of monastic life that had reverberations throughout the whole day.

In the twelfth century, the Carthusian monk Guigo II articulated what is commonly identified as the fourfold nature of *lectio divina*. In a treatise entitled "The Ladder of Monks: A Letter on the Contemplative Life," he writes:

> One day when I was busy working with my hands I began to think about our spiritual work, and all at once four stages in spiritual exercise came into my mind: reading, meditation, prayer and contemplation. These make a ladder for monks by which they are lifted up from earth to heaven. It has few rungs, yet its length is immense and wonderful, for its lower end rests upon the earth, but its top pierces the clouds and touches heavenly secrets.[2]

Having named these stages, Guigo goes on to explore the characteristics of each stage:

> Reading is the careful study of the Scriptures, concentrating all one's powers on it. Meditation is the busy application of the mind to seek with the help of one's own reason for knowledge of hidden truth. Prayer is the heart's devoted turning to God to drive away evil and obtain what is good. Contemplation is when the mind is in some sort lifted up to God and held above itself, so that it tastes the joys of everlasting sweetness.[3]

Guigo further explicates the dynamics of each stage or movement. Notice here the sensate orientation to his understanding, echoing the Hebraic orientation in connecting meditation with the work of the mouth, as when the prophet Ezekiel ate the scroll of the Lord, noting a taste as sweet as honey (cf. Ezek. 3:1-6):

> Reading seeks for the sweetness of a blessed life, meditation perceives it, prayer asks for it, contemplation tastes it. Reading, as it were, puts food whole into the mouth, meditation chews it and breaks it up, prayer extracts its flavor, contemplation is the sweetness itself which gladdens and refreshes. Reading works on the outside, meditation on the pith: prayer asks for what we long for, contemplation gives us delight in the sweetness which we have found.[4]

THE PRACTICE OF *LECTIO DIVINA* AND ITS MOVEMENTS

Historically, *lectio divina* has been a discipline practiced by individuals who lived in communities, namely, monks in monasteries. In this sense, *lectio divina* cannot be considered an individualistic exercise even when taken up as an individual practice. This insight is crucially important for purposes here in applying the principles of *lectio divina* to liturgical participation in Christian assembly when individuals engage the language of liturgy in the company of others. The current interest in spirituality and spiritual practices has resulted in the rediscovery of *lectio divina* as a discipline for all, not just monks. Our day sees a resurgence of interest in *lectio divina*, bringing it out of the monastery. In recent years, numerous books have been published on the practice of *lectio divina*.[5]

During this time, an emphasis on the communal practice of sacred reading has also emerged. It is common now for small groups of people to attend to scriptural passages together, reading, meditating on, praying in response to, and resting in contemplative silence with the Scriptures and with each other. I have participated in and led such groups for a number of years. The movements marked by reading, meditation, prayer, and contemplation consistently result in the experience of deep engagement with the Scriptures, going well beyond the parameters of Bible study, which, though crucially important, is but one way of being present to the Scriptures. Participants in group exercise of *lectio divina* also report livelier experiences of faith and a growing bond between themselves, God, and other members of the group—a wonderful, straightforward way for the Spirit to build up Christ's body in the communal context while also forming people more deeply in faith.

In addition to the four stages of *lectio divina* identified by Guigo, I have added in my own practice two additional movements: time for preparation and occasion for discernment of incarnate mission. That is to say, the practice of *lectio divina* is well served by undertaking preparatory activity to nurture an openness to the divine encounter with the Word. Likewise, the practice of sacred reading is extended and well concluded by consideration of how it is that we will enflesh in our lives and practice of ministry the fruit of the encounter that is sacred reading. That is, how will we in the Spirit's power incarnate a living word in our discipleship and Christian practice? Without this consideration, sacred reading runs the risk of being reduced to a self-serving spiritual practice that is divorced from Christian ethical practice and the church's mission in the world.

Lectio Divina *as an Individual or Group Practice*

Here is what *lectio divina* can look like as an individual or group practice apart from its application to liturgical participation. This kind of exercise can be taken up as an excellent way of preparing for the liturgy.

- *Preparation*: First, engage in simple preparatory activity, sitting in silence, nurturing anticipation of a divine-human encounter soon to be mediated through the Spirit speaking in the Word, and also becoming aware of what you bring to this encounter. That is, what is in your heart and on your mind?
- *Reading*: Then read aloud an appointed biblical passage. In the silence following this first reading, consider what the passage means at an objective or historical level, what the biblical author intends to say. Here the dynamics and content of Bible study are at play. Participants bring their knowledge of the Bible to the encounter and offer their insights and reflections aloud in conversation to other members of the group.
- *Meditation*: Next, read aloud the passage a second time. In the silence following this reading, attempt to discern meanings at a subjective level, the more particularized or personal meanings of the passage for us in our own time and circumstances. What words, phrases, images evoke something within you or are you drawn to as you read and meditate? What might the Spirit be saying to you and to us in our own day? Group participants share their insights aloud in conversation.
- *Prayer*: Then read the text a third time. In the silence following this third reading, consider how the Spirit moves you to pray and then offer the prayers silently or aloud that emerge from having meditated on the reading of the passage.
- *Contemplation*: Read the text a fourth time. Then rest in contemplative silence in response to whatever has occurred in the praying, meditating, and reading, enjoying a sense of communion with God and with others.
- *Incarnation*: Finally, consider what word you may wish to take with you from this time in your life and ministry. What would God have us proclaim, enflesh, and do? Group participants may share aloud their ideas.

While *lectio divina* has characteristic movements and trajectory—reading leads to meditation and then to prayer and contemplation—and it can be a step-by-step spiritual exercise, it is also true that these movements have a certain fluidity and spontaneity and need not be so rigidly prescribed and limited to stages. It is common to experience the dynamics of the distinctive movements of *lectio divina* in each stage of the practice. For example, you might be moved to pray immediately in response to the first reading of the passage, further reflections about the passage may emerge in the quiet time for contemplation, and so on. So, rather than a rigid exercise, *lectio divina* may describe more broadly the movements of spiritual life, even as Guigo offered these stages in terms of the whole of the spiritual life of monks. It will become clear how this broader, more fluid understanding is important in terms of applying *lectio divina* to liturgical participation. However, further exploration of the characteristics of the movements of *lectio divina* is warranted now.

Preparation for *Lectio Divina*

Good preparation makes for good practice. Liturgical participation understood as holy conversation involves the divine voice in the Word and human responsiveness to that Word. This covenantal two-way street also exists in the preparation for *lectio divina* as an individual or group practice. That is to say, consideration needs to be given to what God has prepared and is preparing. We then also engage in our own preparations for sacred reading, considering what we bring to the exchange. In terms of attending to what God has done, echoes from Psalm 23 are evocative: "You prepare a table before me in the presence of my enemies; you anoint my head with oil; my cup overflows" (Ps. 23:5). Recalling God's wondrous intentions and deeds from primordial times can be important for our preparation for sacred reading of the Bible and for our participation in the liturgy, that a table of encounter and nourishment is indeed prepared for us. We are invited to remember God's providential preparatory activity on our behalf, suggested in Paul's explorations of divine ancient wisdom: "But, as it is written, 'What no eye has seen, nor ear heard, nor the human heart conceived, what God has prepared for those who love him'—these things God has revealed to us through the Spirit; for the Spirit searches everything, even the depths of God" (1 Cor. 2:9-10). In our encounters with the Word both in devotional use and in liturgy, we expect the Spirit to be present, revealing the divine gifts to us anew even now. Jesus' own promise along these mystical lines is evocative in helping us recall God's initiative in preparatory activity: "In my Father's house there are many dwelling places. If it were not so, would I have told you that I go to prepare a place for you? And if I go and prepare a place for you, I will come again and will take you to myself, so that where I am, there you may be also" (John 14:2-3). In preparation for holy conversation we anticipate dwelling in the very presence of Christ.

Having recalled that God has prepared for us such a place of meeting, encounter, and indwelling, we then can engage in our own preparatory activity for sacred reading, imitating John the Baptist, whose work is seen as the fulfillment of Isaiah's prophecy: "The voice of one crying out in the wilderness: 'Prepare the way of the Lord, make his paths straight. Every valley shall be filled, and every mountain and hill shall be made low, and the crooked shall be made straight, and the rough ways made smooth; and all flesh shall see the salvation of God'" (Luke 3:4b-6). How best might we smooth the way in our hearts and minds, that our very flesh might witness God's salvation?

Practically speaking, such preparation can involve sitting in silence, doing breathing exercises, or anything that generally has the effect of settling us down for greater focus and attention. Likewise, it is important to consider what it is that we bring to the encounter, what is on our hearts and minds, so that the Spirit's quickening activity offered in the Word may indeed address us in our particularity and unique circumstances.

READING IN *LECTIO DIVINA*

"Reading is the careful study of the scriptures, concentrating all one's powers on it."[6] This dimension of *lectio divina* addresses the Word of God as Revelation, the once-and-for-all nature of this gift, exploring its objective, historical, and intended meanings. This is the time to focus on the primacy of God's speech through the Spirit speaking in the Word. It is time in which the Word is set forth for our obedient and deep listening. Our listening is aided through processes of "careful study." Such study suggests employing the rich tools of exegetical study, the best of historical-critical methods, and other approaches. "Concentrating all one's powers on it" may involve acknowledging and honoring the many traditions of interpretation extant throughout Christian history, and celebrates the fact that we always read and study the Scriptures in a rich and complex communal and culturally diverse matrix, in the company of all the saints.

Such rigorous study lays the foundation for the other movements of *lectio divina* and serves as a tether and a touchstone, lest in the more playful meditative explorations of Scripture's meanings we stray into entirely idiosyncratic and subjectivistic interpretations of biblical passages. Building on this foundation, it is now possible to move into further explorations of Scripture at the level of ongoing revelation, the living Word as it applies to us in our own particular circumstances. But quite importantly, we bring the work of study to both scriptural engagement and liturgical worship. Such study is a crucial dimension of our holy conversation.

MEDITATION IN *LECTIO DIVINA*

"Meditation is the busy application of the mind to seek with the help of one's own reason for knowledge of hidden truth."[7] Guigo's "hidden truth" in the Scriptures is meaning in the sense of ongoing revelation, a living word for us in our time and circumstances. It is the applicability of the scriptural claims to the particularities of our own age based on but extended beyond the objective, intended historical meanings. This is meaning as *sensus plenior*, the fuller sense of the Scripture. This aspect of meaning also has the quality of being a word *pro me*, "for me," and *pro nobis*, "for us." This kind of meaning results from the dynamic, dialogical, that is to say, conversational interaction between readers or hearers and the texts of Scripture. This kind of meaning cannot be reduced to the text, nor can it be reduced to readers or hearers in their own subjectivity. Rather, subjective meanings find expression in the space and energy between readers or hearers and passages, and this is the locus of the Holy Spirit's activity in offering ongoing revelation, the Spirit leading us into all truth (cf. John 16:13a). Crucial here is the quality of having thoughts, feelings, memories, and hopes evoked; meanings for us are called forth in the dialogical interaction between God speaking in the Scriptures and hearers who respond by offering up the fullness of who they are in holy conversation.[8]

Here is where the participatory work of the people of God is indispensable. Created in God's image and baptized into the body of Christ to be that body as church, we have a crucial role to play in the activity from which meanings for us and our time emerge. Our activity in response to the encounter with God's Word centers on attending to the multiple dimensions and fullness of our humanity, recalling the many categories of human experience. This dynamic, dialogical activity has a playful, imaginative, and free-associative quality, thus fully engaging our mental faculties. Thus it is that Guigo refers to meditation as the "busy application of the mind." In the liturgy, this meditative work typically centers on the sermon, but it is also the work of all the people of God in their attentive participation throughout.

Holy conversation based on the interaction between readers or hearers and the texts of Scripture occurs at all levels of human consciousness, ranging from that which claims our focal attention to that which resides in the unconscious aspects of human experience. This interaction can evoke meanings at the level of conscious awareness, or *reminiscence*. Meanings can emerge in relation to previously unconscious material, a phenomenon that is best described by *anamnesis*, a deep and participatory remembrance, a connection with that which otherwise remains hidden and unavailable.

Reminiscence is a term employed in monastic contexts to describe an important feature of monastic life based on *lectio divina*. Jean Leclercq, a scholar of the monastic life, describes reminiscence in this way:

> This way of uniting reading, meditation and prayer . . . had great influence on religious psychology. It occupies and engages the whole person in whom Scripture takes root, later on to bear fruit. It is this deep impregnation with the words of Scripture that explains the extremely important phenomenon of reminiscence whereby the verbal echoes so excite the memory that a mere allusion will spontaneously evoke whole quotations and, in turn, a scriptural phrase will suggest quite naturally allusions elsewhere in the sacred books. Each word is like a hook, so to speak; it catches hold of one or several others which become linked together and make up the fabric of the exposé. . . . The mere fact of hearing certain words, which happen to be similar in sound to certain other words, sets up a kind of chain reaction of associations which will bring together words that have no more than a chance connection, purely external, with one another.[9]

When given free play, the mind naturally works in the way Leclercq describes. We constantly make connections between and among words, phrases, and ideas, connections that the author of a text may not intend but which may result in the evocation of signification, particularly in terms of personal or timely meanings for us.

Language is a vast web of interconnections among words, sentences, narratives, and meanings. We choose words and combine them into sentences. In turn, sentences are linked together to form paragraphs, and paragraphs are joined to generate whole narratives. Words are related to each other based on similarity and difference, words leading to other words (synonyms) and away from others (antonyms). Human consciousness at all levels participates in this web of interconnectivity. In making associations, we remember. This remembrance, this reconnection can occur in our conscious awareness but also in the unconscious (*anamnesis*). The notion of the Freudian slip in speech reveals that unconscious material that we otherwise repress can emerge in unintended ways in our discourse. This dynamic can likewise occur in reading and in hearing in the context of the meditative activity that is part of *lectio divina*.[10] Reminiscence and *anamnesis* occur when we read and engage scriptural passages. But these dynamics are also at play when we worship, when we really pay attention to the language of the liturgy, ever vigilant for a word for us in our own day. To do this meditative work is one of the central features of liturgical worship understood as holy conversation. When the connections are made, new and fresh meanings emerge, the Spirit leading us into truth particular for us.

Meanings Now That the Psalmist Did Not Intend

A personal anecdote may best illustrate the playful, serendipitous nature of meditation in *lectio divina*. Once when engaging in group *lectio divina* with Psalm 32, I was drawn to this verse: "I said, 'I will confess my transgressions to the LORD,' and you forgave the guilt of my sin" (Ps. 32:5b). When the reader uttered these words, I recognized in them the invitation to confession and forgiveness from the liturgy I grew up with. In my mind's eye, I was transported to the nave of First Lutheran Church in Monmouth, Illinois, where so many of my family's major life events occurred—baptisms, confirmations, weddings, funerals, my ordination.

While in that church in my imagination, another verse captivated me: "I will instruct you and teach you the way you should go; I will counsel you with my eye upon you" (Ps. 32:8). With that, a vivid memory came to mind, one that emerged from deep recesses of memory, namely, that of my very young hands reaching out to touch the bald head of the man sitting before me. Informing me of my comparatively minor transgression, my mother gave me perhaps my first explicit theology lesson. She turned me around to look at the center of the beautiful gothic rose window where the all-seeing eye of God was depicted, and she warned me that God is ever watching, even for my misbehavior—an unfortunate lesson, inconsistent with what I now teach and preach, but revelatory perhaps of a theological position I may still hold preconsciously!

Happily, this memory did not conclude my imaginative, meditative work. Other words of the psalm claimed me, such as these: "You are a hiding place for me; you preserve me from trouble; you surround me with glad cries of deliverance" (Ps. 32:7). A living word was given to me in this verse, an opening to the God who is not the judge waiting for me to fall, but rather the God who would watch me in order to guide, to provide safety, to deliver me. Here, I believe, the Spirit speaking in, with, and under the words of Scripture gave me an alternative theology lesson, one that met me in the deep places of early memories and touched me in formative, reformative, transformative ways. This is the Spirit's work of ongoing revelation, of leading us into all truth, far beyond what the psalmist intended when these words were composed in ancient times. This personal anecdote reveals what occurs all the time when we have deep dialogical encounter with the Scriptures in holy conversation. Opportunities for such meaningful encounters abound in liturgical worship from beginning to end.

All of this is crucial to understanding the power of *lectio divina* as a spiritual exercise because it is in the deep places where God in the Spirit most profoundly acts to form and ultimately to transform us. As the psalmist extols of God: "For it was you who formed my inward parts; you knit me together in my mother's womb.... My frame was not hidden from you, when I was being made in secret, intricately woven in the depths of the earth. Your eyes beheld my unformed substance. In your book were written all the days that were formed for me, when none of them as yet existed" (Ps. 139:13, 15-16). Because the unconscious is the location of some of our deepest wounds, *metanoia*, authentic conversion, begins when this material is touched and healed. Deeper still perhaps is our soul, the seat of the will, our true identity in God, that place where as children of God, created in God's image, we experience the Spirit praying in us with sighs too deep for words (cf. Rom. 8:26b). This is the point at which prayer emerges as the expression of our most profound longings and desires.

Prayer in *Lectio Divina*

"Prayer is the heart's devoted turning to God."[11] Prayer is understood variously as petition, intercession, confession, lamentation, expostulation, praise, adoration, oblation, recollection, entreaty, and so on. Prayer in the context of *lectio divina* emerges from meditation in response to reading and hearing scriptural passages and potentially connects us via reminiscence and *anamnesis* to deep-seated dimensions of our identities. When seen this way, prayer is understood as the expression of our deepest aspirations. Prayer involves the Spirit's

quickening work, its effects on us in moving us, acting on us to contribute to
our formation and to our activity and behavior. Prayer in this sense is connected with our breathing—metaphorically but perhaps also literally as *aspiration* relates to the Latin root *spirare*, meaning "to breathe," but also connecting
to "wind" and "spirit." Deep remembrances resulting from the meaning-
making activity of meditation can lead to these prayerful expressions of yearning and desire.[12] Moreover, the winds of the Spirit blowing through our prayers
can change us and propel us into action.

Prayerful remembrance also connects to another important dimension of
the monastic life, *compunction*, which is a piercing-through of defensive strate-
gies, a cutting to the quick that results in full speech, authentic expressions of
who we most deeply are as children of God. Guigo captures well this essence
of prayer in connection with desire in *lectio divina* when he writes and prays:

> So the soul, seeing that it cannot attain by itself that sweetness of
> knowing and feeling for which it longs . . . humbles itself and betakes
> itself to prayer. . . . I seek by reading and meditating what is true purity
> of heart and how it may be had, so that with its help I may know you,
> if only a little. Lord, for long have I meditated in my heart, seeking to
> see your face. It is the sight of you, Lord, that I have sought; and all
> the while in my meditation the fire of longing, the desire to know you
> more fully, has increased. When you break for me the bread of Scrip-
> ture, you have shown yourself to me in that breaking of bread, and the
> more I see you, the more I long to see you, no more from without, in
> the rind of the letter, but within, in the letter's hidden meaning.[13]

Prayer understood in its connection with our deepest yearnings and desires,
our aspirations, and, literally and metaphorically, our breathing, makes for a
richness of interaction with God. Prayer in this sense is our fullest and deepest
breathing, taking in and releasing the very God-given breath of life, the very
Spirit of God. In its authenticity, it is full speech, our real presence, the greatest
extent of full disclosure in holy conversation.

This real presence in holy conversation is, importantly, the Spirit's own
prayer in us. Or to echo again the apostle Paul, "Likewise the Spirit helps us
in our weakness; for we do not know how to pray as we ought, but that very
Spirit intercedes with sighs too deep for words" (Rom. 8:26). Holy conversation in this sense begins with God's speech and is God's speech returning to
God, even as this speech is evidenced in our embodied behavior and activities.
Such a view of prayer goes deeper than the mechanical forms of prayer often
characteristic of liturgical worship. Prayer understood as expressing our most

earnest yearnings can likewise deepen the intercessory dimension of our liturgies, as when we feel compassion in our guts for those for whom we pray, and are motivated to serve them. This plumbing of the depths is when prayer also begins to lead to contemplation.

CONTEMPLATION IN *LECTIO DIVINA*

"Contemplation is when the mind is in some sort lifted up to God and held above itself, so that it tastes the joys of everlasting sweetness."[14] Tasting the joys of everlasting sweetness suggests direct experience of the object of our desire. There is common confusion about the term *contemplation* as it relates to meditation. Sometimes these terms are used interchangeably to refer to the same experience. In the context of *lectio divina*, however, they point to very distinct experiences. While meditation is associated with the active use of the mind, contemplation, in contrast, involves a more receptive, directly experiential mode of presence. Contemplation is resting in the presence of God "apprehended not by thought but by love."[15] It involves an erasing, if just for a moment, of the distinctions between ourselves and God, and between ourselves and others. Contemplation is an experience of reuniting, of communion. In the open and nondefensive posture characteristic of contemplative experience, we catch a glimpse of our deepest identity in God as we also relate to others and to the whole cosmos.

The etymology of the word *contemplation* suggests the depth of the experience. Embedded in *contemplation* is the Latin root word *templum* (from which is derived the word *temple*), which in the most ancient use of the term referred to the place demarcated for the examination of the entrails and viscera of sacrificed animals for signs and omens.[16] In this sense, contemplation as a spiritual experience has everything to do with a return to our core, our pith. In this way also, contemplation involves a return to our embodiment, a reconnection with our physicality and its meanings and messages for us. This is suggested by the consistent use of physically-oriented images and metaphors to describe contemplative experience. Spiritual writers through the centuries often employ the images of both the child at the mother's breast and the lovers' embrace and other earthy metaphors to describe mystical experience.

Guigo himself offers such images in the description of the contemplative state:

> So the soul by such burning words inflames its own desire, makes known its state, and by such spells it seeks to call its spouse. But the

Lord . . . breaks in upon the middle of its prayer, runs to meet it in all haste . . . and He restores the weary soul, He slakes its thirst, He feeds its hunger, He makes the soul forget all earthly things: by making it die to itself He gives it new life in a wonderful way, and by making it drunk He brings it back to its true senses. And just as in the performance of some bodily functions the soul is so conquered by carnal desire that it loses all use of the reason, and man becomes as it were wholly carnal, so on the contrary in this exalted contemplation all carnal motives are so conquered and drawn out of the soul that in no way is the flesh opposed to the spirit, and man becomes, as it were, wholly spiritual.[17]

Flesh no longer opposing spirit, the contemplative state is one of reintegration, of reunion, of knowing unity within ourselves, with God, and with others.

To reinforce the physical orientation of the contemplative experience, tears of catharsis can signal the entry into this state:

Can it be that the heralds and witnesses of this consolation and joys are sighs and tears? . . . When you weep so, O my soul, recognize your spouse, embrace Him whom you long for, make yourself drunk with this torrent of delight, and suck the honey and milk of consolation from the breast. The wonderful reward and comforts which your spouse has brought and awarded you are sobbings and tears.[18]

In its orientation to our reintegration with our embodiment and reconnection with each other, contemplation has deep resonances with Paul's understanding of the church as the body of Christ and the profound extent of interdependence and mutual honoring we know in this body. "For just as the body is one and has many members, and all the members of the body, though many, are one body, so it is with Christ" (1 Cor. 12:12). Contemplation, thus, is not simply an individual experience focused on one's interiority. Rather, contemplation is truly communal.

These contemplative experiences can be and often are short lived, but they can have reverberating effects that ripple through our days, lasting a lifetime. Contemplation is a locus for transformation, when we become more and more like Christ, united with him by faith and in Word and sacraments. As such, contemplation is a gift from God. We cannot confect the state of contemplation. At most, we might nurture in the power of the Spirit an openness to the possibility of the contemplative state.

Contemplation relates significantly to the vision of unity among the disciples and divine interrelatedness offered by Jesus in his high priestly prayer in John's Gospel:

> "As you, Father, are in me and I am in you, may they also be in us, so that the world may believe that you have sent me. The glory that you have given me I have given them, so that they may be one, as we are one, I in them and you in me, that they may become completely one, so that the world may know that you have sent me and have loved them even as you have loved me." (John 17:21b-23)

Note here the ethical and missiological focus and end of this unity: "so that the world may believe . . ."

Contemplation is the deepest reality therapy. It involves our first coming into contact with our mortality and fears of abandonment and disconnection from others. At the same time, contemplation results in a palpable sense of our connection to each other, to the cosmos, and to God. It is healing, not just in a psychodynamic sense, but also in the spiritual sense. Contemplation allows the Word of God to take root in us at the deepest levels and prepares the way for us to birth this Word in our ministry and mission in the world. As I will more fully explore, the most profound experience of contemplation in the Christian tradition is our participation in the Holy Eucharist, where we intimately know Christ in the visible Word contained in, with, and under gifts of bread and wine that we take into ourselves.

INCARNATING THE WORD FOR MISSION IN *LECTIO DIVINA*

If *lectio divina* does not bear fruit in the life of faith, something is amiss, and it is incomplete. The holy conversation between faithful readers and worshipers and the language of Scripture in the liturgy, a holy conversation rooted in reading or hearing Scripture, meditating on it, praying in relation to it, and resting in contemplative experience can result in changed lives, especially when this encounter touches us most deeply. This holistic and integrative experience contributes to our Christian formation, conformation to Christ, reformation, and transformation. Here we can invoke the language of sanctification, being made holy by the power of the Holy Spirit mediated to us through dialogical engagement with God's Word. Here we can also talk about conversion of life, of *metanoia*, the processes involved in the "about-face," the changing and renewing of the mind that occur when we encounter God profoundly. So it is that Paul continues in Romans after his exhortation about offering our bodies as a living sacrifice, which is our spiritual worship: "Do not be conformed to this world, but be transformed by the renewing of our minds, so that you may discern what is the will of God—what is good and acceptable and perfect" (Rom. 12:2). In the next verses, Paul begins to link this activity with our varied ministries in the body of Christ:

> For as in one body we have many members, and not all the members have the same function, so we, who are many, are one body in Christ, and individually we are members one of another. We have gifts that differ according to the grace given to us: prophecy, in proportion to faith; ministry, in ministering; the teacher, in teaching; the exhorter, in exhortation; the giver, in generosity; the leader, in diligence; the compassionate, in cheerfulness. (Rom. 12:4-8)

So, in addition to the themes of formation, conformation, reformation, transformation, sanctification, and conversion, the fruit of *lectio divina* also involves us in ministry according to our varied gifts. It connects up with discipleship and mission, evangelism and social ministries, and advocacy for justice in the world, expressing the ethical and missiological dimensions of spirituality. Here, contemplation and action are importantly linked, a corrective to what otherwise might be a spiritual exercise reduced to individual, interior experience.

As the Word of God was made flesh in Jesus of Nazareth, whom we confess as Christ, so this same Word takes flesh in us. Incarnation comes from the Latin *in caro*, meaning "in the flesh." We, communally as the body of Christ, give birth to the Word of Christ in ministry and mission, the ultimate outcome of *lectio divina*, the holy conversation that is our spiritual worship, our living sacrifice. God in Christ in the power of the Spirit sends us out into the world to accomplish the work we have been called to do.

Lectio Divina and Liturgical Participation

Now it is time to turn more explicit attention to the application of the principles and movements of *lectio divina* to the pattern of Christian worship in Word and sacrament. As much as there is a trajectory in *lectio divina*, so, too, does liturgical worship have a trajectory. These trajectories correspond with each other rather naturally in my experience, practice, and understanding. In short, the rhythms of sacred reading (preparation, reading, meditation, prayer, contemplation, incarnation for mission) parallel the patterns of the principal liturgical assemblies of Western Christians in terms of their movements: gathering to hear and prayerfully respond to the Word, sharing the meal, and being sent into the world for mission.

In the gathering, we *prepare* for the divine-human encounter. Next, we *hear the public reading* of Scripture and *meditate* in response to it in our deep listening and in the form of a sermon and other responses to the proclamation of the Word. We then offer *prayers* of intercession in response to the reading and meditations on the Word and likewise offer material gifts for the church's mission, exchanging Christ's peace. We proceed next to share in the eucharistic meal, our sacrifice of thanksgiving that merges with Christ's sacrifice, the movement in liturgy where I locate the theme of *contemplation*, our intimate participation in Christ. Finally, we are *sent* into the world to do the work God has called us to do in ministry and in *mission*, incarnating God's saving Word in us through the power of the Spirit for the sake of the world. So the liturgical assembly meeting around Word and sacrament, from the vantage point of this book, is an exercise of corporate *lectio divina*, a communal holy conversation.

Liturgical scholarship has made much of the shape or patterns of liturgical worship in recent years, noting that the *ordo* is eminently cross-cultural and that the shape of the rite can accommodate a variety of particular expressions. Explorations connecting *lectio divina* with the pattern of the rite offer much to further an understanding of the *ordo* itself, making it possible to experience its rhythms at a deeper, experiential level.

Examining the overlap between *lectio divina* and liturgy advances the importance of the trajectory of the *ordo*; it is not enough to maintain simply the elements or pieces of liturgical worship. Rather, the pattern, the flow, the logic of the movements are critically important as, for example, we gather to encounter the Word, prayerfully respond, share contemplatively in the meal, and are sent out into the world to do our work. Without this flow, the rite is deprived of its central logic.

Furthermore, each movement of both the *ordo* and *lectio divina* involves distinct ways of being present to God in holy conversation, helping us to participate deeply in the Spirit's activity in liturgical worship. In terms of the *ordo*, the duality implied by *Gottesdienst* is operative in each movement of the liturgy. God acts; we respond. Martin Luther suggested that the human response to God consists of prayer and praise. For twentieth-century theologian Peter Brunner, the human part of the conversation involves prayer, confession, thanksgiving, and praise. In terms of the movements of *lectio divina*, the human side of the equation involves us in preparation, reading, meditation, prayer, contemplation, and sending:

- In the gathering, the Spirit calls us together and we respond by assembling and preparing ourselves for holy encounter.
- In the movement focusing on the Word, the Spirit of God speaks to us through the Word and we respond by listening attentively to and meditating on that Word and also by praying and offering ourselves in relation to that Word.
- In the meal, Christ hosts us and we host each other in Holy Communion, contemplatively enjoying both Christ's presence in our midst and our unifying presence with and to each other.
- In the sending, God propels us forth in the power of the Spirit and we go, having discerned what God would have us do in our mission in the world.

In terms of *lectio divina* as it is applied to the movements of the *ordo*, each movement expresses a different dimension of holy conversation.

- In preparation, we renew our acquaintance with ourselves and each other, attending to what is on our hearts and minds as the Spirit calls us together for worship, meanwhile heightening our anticipation of sacred encounter.
- As we hear the public reading of the Word, God's Spirit speaks to us, and we listen attentively and obediently.
- We also begin to respond in meditation, asking ourselves what God intends to proclaim, discerning a particular living word for us in our own circumstances: "Hear what the Spirit is saying to the churches."
- This meditation leads to prayer, another dimension of conversational presence, as we intercede for the needs of the world and prayerfully offer ourselves more fully to God in Christ in the power of the Spirit and to each other in the peace of Christ and in the giving of gifts.
- Then Christ calls us to intimate participation in his real presence, his body and blood known to us in, with, and under the signs of bread and wine. The union experienced in this table fellowship is our contemplative encounter, our wordless conversation with Christ, our friend, our brother, our lover.
- In the empowerment that is Christ's gift of himself to us, we then get up from the table to go into the world to do the work God has called us to do, to incarnate the very Word of God in ministry and mission, to be the enactment of our holy conversation in public witness. Or, as St. Francis of Assisi is believed to have said and by way of exhortation in the sending, "Preach the gospel at all times; if necessary use words."

This way of experiencing the liturgy, applying the sensibilities of *lectio divina* to the *ordo* and thereby striking up holy conversation, is a way of providing structure and discipline to our mental participation in the liturgy, a way of keeping our minds focused when otherwise our attention might wander. The discipline of connecting *lectio divina* to the rhythms of the liturgy can guard against the extraneous, less-than-holy conversations that inevitably occur while we worship. Most significantly, engaging the liturgy in the spirit of *lectio divina* is a way of plumbing the depths, going well beyond the mechanics of "doing the liturgy," standing and sitting, singing and praying, following along with the "script." Through this deep, mindful participation, the Spirit of God in Christ can form us, conform us to God's will and to the mind of Christ, reform us, and ultimately, over the long haul, transform us into the people God has called us to be. When we are deep conversation partners with the Spirit of the living God in our liturgical worship, we grow to resemble the very One who has called us, and we become more fully and authentically what we are, children of God, heirs with Christ. The stories we tell about ourselves come to grow in harmony with God's story of salvation. This is how the Spirit builds up the body of Christ for the work of ministry. In short, every act of liturgical worship conceived as holy conversation is Pentecost all over again, when the Spirit births proclamation of God's deeds of power for resurrection life and thereby changes people, making them disciples and members of Christian community. The opportunity before us is to claim the extraordinary gift that is ever before us when we gather for liturgy, often hidden in plain sight in the ordinary things we do. *Lectio divina* applied to the *ordo* gives focus and logic to this Spirit-inspired work of worshipful holy conversation.

Part Two

MEDITATIONS ON THE MASS

The second part of this book is in large measure an application of the princi-ples explored thus far to a particular liturgy: a *Mass for the Day of Pentecost*. In addition to being a common term for worship on the Lord's Day, the word *mass* also carries artistic overtones—think of the many musical masterpieces that are masses. In my own holy conversations about *Holy Conversation*, I will explore the artistry of particular texts and narrative trajectories and the spiritu-ality of the liturgical activities surrounding them as they interweave and blend together to create a lovely symphony of inspiration, many voices and sounds (*phone* in the Greek) coming together (*syn*) for renewed, broadened, and deep-ened understandings of liturgical worship. Mass also is a convincing designation for our considerations because it links liturgy to the mission of the church, *mass* deriving from the Latin *missio* and *mittere*, having to do with being sent off, dis-patched in the power of the Spirit for the work God has called us to do.

Reflecting on a specific mass gives a liturgical anchoring to the further explorations of spirituality for worship as I apply the movements of *lectio div-ina* to a particular liturgy, illustrating by way of concrete examples how these movements serve as another overlay for the *ordo*, further deepening our under-standing of liturgical worship and our participation in that worship. There is no liturgy in the abstract. Rather, liturgy is always contextualized in terms of specific days, seasons, places, cultures, circumstances, and ecclesial traditions. It is compellingly appropriate, given the thematic focus of this work on spirituality for worship, to offer reflections on a liturgy for the day of Pentecost to carry our holy conversation.

A word about the day of Pentecost as a liturgical festival. Easter, the day of resurrection, was the celebratory focus for the most ancient Christians. The day of Pentecost was less a separate festival than a culmination of Eastertide. Indeed, Pentecost is intimately tied to resurrection, especially in John's Gospel where it is the resurrected Jesus himself who imparts the gift of the Spirit. Furthermore, the Holy Spirit makes possible the proclamation of the resurrection in the book of Acts. In the Christian calendar, Pentecost is the fiftieth day of the Easter season—in the Greek, *pentekoste* literally means "fiftieth day." Like Easter, Pentecost had been a day for baptisms, especially for those unable to be baptized at the Easter Vigil. The baptismal association with Pentecost is suggested by an older name for the day, namely, Whitsunday—White Sunday—an allusion to the white garments worn at baptism. By the fourth century, Pentecost and Ascension Day came to be separate liturgical festivals with their own elaborations.

Recent years have seen renewed interest in the day of Pentecost as a significant festival in the liturgical year. Some congregations celebrate confirmation, or affirmation of baptism, on Pentecost. As the liturgical color for the day is red, popular devotion is expressed on the day of Pentecost sometimes by wearing red garments, adorning the church with red flowers and banners, and so on. In some settings, the liturgical celebration of the Vigil of Pentecost is observed. Perhaps this renewed focus on the day of Pentecost is in some measure connected with the current fascination with spirituality and the experience of the Holy Spirit.

What follows is an order of service that uses the lessons and propers appointed for the day of Pentecost, Year A, in the three-year cycle of the Revised Common Lectionary, along with hymns, musical selections, and other rites appropriate for the liturgical day, making the most of the connections among Easter, Pentecost, baptismal themes, and the mission of the church. The content of this order of service is consistent with current Lutheran practice as the texts are drawn primarily from a contemporary North American resource, *Evangelical Lutheran Worship*. Note, however, that the demarcation of the segments of the liturgy follows the trajectory of liturgical holy conversation inspired by the movements of *lectio divina*:

Mass for the Day of Pentecost

Praeparatio—Preparation

Gathering Conversation
Gathering Music: *Veni Sancte Spiritus*, Pentecost Sequence, Taizé
    Community
Thanksgiving for Baptism
Entrance Hymn: "God Is Here!"
Greeting
Kyrie Eleison—Lord, Have Mercy
Hymn of Praise: *Gloria in Excelsis Deo*
Prayer of the Day

Lectio—Reading

First Reading: Numbers 11:24-30
Psalm 104:24-34, 35b
Second Reading: Acts 2:1-21
Gospel Verse and Acclamation
Gospel: John 20:19-23

Meditatio—Meditation

Sermon
Hymn of the Day: "God of Tempest, God of Whirlwind"
Nicene Creed

Oratio—Prayer

Prayers of Intercession
Peace
Gathering and Presenting Gifts
Offertory Music: "Come Down, O Love Divine"
Offertory Canticle: "Let the Vineyards Be Fruitful"
Offertory Prayer

CONTEMPLATIO—CONTEMPLATION

Great Thanksgiving:
    Preface Dialogue
    Preface for Pentecost
    Sanctus—Holy, Holy, Holy
    Eucharistic Prayer
    Lord's Prayer
    Breaking Bread
    Agnus Dei—Lamb of God
The Communion
    Invitation to Communion
    Hymn during Communion: "Soul, Adorn Yourself with Gladness"
Postcommunion Canticle: *Nunc Dimittis*—Now, Lord, You Let Your
    Servant Go
Prayer after Communion

MISSIO—SENDING

Sending of Eucharistic Ministers
Affirmation of the Vocation of the Baptized in the World
Conversation Concerning the Church's Mission
Blessing
Sending Hymn: "The Spirit Sends Us Forth to Serve"
Dismissal

While this order of service is located in a particular tradition, namely Lutheranism, it points beyond itself to general principles and features of the liturgy of the Western church. That is to say, this *Mass for the Day of Pentecost* is common, rather ordinary, and ecumenically recognizable, and will thus be useful in guiding the reflections of readers representing a wide variety of Christian traditions that follow the *ordo* of the Western Rite. Lutherans share with many Christians a devotion to the basic patterns for liturgical celebration on the Lord's Day. Any number of musical, textual, and ceremonial styles—all reflecting the beautiful cultural and ethnic diversity of Christian churches—could be chosen and employed for a Pentecost mass. The principles of holy conversation persist and are applicable cross-culturally and ecumenically.

The following chapters take each movement of the liturgy in turn, concretely illustrating with particular hymn texts, biblical passages, and other regular features of the rite the principles of worshiping in the spirit of *lectio divina*. Again, this is a work about holy conversation, and the meditations that follow are themselves holy conversation, giving expression to the very kind of dialogue that is a central feature of spiritual worship.

In what follows, there is significant focus on *what* we do in liturgical holy conversation, but also attention to *how* we worship for deeper holy conversation. As I also reflect on how this liturgy might be undertaken in terms of exploring in some depth the dynamics of preparation, reading, meditation, prayer, contemplation, and sending, you will note a call for more silence in liturgy, allowing time, a kind of leisure and spaciousness, to accommodate our response in holy conversation. Likewise, there will be suggestions for how liturgical leaders and other worshipers can make the most of our internal and communal processes of holy conversation, following the distinctive ways of being present to the language of liturgy according to the logic of the movements of *lectio divina*. There will be suggestions about the judicious use of nonscripted discourse in the liturgy—while people gather and prepare for worship, in the context or in place of a traditional sermon, during the prayers of intercession, and during the sending as people discern their calling to embody the Word in mission—that holy conversation may explicitly and publicly involve the whole assembly.

I invite you as reader to think about how you engage in liturgical holy conversation in your place in ways consistent with your spiritual tradition, using the meditations that follow to inspire your own reflections, your own holy conversation. I have had the luxury over the course of an extended time period to explore the greater fullness of this *Mass for the Day of Pentecost*, dwelling with its particular texts and musing on how it might be offered in practice. In the actual hour or more that it would take to do and to experience this liturgy, there is no way for worshipers to plumb the depths that I have here explored in my greater, studied leisure. This is simply in the nature of divine-human phenomena—each and every liturgical event is far richer and fuller than we can consciously be aware of and experience in the moment.

It is also true that at any given liturgical assembly, there will be a wide diversity of people with varying levels of experience with the Christian tradition, ranging from first-time seekers to persons steeped in faith formation for decades. A wonderful thing about *lectio divina* in general, and in its application to liturgical participation in particular, is that it tends to democratize experience, as the evocations, insights, and experiences of each participant are all on a level playing field, each equally valued. Consider that reality as you read and engage in your own dialogue with me, thinking of your places of worship and the people with whom you worship.

When it is all said and done, though, a principal goal in offering the meditations that follow is this: to begin to lift the veil to reveal the greater depths of liturgical worship as a divine-human phenomenon, that when we gather in Christian assembly we may be moved to exclaim worshipfully with the apostle Paul, "O the depth of the riches and wisdom and knowledge of God! How unsearchable are [God's] judgments and how inscrutable [God's] ways!" (Rom. 11:33).

Chapter 4

PREPARATION

Just as practitioners prepare for divine encounter in *lectio divina*, worshipers also prepare themselves in parallel fashion for such encounter in liturgical worship. Liturgically, the gathering constitutes the assembly's activity in preparing to meet Christ in Word and sacraments. Spiritually speaking, gathering and preparation have to do with nurturing an openness to the presence of the living God made known to us through the means of grace. Practical enactments can serve to evoke a spirit of anticipation. Whatever we do in preparation for liturgy, practically and spiritually, serves to build the expectation that we will meet the living Christ in the liturgy, not unlike the encounter between the risen Jesus and the two disciples on the road to Emmaus, when he interpreted for them the Scriptures, when he sat at table with them, breaking bread, that they might recognize him (cf. Luke 24:13-35). Christian assembly is a liminal time, a time to be on the threshold between things human and things divine. It is a time to know the transcendence of God in the imminence of our communities. This time in assembly is characterized as *kairos*, popularly understood as decisive time, the high point of the Christian week when God breaks in upon us in our ordinary routines. Thus, gathering is not just a mechanical activity of getting people to their places on time.

GATHERING AND PREPARATION: BEFORE THE APPOINTED HOUR

The dynamics of gathering and preparation begin long before the appointed hour for the liturgy. Practically speaking, many people undertake a variety of activities. Musicians practice their music. The preaching minister prepares a sermon. Members of the altar guild attend to their particular preparations for the Holy Communion. Church office administrators print worship bulletins. And the list goes on. Think of your own setting and the significant number of people who share in the work of preparing for and implementing any given worship service. When worship goes well according to a routine, we may not be aware of the many hands that make for light work for the worship of God.

Additionally, various everyday preparations are undertaken that, with some imagination, can be viewed in connection with liturgy. We wake up, eat breakfast, get dressed, perhaps attend to the needs of other members of the family, and so on, and then find our way to the church. Is this not also part of the gathering rite, our preparation for liturgy by imaginative extension? I find evocative the vision of people driving, walking, and taking public transportation to the church, and see this as an aspect of the liturgical procession, formalized in the liturgy when worship leaders proceed into the chancel down a center aisle.

In terms of taking up liturgy as holy conversation, we have an opportunity to transcend the compartmentalizing tendencies common in our society where religious activity for an hour on Sunday is thought to be radically distinct from the rest of the week. This view proceeds in part from a belief that religion is a private affair separate from public life. Indeed, the principal assembly of Christians that typically occurs on Sunday is a pinnacle time, a high time, a fulcrum period. But it is also intimately related to the rest of the week and the whole lives of the people of God individually and communally. Human lives and circumstances can change dramatically in the course of a single week. The people of God bring with them to the liturgical hour tremendous amounts of experience at various levels of consciousness that can be considered and offered up to God in liturgy understood as holy conversation. In short, we bring long lists of potential conversation topics when we arrive at the threshold of the place for worship. Gathering rites at their best address aspects of experience beyond the mechanics of assembling people in the worship space, and are planned in such a way as to call attention to what is on our hearts and minds as we prepare for worship, building anticipation for sacred encounter.

Worship Planning as a Dimension of the Assembly's Gathering

The planning of worship services is a crucial aspect of preparation for worship. These planning activities, taken up during committee meetings and in other contexts, involve the preparatory tasks of presiding and assisting ministers or deacons, preachers, readers, acolytes, musicians and choristers, greeters, ushers, members of altar guilds, and others. A high percentage of the assemblies in smaller-membership congregations can be involved in the planning of, preparation for, and implementation of any given liturgy. This breadth of participation gives flesh to the understanding of liturgy as the work of the people.

Just as true worship involves going beyond the mechanics of "doing the liturgy," liturgical planning can at its best be more than a constellation of professional tasks to accomplish. That is to say, liturgical planning can itself be a spiritual discipline, a form of worship. When I served as a pastor of a congregation, I delighted in doing *lectio divina* with the lectionary texts appointed for the upcoming Sunday. This spiritually oriented, prayerful process informed not only the sermon I felt called to preach but also the selection of hymns for the day. The entire week, then, involved dwelling with the Word in anticipation of the Sunday assembly. In other words, my worship as holy conversation began early in the week and continued throughout the week only to find its culmination in the liturgy itself at the appointed hour on the following Sunday. Such preparatory activity is a wonderful way to redeem the burden of busy tasks to perform, turning them into occasions for spiritual refreshment and inspiration, a centerpiece of one's own spiritual life. This is a perspectival gift consistent with a view of Christian spirituality that emphasizes the sacredness of ordinary routine.

Viewing worship planning as a spiritual discipline can have the effect of freeing the mind for a kind of holy leisure that makes room for creativity—the kind of creativity that opens up fresh possibilities for choosing hymns and choral music, ceremony, and other liturgical activities to reinforce in complementary fashion the proclamation of the Word, each element of the liturgy building on others. Creative opportunities can be missed when worship planning consists of tasks to cross off a to-do list. Think of the meetings of worship committees as occasions for group sacred reading of, meditation on, and praying with appointed texts, a gathering around the seasonal themes for the day that is itself worshipful and less task oriented. Imagine meetings that include sitting in contemplative silence and simply being still with each other around the Word—a countercultural, life-giving witness in our results-oriented age.

In a similar vein, worship leaders may wish to reframe and view rehearsals for liturgy as themselves occasions for spiritual preparation for worship, and indeed, as worship itself. When lay readers examine the biblical texts they will read on Sunday, rehearsing their part in the holy drama, looking out for words that are difficult to pronounce, and so on, they can also transform this time, viewing it as part of their own prayerful preparation for liturgy, thus perhaps taking the edge off performance anxiety. Rehearsal thus conceived and reclaimed can result in liturgical leaders who are more fully present, authentic, and worshipful in their leadership. Holy conversation is well served by leaders who are themselves worshipers, holy conversationalists, and not merely performers.

Preparation for All of God's People

As liturgy is the work of all of God's people, the specific role of congregants who worship but who do not serve as worship leaders calls for renewed and full attention. How do all of the people of God prepare for liturgy as holy conversation, their living sacrifice, their spiritual worship? A critical dimension of that preparation involves programs of education about liturgy and worship, especially its spiritual aspects in going beyond the mechanics of doing liturgy, standing and sitting, and following along "in the script." Here is an opportunity—in adult forums and other educational settings—to claim teachable moments to remind ourselves that we bring all of who we are—consciously, preconsciously, and unconsciously—to the act of worship, our thoughts and feelings, memories and hopes, all of our experiences, relationships, the events of our lives. Most of this remains hidden to our conscious awareness. But there may be something in the language of the liturgy that will evoke memories that in connection to the Word of God make for our spiritual growth and formation in faith. It is the work of the people, all worshipers, to be prepared for such possibilities and thus to be attentive to what we bring to holy conversation.

As one of the preparatory activities in the time before liturgy or in the context of the gathering rite itself, consider what is on your heart and mind, what events of the previous week preoccupy you, that you hope God's Word will address in the day's liturgy. You may also wish to consider that which may hinder and inhibit your worship. What do you wish to leave at the door of the worship space that may interfere with the day's holy conversation? Also, consider these questions:

- How do you routinely prepare to come to church?
- Do you allow enough time to get ready in the morning?
- Are you rushed and thus bring that hurriedness with you to liturgy?
- In short, do your routines at home allow you to begin to be attentive to the divine possibilities of liturgical worship?
- Do they heighten your expectation that God in Christ in the power of the Holy Spirit will be made known to you in the means of grace?

Know, however, that God's Spirit, speaking through the language of liturgy, can break in and surprise even the harried and otherwise unprepared worshipers.

All of this preparatory and anticipatory activity has individual and communal dimensions. Individually we are members of the body of Christ, the church. In addition to remembering what we bring to liturgy as individuals, we also have the opportunity to consider the shared aspects of congregational life that we bring to liturgy together as a community. The experience of any given liturgy is affected by individual and communal experience prior to the worship hour. What has happened in the world in the prior week and in the local community where you live? What has happened in the congregation? What is the mood of the congregation? Are we in grief, or are we celebrating joys and hopefulness? The multiplicity of individual and shared experiences will affect worship and should be taken into consideration when preparing for holy conversation.

In personal preparations for liturgy, worshipers may want to engage in individual *lectio divina* or participate in congregational Bible studies on the appointed scriptural texts during the week prior to attending worship. Consider doing devotional exercises at home, such as silent prayer, prior to coming to liturgy. Pray through the order of the worship service in advance of coming to church. Any number of practical activities can prepare us for holy conversation. The main point is to engage in those practices that, again, heighten our expectation of the divine-human encounter and to call to mind what we bring to the act of worship, conceived as holy conversation.

Gathering: Silently or Aloud?

One of the compelling challenges of gathering rites as they are commonly enacted is the difficulty of attempting to address individual and internal dimensions of preparing for worship alongside the communal and external dimensions. Do we gather silently or with boisterous conversation? This challenge can generate a cognitive dissonance in the assembly, revealed in the common lament of many that people talk during prelude music when that time is intended for silently meditating and listening to carefully prepared music. This dilemma points to two crucial movements of the gathering: first, that worshipers are called to be attentive to their interior lives, and second, that they also are invited to attend to the communal dimensions of the gathering. We cannot easily do these activities simultaneously.

Gathering that makes the most of both individual and communal movements of the rite separates these two divergent but crucially important activities chronologically or spatially. There is indeed a place for actual conversation, if not to say exuberant chattiness, as members of the body of Christ gather to reacquaint themselves with one another again. We want to catch up with one another. We want to hear reports about how the surgery went for a loved one, about how others are doing in the hospital. We desire to learn about the outcome of the job interview, and so on. These streams of conversation are not trivial. Rather, they contribute concretely to the re-membering of the body after a week's diaspora in life, having been sent into the community in mission and ministry at the conclusion of the previous liturgy. Our conversations before the service may, for example, contribute content to the prayers of intercession later during the day's liturgy. These gathering conversations also can contribute to setting the agenda for the mission of the church in terms of, for example, identifying who in the assembly may need pastoral care.

In addition to these extroverted and communal aspects of gathering and the place of perhaps exuberant conversation, there is a legitimate call for silent spaciousness to allow room for worshipers to attend to their individual and interior lives. A prelude or other gathering music may nurture openness to these interior dimensions. The challenge and opportunity is to separate these activities and dynamics. Rather than perpetuating extended disagreements over conversations that take place during the musical prelude, let the people of God have conversation. Such conversation may even be scheduled by making time in nonscripted discourse for members of the church to share what in fact is on their hearts and minds this week. Then bells may be tolled, music played, silence observed, and the interior and individual aspects of the gathering can be incorporated into the gathering. The rite itself can then begin in earnest.

What follows are my own meditations on the potential meanings of elements of the gathering rite, exemplifying the kind of reflective work that all worshipers can undertake as expressions of their holy conversation, their spiritual worship. These reflections are intended to be evocative, leading you into deeper holy conversation and to your own reflections on the meanings of what we do when we gather.

PROCESSION: THE BODY'S MOVEMENT IN GATHERING

How the people of God physically gather and assemble is another crucial feature of preparation involving matters of ceremonial, choreography, staging, and movement. The actual gathering invokes the kinetic or physical dimensions of spirituality as lived, embodied, and enacted theology—spirituality and proclamation in motion, if you will. What specific physical activities might we employ to gather and assemble the people of God for liturgical worship understood as holy conversation? Often we imagine that worship leaders are solely responsible for the physical aspect of gathering, confining it to the procession of public ministers and choristers. Such processions can offer beautiful and evocative visual images to worshipers and can be wonderfully symbolic and iconic, thus aiding holy conversation. To reduce the question of physical gathering to the matter of a liturgical procession, however, is to compartmentalize a part of the whole worshipful experience, thus excluding other worshipers from an important aspect of liturgy as holy conversation. How is it, then, that the whole body gathers, not just liturgical leaders? How might everyone's bodies be used for worship? In Tanzania, for example, whole villages gather to greet honored guests on the outskirts of town, and the entire assembly dances its way to the place of meeting, accompanied by singing and drumming. Perhaps we would do well to emulate such traditions in our celebratory liturgical assemblies.

In terms of the relatedness of movement and physicality to the gathering of the whole assembly for worship and how this advances holy conversation, it is important also to consider how people physically greet one another to begin ordinary conversations. In some traditions, shaking hands is customary. This habit finds important parallels in our own liturgical assemblies when congregants greet one another and ministers as they enter the church building. In many non-Western cultures, people greet by bowing to one another. This, too, can be a meaningful expression of symbolic greeting when worshipers genuflect or bow to a cross passing in procession, for instance. Other traditions may include the lifting of hands in praise and honor of the Holy One.

Bowing, making the sign of the cross, kneeling in prayer in preparation for liturgy, and lifting hands in the *orans* position are all excellent and traditional ways of honoring the presence of the holy in worship. These gestures relate to worship understood as *proskynesis*, bowing down before holiness. However, there are other important forms of embodied worship that all worshipers, not just the leaders, might be encouraged to employ toward engaging all physical senses in worship. What do you see, hear, and smell? How is the sense of touch employed? What do you in fact taste or anticipate tasting—literally or metaphorically? Moreover, pay attention to your breathing; think of it as the Spirit of God in you, the very breath of life, the very breath of God. Attend to where in your body you carry stress, and pray that God would be present there. The more physically relaxed you are, the more open you are to the encounter with God in Word and sacraments.

GATHERING CONVERSATION:
ANNOUNCEMENTS AND NONSCRIPTED DISCOURSE

The Holy Spirit's presence and activity in the language of liturgical worship are not limited to words on the page. That is to say, nonscripted discourse in the form of announcements and other exchanges is important for advancing holy conversation. Worship planners and leaders often struggle over the place of verbal announcements and other forms of nonscripted language in the liturgy. I often hear colleagues comment on the awkwardness of verbal announcements, how they can interrupt the flow of liturgy, and how there is no easy solution to this dilemma. While I share similar views and have experienced such frustrations, I am convinced that the dilemma can be addressed by greater attention to the purpose of announcements specifically and the place of nonscripted language generally in the liturgy, and how this language serves the movements and trajectory of holy conversation. Think of these simple questions: How do verbal announcements fit the logic and the flow of the rhythms of worship? How do they advance and enhance worship as holy conversation? How might they inhibit holy conversation? What end do they serve?

In response to such questions, I would suggest that announcements pertaining to the programmatic activities of the church do not have a compelling place in the gathering rite. Calling attention to the mission and ministry-related efforts of the church makes far more sense in the context of the sending rite, at the conclusion of the worship service. If there are to be any announcements at the beginning of the liturgy during the gathering rite, I advocate for conversation or statements that seek to heighten expectation of the holiness of the encounter about to take place alongside comments that invite worshipers to explore and be attentive to what is on their hearts and minds as they come to liturgy. Moreover, actual conversation among those in the assembly might be formalized in place of programmatic announcements, so that the communal nature of the self-offering of worshipers might be heightened. The people of God may be encouraged to state publicly what is on their hearts and minds as the gathering begins.[1]

Regarding other expressions of nonscripted language here and at other points in the service, it is important for the presiding minister and others to exercise restraint in offering commentary. Less is more in this regard. The question should always be asked: What end does the offering of nonscripted comments serve? If it serves to showcase elements of performance or to advertise an event that mimics popular culture, it may not serve the end of holy conversation.

GATHERING MUSIC

The experience of the presence of God in the power of the Spirit can give birth to singing. Spirituality and music making have been deeply connected throughout the centuries. Upon their deliverance from the Egyptians in the safe passage through the waters of the sea, Moses and the Israelites erupted into song: "I will sing to the LORD, for he has triumphed gloriously; horse and rider he has thrown into the sea" (Exod. 15:1ff.). Singing is a natural response of thanksgiving for what God has done. Singing likewise is among the practices for which the apostle advocates in the letter to the Colossians: "Let the word of Christ dwell in you richly; teach and admonish one another in all wisdom; and with gratitude in your hearts sing psalms, hymns, and spiritual songs to God" (Col. 3:16). Singing, finally, is a feature of that time when we will gather around God in the heavenly realm as suggested by this vision in the Revelation to John:

> Then I looked, and I heard the voice of many angels surrounding the throne and the living creatures and the elders; they numbered myriads of myriads and thousands of thousands, singing with full voice, "Worthy is the Lamb that was slaughtered to receive power and wealth and

wisdom and might and honor and glory and blessing!" Then I heard
every creature in heaven and on earth and under the earth and in the
sea, and all that is in them, singing, "To the one seated on the throne
and to the Lamb be blessing and honor and glory and might forever
and ever!" And the four living creatures said, "Amen!" And the elders
fell down and worshiped. (Rev. 5:11-14)

This vision from Revelation conveys the spirit of our own gathering, when
our singing in assembly parallels and points to the singing assembly in
heaven.

Music serves to deepen the life of prayer, our holy conversation. Recall
again the popular saying "The one who sings prays twice." This proverb seems
to suggest that music carries prayer effectively from deeper levels to higher
and perhaps back again. Martin Luther also noted the power and centrality of
music in proclaiming the gospel:

> Thus it was not without reason that the fathers and prophets wanted
> nothing else to be associated as closely with the Word of God as music.
> Therefore, we have so many hymns and Psalms where message and
> music join to move the listener's soul. . . . After all, the gift of language
> combined with the gift of song was only given to man [sic] to let him
> know that he should praise God with both words and music, namely,
> by proclaiming [the Word of God] through music and by providing
> sweet melodies with words.[2]

Music and spirituality, then, are quite intimately associated. The embodied
qualities of making music carry the Word into ourselves and employ multiple
dimensions of our physicality and experience. Music making also involves
memory in profound ways. The associations we make linking certain texts
and tunes can evoke deep memories. These qualities suggest that music carries
divine voice and Word effectively for our authentic and deep apprehension
of that Word and of sacred experience. In short, music makes for deeper holy
conversation.

Moreover, the varieties of music styles, as well as different kinds of instru-
mentation and accompaniment, can carry us in our imaginations and experiences to the ends of the earth such that we can grow in appreciation for the
gift of cultural diversity. Music is wedded to our particular cultural and ethnic
traditions. Liturgies that employ various of kinds of musical traditions create
a symphony that conveys a sense of the rich tapestry that we are as human
family.

Given the power of music in connection with human experience and spirituality, and given the pervasive presence of music in Christian worship, music can be a significant tool in serving liturgy as holy conversation throughout the liturgy, from beginning to end. As we gather for the day's encounter, musical preludes can nurture the affective climate appropriate for the liturgical season and day. This music can deepen worshipers' meditative considerations and prayer as the people assemble for liturgy. We can apply the principles of *lectio divina* to our intentional listening to music (*audio divina*, if you will, or sacred listening), and through these means music can draw us into meditation, prayer, and contemplation.

Turning attention now to the particular service for the day of Pentecost, for example, as we gather on this festival day to prepare for the Spirit's visitation, music representing ethnic and cultural traditions from around the world is offered as the people assemble, calling attention to the multilingual, multicultural nature of the Pentecost event. After the gathering conversation, to finally and fully bring us together for worship, a choral ensemble sings a sequence for this day from the ecumenical and multinational Taizé community *in ostinato*, repeating this invitation again and again: *Veni Sancte Spiritus*—"Holy Spirit, come to us," an invitatory prayer that calls us together, expressing our shared yearnings on this festival day. The assembly spends this time in sacred listening, meditating on the words in repetition, being drawn to offer prayer, and resting in stillness as the ensemble sings on our behalf. This music contributes to bonding us together as the body of Christ, as we re-member each other and remember why we have assembled.

THANKSGIVING FOR BAPTISM

In many current liturgies, a great emphasis is placed on the remembrance of and thanksgiving for baptism in the gathering rite. Baptism is our initiation, our point of entry into holy conversation with God in Christ in the power of the Spirit. Baptism formally and organically begins the relationship with God as we are baptized into Christ's death and resurrection and receive the gift of the Holy Spirit. Liturgical rites for baptismal remembrance typically begin by invoking the trinitarian name of God; they then review salvation history, calling attention to the prominence of water as a symbol in creation and throughout this history. They may take place at the baptismal font, or they may use water when members of the assembly are sprinkled, as in the practice of asperges. When participants in the assembly are sprinkled, they may make the sign of the cross in remembrance of their baptism.

In order to engage the language and themes of rites of thanksgiving for baptism, make the most of personal associations with baptism in the spirit of meditation inspired by *lectio divina*, seeking personal meanings in response to baptismal themes. If your baptism happened in infancy, note that while you may not consciously remember your baptism, your young ears did indeed hear the trinitarian name of God invoked in connection with your own given name. Reflect that indeed water touched the very same flesh that you have now grown into and that your same nervous system responded to the stimulation of the water. Perhaps at some unconscious level or in a region of the mind, there is a memory of the experience of baptism, though that memory is inaccessible to your conscious mind. Recall other baptisms you have been present for, those of brothers or sisters, sons or daughters, and other friends and loved ones, highlighting the communal nature of baptism.

Anniversary of Baptism: A Personal Thanksgiving

As was my custom when I was a pastor in Pittsburgh, Pennsylvania, I took a break between Christmas and New Year's to visit family in Illinois. On one such occasion, I happened to be in my hometown for a family funeral. While I was milling about the nave after the service and luncheon, listening to one of my father's cousins play an impromptu recital on the newly renovated pipe organ, it suddenly struck me that it was thirty years ago to the day that I was baptized in that very room, at the very font at which I was looking, and some of the very people in the room at that moment of thankful remembrance were also present thirty years prior. It was remarkable serendipity of the Spirit to come to that realization. This occasion was one of my first realizations of the objective reality and objective claims of my baptism. In that room, at that font, with those family members, my head felt the splash of water and my infant ears heard the words, "Jonathan, I baptize you in the name of the Father, and of the Son, and of the Holy Spirit." Though I have no conscious memory of my baptism, the thirtieth anniversary remembrance made it experientially real for me for perhaps the first time. Perhaps you have had similar occasions of serendipitous, joyous remembrance. With thanksgiving, bring those to mind.

Water is a primordial human symbol and sign. Meditate on ordinary uses of water, for bathing, for recreation, for drinking, and so on, connecting these ordinary uses with the themes of baptism. Think of controversies surrounding water currently: water shortages in many regions of the world and the fact that a majority of the human population does not have adequate access to clean water. This awareness is fodder for meditative activity in connection to the mission of the church to serve the needy, the thirsty, in the living out of our baptismal covenants.

These invitations to reflection illustrate the kind of imaginative or meditative dialogue that is possible in the language and symbolism of rites of thanksgiving for baptism. It is this kind of imaginative work that deepens liturgy as holy conversation leading to the experience of meaningfulness that can result in worship, our awe-filled praise and thanksgiving for the immeasurable gifts known to us in water and the Word.

Turning attention again to the gathering for our service on the day of Pentecost, people make the sign of the cross, recalling that same sign applied to foreheads with the oil of chrism at baptism, as the presiding minister gathers the assembly "in the name of the Father, and of the Son, and of the Holy Spirit." The presiding minister next invites the assembly's thanksgiving for baptism: "Joined to Christ in the waters of baptism, we are clothed with God's mercy and forgiveness. Let us give thanks for the gift of baptism." Here in preparatory holy conversation as we gather as the people of God, we may pause to "fill in the blanks" with our own particular petitions of thanks for baptism, our own and that of loved ones. The presiding minister then continues with this address and thanksgiving while water is poured into the font:

> We give you thanks, O God, for in the beginning your Spirit moved over the waters and by your Word you created the world, calling forth life in which you took delight. Through the waters of the flood you delivered Noah and his family. Through the sea you led your people Israel from slavery into freedom. At the river your Son was baptized by John and anointed with the Holy Spirit. By water and your Word you claim us as daughters and sons, making us heirs of your promise and servants of all. We praise you for the gift of water that sustains life, and above all we praise you for the gift of new life in Jesus Christ. Shower us with your Spirit, and renew our lives with your forgiveness, grace, and love. To you be given honor and praise through Jesus Christ our Lord in the unity of the Holy Spirit, now and forever. Amen.[3]

How does this rite of thanksgiving for baptism serve to gather us in holy conversation? It sets our baptism in the context of the whole fabric of God's salvation history, God's participation in human events, thus calling attention to the fact that we participate even now in an extraordinary divine reality as we come together in God's trinitarian name. This serves to build anticipation for what is yet to come in the liturgy as that same God is present to us in Word and sacrament.

On the day of Pentecost we remember in particular the presence of God's Spirit in connection to water throughout salvation history. The Spirit broods over the waters at creation. The waters of the flood had a purgative effect as Noah and his family were delivered from devastation. In that story, the dove— later a sign of the coming of the Spirit at Jesus' own baptism—was a sign of promise that the flood was over, that it was safe to return to dry land. The people of Israel were led through the waters of the sea in the exodus, guided also by a pillar of fire, fire itself a sign of the Spirit's presence, as in the tongues as of fire on the day of Pentecost. The Spirit is present again at Jesus' baptism in the waters of the river Jordan to anoint him and commission him for his ministry and mission. "In those days Jesus came from Nazareth of Galilee and was baptized by John in the Jordan. And just as he was coming up out of the water, he saw the heavens torn apart and the Spirit descending like a dove on him. And a voice came from heaven, 'You are my Son, the Beloved; with you I am well pleased' " (Mark 1:9-11).

All of these events of divine intervention connect up with our own baptisms, our own visitations from the Spirit—"You are my sons, my daughters, the beloved"—our own experience of Pentecost, the Spirit gifting us for proclamation of the Gospel. As the rite of Thanksgiving for Baptism acknowledges before God, "By water and your Word you claim us as daughters and sons, making us heirs of your promise and servants of all"—we are heirs and servants, qualities suggestive of covenant relationship. Indeed, thanksgiving for baptism implies that with thanks we again pledge to live according to the baptismal covenant that we affirm, "to live among God's faithful people, to hear the word of God and share in the Lord's supper, to proclaim the good news of God in Christ through word and deed, to serve all people, following the example of Jesus, and to strive for justice and peace in all the earth."[4] In other words, we pledge to live according to the principles of the Spirit-led community outlined in Acts 2. In the preparatory holy conversation on the festival of Pentecost, we again seek the Spirit's visitation: "Shower us with your Spirit, and renew our lives with your forgiveness, grace, and love." Worship continues as the assembly is sprinkled with the waters of spiritual renewal.

Confession and Forgiveness

In many traditions, worship services often begin with an order for confession and forgiveness that can be understood as a preparatory rite undertaken in advance of the actual service. The use of this rite can be seasonal, especially those liturgical seasons and occasions that are more penitential in nature. The celebratory tone of the rite of Thanksgiving for Baptism is more appropriate on a festival such as the day of Pentecost. Like Thanksgiving for Baptism, the rite for confession and forgiveness has its contextualization also in baptismal themes and can take place at the font. The assembly invokes the trinitarian name of God, the people make the sign of the cross in baptismal remembrance, a minister invites confession and the people stand or kneel, and after a period of silence for reflection, the people share together in a general confession of sins that covers a multitude of possible transgressions, sins in "thought, word, and deed . . . what we have done . . . and have left undone," and so on. Then an ordained minister offers absolution.

Common experience suggests that many people do plenary confession and forgiveness by rote, speaking the well-known and perhaps memorized words without giving significant thought to the specificity of sins confessed. Here, then, is an opportunity to engage in deep conversation and dialogue with God. Each word of the confession can be a linguistic icon, a sign pointing beyond itself to particular circumstances in our lives when we give voice to the words, confessing sins in thought, word, and deed. What are the particular thoughts that we count as sinful? What specific words have we spoken that have offended and contributed to broken relationships? What deeds have we in fact done and what things have we refrained from doing that we would name as our particular sins of the day, of the week? The silence for reflection invites very specific responses to these questions, that we may fill in the blanks, so to speak, taking our conversational engagement with the language of worship to a deeper level. This two-way interaction mirrors the movements of *lectio divina*. We read the words of the confession, meditate on their particular meanings for us, and pray the prayer of confession, which then becomes a prayer of the heart when we apply the words to our own lives. In the words of absolution that follow, we may know a sense of contemplative reconnection to God through Christ in the Spirit, contemplation involving our being reunited to God and to others. Implicit in the dynamics of confession and absolution is the call to do our part in reestablishing and incarnating right relationships with the ones we have wronged, to do our part in the hard work of reconciliation, after having known reconciliation with God through this rite for confession and forgiveness.

Entrance Hymn

Music at the gathering may include an entrance hymn during which the assembly is sprinkled with the waters of baptismal thanksgiving and remembrance, and liturgical ministers take their places to lead the service. Such a hymn can heighten the people's anticipation of the sacred encounter about to take place, as recounted in the following hymn text by Fred Pratt Green, a twentieth-century English Methodist bishop. This poetry, appropriate for the day of Pentecost, is both proclamation and prayer addressed to God, and describes well the dynamics of gathering as preparation for a sacred meeting:

> God is here! As we your people
> meet to offer praise and prayer,
> may we find in fuller measure
> what it is in Christ we share.
> Here, as in the world around us,
> all our varied skills and arts
> wait the coming of the Spirit
> into open minds and hearts.
>
> Here are symbols to remind us
> of our life-long need of grace;
> here are table, font, and pulpit;
> here the cross has central place.
> Here in honesty of preaching,
> here in silence, as in speech,
> here, in newness and renewal,
> God the Spirit comes to each.
>
> Here our children find a welcome
> in the Shepherd's flock and fold;
> here as bread and wine are taken,
> Christ sustains us as of old.
> Here the servants of the Servant
> seek in worship to explore
> what it means in daily living
> to believe and to adore.
>
> Lord of all, of church and kingdom,
> in an age of change and doubt,

keep us faithful to the gospel;
help us work your purpose out.
Here, in this day's dedication,
all we have to give, receive;
we, who cannot live without you,
we adore you! We believe![5]

God is here! Twelve times in these four stanzas "here" is used to emphasize the specificity of sacred space and the immanence of God's presence in our particular places for assembly, especially when those places involve people assembling around table, font, pulpit, cross, preaching, bread and wine, silence, and speech—means through which the Spirit of God in Christ "comes to each" in "open minds and hearts." This hymn text in the evocative medium of poetry conveys the tone of the gathering rite particularly in building anticipation for sacred encounter in the means of grace to follow, and also conveys that this encounter will indeed happen *here*, not in the abstract, but in the particularities of our lives in this community now.

Fred Pratt Green's text suggests a desire to go deeper in our worship as we gather: "As we your people meet to offer praise and prayer, may we find in fuller measure what it is in Christ we share." It is the Spirit for whom we wait who will take us to these deeper, worshipful places through the means of grace and through our own discerning holy conversation as "servants of the Servant seek in worship to explore what it means in daily living to believe and to adore." Through our meditation on God's Word and on the symbols of faith, we seek to discern God's will for us—"help us work your purpose out." Our Spirit-led liturgy ends in the posture of worship, *proskynesis*, and in our confession of faith, as we trustingly offer as a living sacrifice to God all that we are, which itself, we realize, is God's gift to us—"Here, in this day's dedication, all we have to give, receive; we, who cannot live without you, we adore you! We believe!"

THE GREETING

There are certainly a variety of ways of greeting the assembly as people gather for worship—invocations, acclamations, calls to worship that are specifically written or locally composed and may relate specifically to the liturgical calendar—but the main point is to greet those gathered and to note in whose name we gather. Our liturgy for the day of Pentecost echoes the words the apostle Paul used to conclude his second letter to the Corinthians: "The grace of our Lord Jesus Christ, the love of God and the communion of the Holy

Spirit be with you all." In the context of the liturgy, this exchange is itself conversation between the presiding minister and the whole assembly as they reply,
"And also with you," and expresses a most profound wish that all may know
the grace, love, and communion of the Triune God. A simple greeting contains
the depth of Christian theological affirmations. As liturgical theologian Philip
Pfatteicher suggests:

> The grace of Christ leads to the love of the Father, which yields par-
> ticipation in the Spirit and produces communion between God and
> people. It is thus a summary of the principal gifts of the three persons
> of the Holy Trinity which will be unfolded as the liturgy progresses.
> Like an overture to an opera, this verse of apostolic greeting intro-
> duces the themes which will be developed as the work proceeds and
> by this statement prepares the assembly for what follows, alerting
> them to the significant themes.[6]

KYRIE ELEISON—LORD, HAVE MERCY

"Lord, have mercy"—in the Greek, *kyrie eleison*—is an ancient cry that predates Christian times and usage. It was a plea for favor from the emperor. It
was an exclamation to the sun god at dawn. "Lord, have mercy" is akin to
"Hosanna" in the Hebrew, "Save now." It appears in the psalms: "To you I lift
up my eyes, O you who are enthroned in the heavens! As the eyes of servants
look to the hand of their master, as the eyes of a maid to the hand of her mis-
tress, so our eyes look to the LORD our God, until he has mercy upon us. Have
mercy upon us, O LORD, have mercy upon us" (Ps. 123:1-3a).

Jesus heard the pleas from those whom he encountered along the roads
who sought healing. "Bartimaeus son of Timaeus, a blind beggar, was sitting
by the roadside. When he heard that it was Jesus of Nazareth, he began to
shout out and say, 'Jesus, Son of David, have mercy on me!' Many sternly
ordered him to be quiet, but he cried out even more loudly, 'Son of David, have
mercy on me!'" (Mark 10:46-48). His cries got Jesus' attention and compassion: "'Go; your faith has made you well.' Immediately he regained his sight
and followed him on the way" (Mark 10:52). The insistent cries of Bartimaeus
and other figures from the Bible echo through the centuries in our own pleas,
"Lord, have mercy." In our liturgies we, too, gather anticipating healing, only
then in the end also to be sent to follow on the way.

By the fourth century, the *Kyrie Eleison* found its way formally into the
church's liturgy in the East in the form of a call and response between deacons

and the assembly. This ancient pattern is evident in this litany adapted from the Byzantine Great Litany where leader and assembly reply to each other in dialogue:

> In peace, let us pray to the Lord.
> *Lord, have mercy.*
> For the peace from above, and for our salvation, let us pray to the Lord.
> *Lord, have mercy.*
> For the peace of the whole world, for the well-being of the church of God, and for the unity of all, let us pray to the Lord.
> *Lord, have mercy.*
> For this holy house, and for all who offer here their worship and praise, let us pray to the Lord.
> *Lord, have mercy.*
> Help, save, comfort, and defend us, gracious Lord. *Amen.*[7]

This call-and-response quality binds leader and assembly to each other, especially when this litany is sung and "... Lord. Lord ..." overlaps, blending into one cry of all. Holy conversation here is invited by the leader—"Let us pray to the Lord"—and the assembly then replies by addressing God—"Lord, have mercy." Our eyes look to each other and then to the heavens. Moreover, there is power in the fourfold repetition, as we *re-petition* God, again and again, seeking God's favor. *Petition*, as it emerges from the Latin *petere*, captures the multivalent spirit of our anticipatory prayer: to head for, strive after, aim at, demand, require, exact, claim, sue for, beg, entreat, search for, run after, and chase. Such is the spirit in which we gather.

In this version of the *Kyrie Eleison*, we seek heavenly peace for our varied contexts, all of which we share in simultaneously: our global and local contextualizations—"For the peace from above . . . For the peace of the whole world . . . For this holy house, and for all who offer here their worship and praise . . ." We call to mind varied needs concerning peace, salvation, world, church, unity, and the particular concerns of the local assembly. The day—the festival of Pentecost and the needs specific to the calendar and year in human history—carries plenty of concerns that we may fill the imaginative space in our praying and plea-making for world and church and the local assembly.

Each word of petition in this litany-style *Kyrie* can bring to mind particular situations that call for us to implore God for mercy. In asking for peace for the whole world, think of the many situations throughout the globe that cause people to cry out for peace. Praying for the well-being of the church evokes thoughts of those many situations in which the church is not as healthy and whole as it might be. Calling for unity provokes attention to that which is divided. "For this holy house, and for all who offer here their worship and praise"—here is occasion to fill in many particular imaginative blanks in the life of your own congregation and in the lives of those who are in fact gathered with you for the liturgical assembly. We sing and pray the *Kyrie* quickly in gathering, but it may be that on a particular day something or someone will come to mind as you sing. This is the work of meditative dialogue that reveals liturgy as holy conversation.

We make our plea for peace, God's *shalom*, that holistic, all-encompassing well-being that is not just the absence of strife but a condition that benefits everyone in all circumstances. It is this gift of peace that we anticipate later in the liturgy, the sharing of Christ's peace, which itself forms a centerpiece of the coming of the gift of the Holy Spirit in John, the Gospel passage appointed for the day of Pentecost: "Jesus said to them again, 'Peace be with you. As the Father has sent me, so I send you. . . . If you forgive the sins of any, they are forgiven them; if you retain the sins of any, they are retained'" (John 20:21, 23). In this gathering moment of holy conversation, as we beg for God's mercy, we recognize that indeed we, too, shall be empowered by Christ's presence in the Spirit and through his own gift of peace to share in the reconciling work of ministry and mission that will contribute to the world's knowing some measure of God's *shalom*.

GLORIA IN EXCELSIS DEO—THE HYMN OF PRAISE

Gathering music may include any number of texts for a hymn of praise. In the traditional Western Rite of the church, the *Gloria in Excelsis Deo* follows the *Kyrie* on many festival days. *Gloria in Excelsis*, known as the angelic hymn and also as the greater doxology in contrast to the *Gloria Patri*, the lesser doxology, has been used as a canticle in the church's liturgies since the patristic period. One tradition has it that in the second century, Pope Telesophorus was the first to use this canticle at Midnight Mass at Christmas. By the end of the eleventh century, its use was common in festival masses. We thus sing now in the long tradition of and in company with the saints through the centuries.

The exclamation of "Glory to God in the highest, and peace to God's people on earth" paraphrases the angelic song to the shepherds' announcement of the birth of Jesus, "Glory to God in the highest heaven, and on earth peace among those whom he favors!" (Luke 2:14). This cry of the angels brings to mind themes of Christmas, of the incarnation, when through the intervention of the Holy Spirit at the annunciation, the virgin Mary came to be with child. On the Feast of the Nativity, the very Word of God became flesh, marking the entry of the spiritual realm into embodied human reality, its own pentecostal, en-Spirited moment.

The antiphon also anticipates Passiontide in the cry of the crowds when Jesus entered Jerusalem at the end of his earthly life:

> As he was now approaching the path down from the Mount of Olives, the whole multitude of the disciples began to praise God joyfully with a loud voice for all the deeds of power that they had seen, saying, "Blessed is the king who comes in the name of the Lord! Peace in heaven, and glory in the highest heaven!" Some of the Pharisees in the crowd said to him, "Teacher, order your disciples to stop." He answered, "I tell you, if these were silent, the stones would shout out." (Luke 19:37-40)

With the whole salvation event of Christ in mind, from birth to its conclusion, when things human were joined to things divine, we shout and we sing, "Glory to God in the highest, and peace to God's people on earth."

This antiphon is followed by a text that is not from the Scriptures, but which resembles biblical psalms and canticles and addresses both God and Jesus Christ with the Holy Spirit in trinitarian relationship:

> Lord God, heavenly King, almighty God and Father, we worship you, we give you thanks, we praise you for your glory. Lord Jesus Christ, only Son of the Father, Lord God, Lamb of God, you take away the sin of the world: have mercy on us; you are seated at the right hand of the Father: receive our prayer. For you alone are the Holy One, you alone are the Lord, you alone are the Most High, Jesus Christ, with the Holy Spirit, in the glory of God the Father. Amen.[8]

This whole hymn serves as an extension of and a trinitarian elaboration on the biblical antiphon "Glory to God in the highest." With its naming of God and indications of the divine titles—"Lord God, heavenly King, almighty God and Father . . . Lord Jesus Christ, only Son of the Father . . . Lamb of God . . . Holy One . . . Lord . . . Most High . . . with the Holy Spirit"—we have still greater clarity about the name in which we gather. The spirit of the *Gloria in Excelsis* likewise has parallels in the affirmations of the Christ hymn, itself perhaps an early liturgical text, found in Paul's letter to the Philippians. To call attention to this parallel deepens our engagement with the *Gloria* itself: "Therefore God also highly exalted him and gave him the name that is above every name, so that at the name of Jesus every knee should bend, in heaven and on earth and under the earth, and every tongue should confess that Jesus Christ is Lord, to the glory of God the Father" (Phil. 2:9-11). This worshipful end is also conveyed in the *Gloria*: "We worship you, we give you thanks, we praise you for your glory." The *Gloria in Excelsis* is itself an expression of worship. When we sing it we do our own *proskynesis*, bending the knee, bowing before the one whom we confess as Lord, anticipating the further encounter with this one in the day's festival gathering around Word and sacrament.

Furthermore, the *Gloria* draws our attention in anticipation to a later segment of the liturgy, the hymn at the breaking of the bread, *Agnus Dei*: "Lamb of God, you take away the sin of the world: have mercy on us." So it is also in the *Gloria* we make our requests known: "Have mercy on us . . . receive our prayer." We have before us a vision of the greater trajectory of the liturgy that itself points to the whole Christ event.

As we sing the *Gloria* in our own day, in addressing and petitioning God, we also share in holy conversation with the angels and the shepherds at Christmas, and with the multitudes in Jerusalem during Jesus' last days. Likewise, we join our voices with millions of Christians who have sung these very same words in various tongues, and in numerous nations and cultures, carried by varied styles of music throughout the centuries, a poignant reminder in shared text that we do not engage in liturgy as holy conversation by ourselves. Indeed, we are joined in song by countless hosts in heaven and on earth.

THE PRAYER OF THE DAY

The Prayer of the Day, often appropriately called the Collect (pronounced "KA-likt"), serves to gather or "collect" our thoughts toward the seasonal and scripturally thematic focus for the day. This brief prayer calls attention to themes for the day's holy conversation. After perhaps a few moments of silence, the presiding minister on behalf of all collects the self-offering of all the people in what they have brought with them to this holy day as they now have assembled for worship, for holy conversation. With this summary prayer, the people of God have been called by God, have gathered, and are now prepared to be attentive to meet God in the Word in the readings appointed for the day.

The Prayer of the Day often follows a set pattern that includes an initial address to God, calling attention to particular attributes or activities that God has done, petitioning God to address human need, and concluding with a doxology or thanksgiving. A Christian theology of prayer is embedded in the common way of structuring this prayer form. We pray to God, through Jesus Christ, with or in the power of the Spirit. Our *Amen* is joined by all the faithful, as we recognize that we pray also in the communion of saints. This common pattern and these theological sensibilities are identifiable in this classic prayer for the day of Pentecost:

> O God, on this day you open the hearts of your faithful people by sending into us your Holy Spirit. Direct us by the light of that Spirit, that we may have a right judgment in all things and rejoice at all times in your peace, through Jesus Christ, your Son and our Lord, who lives and reigns with you and the Holy Spirit, one God, now and forever. Amen.[9]

This particular prayer originated in a sacramentary attributed to Pope Gregory I, who was bishop of Rome from 590 to 604 C.E., and was appointed for use during the Morning Mass on Pentecost at St. Peter's Basilica. With ancient origins, this prayer, like many traditional collects, has an ecumenical history of usage as it has been a collect appointed for the festival of Pentecost in a number of versions of prayer and service books in the Latin churches of the West.

The prayer recognizes God's action in opening the heart, the seat of the will and our deepest identity, but often hardened due to our stubborn resistance, through the sending of the Holy Spirit at Pentecost. It was this opening of hearts that also led to unstopping of tongues and opening of mouths for the proclamation of the gospel on the day of Pentecost, recalling and anticipating the hearing of the story in Acts. Now we pray again for the Spirit's direction in guiding our discernment—"that we may have a right judgment in all things." We likewise pray that the light of the Spirit will be the cause of our rejoicing at all times in peace. The apostle Paul recognizes the importance of the Spirit's activity in making for joy, even in the circumstances of his imprisonment, as he addresses the Philippians: "Yes, and I will continue to rejoice, for I know that through your prayers and the help of the Spirit of Jesus Christ this will turn out for my deliverance" (Phil. 1:18b-19). So it is that Paul, in the power of the Spirit, can exhort the assembly at Philippi, "Rejoice in the Lord always; again I will say, Rejoice" (Phil. 4:4), concluding that "the peace of God, which surpasses all understanding, will guard your hearts and your minds in Christ Jesus" (Phil. 4:7). It is this joyful peace which we, in large measure, celebrate on the day of Pentecost, when Jesus breathes on his disciples to impart the gift of his Spirit and when the tongues as of fire descend to generate the proclamation of good news. Through this collect our minds and hearts are drawn to attend to the public reading of the stories for the day's festivities. It is to this service of readings and the dynamics of spiritual reading that we now turn.

Chapter 5

READING

R eading is a basic Christian spiritual discipline, as our faith is a tradition of the book, the Bible. As a corollary to this fact, listening attentively to the Word of God read aloud in assembly is also a central feature of Christian spirituality. Our liturgical practice reverberates with the age of oral tradition, when texts were scarce and communities had to rely on the aural experience of the public reading of Scripture. Indeed, our liturgical service of readings relates intimately to the ancient practice of the Jewish synagogue, the liturgy of which was centered on attending to God's scriptural Word.

Reading is a kind of listening to texts even as listening to texts read aloud is a kind of reading, a practice that predates the age when most people could in fact actually read. As is the case when people read texts on the printed page, the aural experience involves seeking understanding, listening for the meanings of what is heard. This activity of seeking understanding and meaning constitutes a crucial feature of God's Word understood as living and active (Heb. 4:12), offering to us an ongoing revelation centered in the once-and-for-all Revelation of Scripture, and applicable to our day. Our Spirit-inspired, active engagement in listening for what God intends to say through Scripture, and then discerning what that means for us in our own circumstances, is perhaps part of

what Jesus meant when he promised in the Gospel of John that the Holy Spirit
will lead us into all truth (John 14:26; 16:12-13).

Beyond the mechanics of reading lessons aloud, God's Word here begins
to make its claim on us as obedient (*obedience* has a Latin root, *audire*, meaning "to hear") and faithful listeners, particularly as the Word begins to intersect with the particularities of our circumstances, attention to which has been
drawn in the time of preparation at the gathering rite—What have we brought
with us to this assembly? What is on our hearts and minds? We may not even
be consciously aware of the Spirit's quickening activity, but at perhaps preconscious levels, holy conversation begins to happen in the intersection between
biblical narratives and our lives. This dialogical activity lays the foundation
for the more intentional work of meditation to be taken up in the next movement of the liturgy, when a sermon or another form of interpretive discourse is
undertaken. First, we carefully attend to the public reading of Scripture as God
takes the lead in speaking in holy conversation.

God's Spirit is carried on the pages of Scripture and as the biblical stories
are told anew in our public assemblies. In this movement of liturgical holy conversation, God's voice in the Word, particularly the Spirit's speaking through
that Word, is primary. That is to say, God is the primary conversation partner
at this point in the liturgy. The human role is secondary and focused on obedient listening toward receiving the fullness of this proclamation; we attempt to
discern what God intends objectively to communicate. Human participation
in this aspect of holy conversation is not absent, however. Those who read
scriptural passages aloud are also partners in conversation, as are all the others
in assembly who hear the Word and listen attentively.

THE ROLE OF READERS IN HOLY CONVERSATION

The act of public reading lays before the assembly the very Word of God, thus
continuing the holy conversation and providing the most profound content of
that conversation. The role of the lectors is thus a crucial one, and cannot be
underestimated, for they serve as vessels through which God's voice mediated
in the Scriptures is heard, and they share in the work of nurturing deepened
holy conversation on behalf of the whole assembly. That the Holy Spirit would
so employ public readers of Scripture is a remarkable gift indeed and might
cause us to tremble in a posture of true worship, bowing before the Almighty
in this sacred moment.

Public reading of Scripture also anticipates the work of meditation when
hearers discern what God intends to say and we begin to seek meaning for our

time in the sense of ongoing revelation. Reading aloud contributes to this discernment as an act of interpretation in terms of pacing, tone of voice, emphasis, and so on. Calling attention by way of emphasis to a particular word in public reading can suggest the importance of that word in contrast to others, and this, then, is an interpretive act.

The Spirituality of Public Reading

The power and significance of the presence of public readers call for attention to the formation of those readers. We might think more in terms of the formation of readers rather than their training, though training in the technicalities of public reading is important. Attention to the spirituality of public reading suggests encouraging times for dwelling with the Word and not simply rehearsing for a kind of public performance. The spirituality of public reading suggests a call to slow down, to be more fully present to the Spirit speaking in the Word in such a way as to invite more active listening on the part of members of the assembly. The spirituality of public reading suggests that the reader is an iconic figure pointing beyond the self to the divine voice that uses the reader as vessel. What, then, is the extent to which public reading should be dramatic? An overly dramatic presence can point to itself and less to the sacred voice. Yet an understated presence or one that is not sensitive to the drama of public reading in the sense of the divine voice being carried in the act of reading can likewise inhibit the assembly's apprehension of the sacredness of public reading. A faithful goal may be for readers to get out of the way of themselves, nurturing as transparent a presence as possible, that the assembly's attention remains clearly focused on the biblical narrative.

THE ROLE OF LISTENERS

In the service of deepening the experience of liturgy as holy conversation, listeners also have a crucial role, particularly at this point in nurturing their openness to receiving the fullness of revelation that God offers in the public reading of biblical narratives. We who listen, then, are invited to attend to the Word in the spirit that characterizes our love for God, that is, with our whole heart, soul, mind, and strength (Mark 12:30). Strive to discern what God intends to communicate and reveal in the passage. Bring to the encounter your study of biblical texts. Lifelong participation in Bible study deepens holy conversation.

Also listen for particular words, phrases, ideas, and images that evoke your thoughts, feelings, memories, and imaginations, features of the story that speak to you in special ways and to which you are drawn. These evocations may be a sign of the Spirit's quickening work, the Spirit thereby speaking a word to you in our own time. This proclamation can be an expression of God's living Word to us so that we might know continued formation in that Word and perhaps also transformation by that Word. Through such engagement with the Word, we are on holy ground indeed. If we as the people of God can claim liturgy as holy conversation, we all, each one of us, can be actively engaged in meditative response to the readings, can hang on every word, and can relish the echoes of the Word in meditative silence as if our very lives depend on the deep listening. This is in fact what we confess: that our lives do indeed depend on this life-giving Word from God.

Making Room for Holy Conversation with the Word

A challenge in our age, when we are constantly bombarded with information and verbiage, is how to make the most of the multiple scriptural passages present in typical liturgies, and to do so meaningfully. This can seem like a lot of Scripture in the space of what is commonly an hour-long service. How do we guard against feeling inundated by too many words in a society beleaguered with too much information? How do we meaningfully attend to the Scriptures when many in our assemblies do not have extensive familiarity with the Bible? Liturgical worship understood as holy conversation calls us to listen attentively to the Scriptures, and invites practice that makes room for meditative considerations.

If, indeed, attending to the public reading of Scripture is a centerpiece of liturgy as holy conversation, then we do well to make room and give time for that conversation to happen. This claiming of time calls for more generous use of silence in our liturgies. The public reading of each passage of the lectionary can be followed by time for silent meditation. This silence is not empty space, however. Rather, it is filled with the echoes and the reverberations of the Word that was just read.

Maintaining space for silent reflection after each reading is countercultural in this season of our own mainstream culture's existence. Many in the assembly might be uncomfortable with this silence, finding it anxiety provoking. Yet one of the central features of the church's current mission in a culture that is overstimulated with noise and constant verbiage is the call to make room for silent spaciousness. A calling of our age is to live more comfortably with silence, engaging silence for deeper spiritual encounter as the Word continues to echo in our minds, sinking into the deeper levels of our consciousness.

The Lectionary and Holy Conversation

In traditions that follow the lectionary, that is, regular cycles of biblical texts read on particular days, the liturgy of the Word usually includes readings from the Hebrew Bible, a psalm or other responsive reading, a passage from New Testament literature, and a reading from one of the Gospels. The use of lectionaries is an ancient Christian practice. By the fourth century, it was common for liturgies to include readings from the Old and New Testaments and the Gospels, and likewise during this period, particular Sundays in the church year came to have specially appointed texts. The first complete lectionaries date from the seventh century. Lectionaries that feature three-year cycles of texts, in common ecumenical use today, emerged out of the era of the Second Vatican Council. Its concern was that the people of God should have a broader exposure to biblical material—exposure to a cross-section of Scripture, including varieties of literature types, and central biblical stories.

When a Sunday liturgy contains readings from both testaments, a psalm, and a passage from one of the Gospels, God's voice and speech are conveyed by the Spirit in profound and extensive ways. The movement of the liturgy during which these passages are publicly read is full of divine presence, sometimes overwhelmingly so if indeed we attend to the textual interconnections deeply. The sheer weight of God's Word may inspire us to bow down before God in the holiness of these moments in true worship. If we confess that God speaks through means and a principal means of this speech is the word of Scripture, then including multiple readings from the Bible provides an extensive, broad, and deep exposure to the divine voice, more perhaps than in liturgies where the Bible has a diminished presence, perhaps in the form of a single passage. It may be simplistic to suggest that God is more present when liturgies include more Scripture. After all, how can you measure the weight of God's Word in relation to numbers of texts or words on the page? But it can be cause for concern when Scripture is minimally present in some worship movements in our day.

The full range of readings gives us a sense of God's presence throughout human history. Readings from the Hebrew Scriptures reveal Christian continuity with the Jewish tradition. Singing psalms anchors us in the primary hymnbook of both Judaism and Christianity, and evokes a sense of connectedness also with the long history of Christian monasticism, since monastic life focuses on praying through the psalter regularly. Readings from Acts and New Testament letters link us with the earliest followers of the way, our forerunners in the nascent church. The service of readings builds in crescendo to its climax in the reading from one of the Gospels, when Christ is present in our midst via that reading, and we surround that reading with greater ceremonial devotion, including the assembly's standing for the Gospel reading.

Furthermore, when we use a lectionary, such as the Revised Common Lectionary, we stand with other Christians who also use it. Awareness that other Christians in differing ecclesial traditions, nations, and cultures throughout the world share the same lectionary readings for any given Sunday builds a palpable sense of Christian unity.

In short, the use of the lectionary is a great gift and seldom fails to offer up passages from Scripture that evoke rich meanings for particular settings and contexts, a living word readily applicable to our circumstances. Such meaningfulness can erupt in the serendipity of the Spirit, particularly when we actively and meditatively engage the Scriptures of the lectionary, listening for intersections between readings and our lives and circumstances. With such attentive listening, the lectionary can deliver a word via the workings of the Spirit in our holy conversation. So it is that the Word of God is living and active.

The Lectionary and the Coincidence of Time and Place

Some years ago I was invited to be a member of a delegation to visit ecumenical partners in Geneva, Istanbul, and Rome. I was given the privilege of being the chaplain for the group and had the responsibility of compiling a daily devotional booklet that followed our church's calendar of commemorations. We worshiped together when we could, given our busy travel schedule and the claims of many meetings and tours. One occasion convinced me that the lectionary has an uncanny ability to give a living word, despite the givenness of set texts. We had just toured the Basilica in Rome where the remains of the apostle Paul are believed to rest, and we decided to claim a devotional moment. Curiously, the day's commemoration was Jonathan Edwards. Serendipitously in the Spirit, the passage was from 1 Corinthians 3 and included this from Paul himself: "What then in Apollos? What is Paul? Servants through whom you came to believe, as the Lord assigned to each. I planted, Apollos watered, but God gave the growth. So neither the one who plants nor the one who waters is anything, but only God who gives the growth" (1 Cor. 3:5-7). This passage in the place where Paul's mortal dust remains! It was spectacular as poignant meaningfulness exploded onto the scene. Divine coincidence, as in the coinciding of Scripture with our lives. When we are poised and open in holy conversation with the lectionary passages, looking for intersections between God's Word and our circumstances, the lectionary is full to overflowing with potential meanings, living words for us in our day.

First Reading

Again, the reading from the Hebrew Scriptures allows us to see our continuity with the Jewish tradition and thus to gain a fuller picture of God's involvement with humanity through the centuries. In the case of the reading from Numbers 11 on the day of Pentecost, this passage suggests that the work of God's Spirit is not limited to Pentecost as a particular Christian festival, the story of which is told in Acts 2. In terms of the rationale for selections of particular readings in the lectionary, the first reading often relates to or anticipates the Gospel reading. In this case, there may be more connection with the second reading from Acts.

Employing a custom that dates from the twelfth century, the reader announces, "A reading from Numbers, chapter 11, beginning with the twenty-fourth verse." Listeners in the assembly prepare to attend closely to the reading of this passage, seeking to understand what God has to say, and also to listen for words, images, phrases that call out to them, a sign perhaps of the Spirit's quickening work. The reader continues, present to the narrative, and with subtlety naturally calls attention to certain words or phrases through emphasis, inflection, tone, nurturing the possibility for the Spirit to speak a living word for us:

> So Moses went out and told the people the words of the LORD; and he gathered seventy elders of the people, and placed them all around the tent. Then the LORD came down in the cloud and spoke to him, and took some of the spirit that was on him and put it on the seventy elders; and when the spirit rested upon them, they prophesied. But they did not do so again.
>
> Two men remained in the camp, one named Eldad, and the other named Medad, and the spirit rested on them; they were among those registered, but they had not gone out to the tent, and so they prophesied in the camp. And a young man ran and told Moses, "Eldad and Medad are prophesying in the camp." And Joshua son of Nun, the assistant of Moses, one of his chosen men, said, "My lord Moses, stop them!" But Moses said to him, "Are you jealous for my sake? Would that all the LORD's people were prophets, and that the LORD would put his spirit on them!" And Moses and the elders of Israel returned to the camp. (Num. 11:24-30)

This public proclamation of God's Word can appropriately be followed by silence, a spaciousness allowing for the story to continue to reverberate, lasting perhaps thirty seconds, a minute, in some settings even a few minutes. In our culture, even thirty seconds of silence can seem like an extended period.

Participants in holy conversation use this time to allow the story and its main points to soak in, dwelling with this Word from God, trusting that this silence is not empty space but is full of the Spirit's presence in proclamation. Imagine yourself in that assembly. If the text is before you on a printed page, in a bulletin leaflet or pew Bible, you may be drawn to return to it, looking for the evocative words. If you happened to be at a midweek Bible study on the texts appointed for this day, return to that study in your mind's eye. What did you learn that informs your understanding now? You may have undertaken the individual practice of *lectio divina* with this passage. What emerges for you from having spent other time in meditation and prayer with this passage? In some settings, electronic visual images may be projected to reinforce themes associated with the text. The intent of this silence is to make room for deeper engagement with the biblical readings, that we might be in a better position to hear more fully what God objectively reveals to us. This is time also to begin to consider how this Word speaks for you in particular, especially in connection to what has been on your heart and mind. What evokes or provokes your thoughts and feelings, your memory and imagination even now as you have read this passage on the previous page? What words, ideas, and images draw you in, captivate you? Where is the spiritual energy for you?

A Living Word from the First Reading

The following meditations illustrate my own musings on the text, the work of dialogue, of holy conversation. The context for this story in Numbers is the complaint of the people in the desert: "If only we had meat to eat! We remember the fish we used to eat in Egypt for nothing, the cucumbers, the melons, the leeks, the onions, and the garlic; but now our strength is dried up, and there is nothing at all but this manna to look at" (Num. 11:4b-6). Moses is frustrated with their complaining and with the burden of leadership as he expresses to the Lord, "Why have you treated your servant so badly? Why have I not found favor in your sight, that you lay the burden of all this people on me?" (11:11). In reply, the Lord instructs Moses to gather the seventy elders, that the Lord might address them in assembly at the tent of meeting: "I will come down and talk with you there; and I will take some of the spirit that is on you and put it on them; and they shall bear the burden of the people along with you so that you will not bear it all by yourself" (11:17).

The elders assemble. The promised spirit is placed on them, and they prophesy. What is this spirit? The divine power. What does it mean to prophesy? In this case, as some commentators suggest, it was to engage in ecstatic behavior, raving even, to demonstrate outward signs of the divine power of the spirit. Eldad and Medad, though registered, prophesy out of bounds apart from the tent, but in the camp. This perceived transgression of the parameters of the assembly provokes Moses' assistant to exclaim, "My lord Moses, stop them!" Then Moses offers the response that becomes evocative for our discerning purposes and what all this might mean for us in terms of the day of Pentecost: "Are you jealous for my sake? Would that all the LORD's people were prophets, and that the LORD would put his spirit on them!" (11:29).

By way of meditative reminiscence, one scriptural passage calling to mind another, we may well recall moments from the prophet Joel, as quoted in the Pentecost passage from Acts 2: "Then afterward I will pour out my spirit on all flesh; your sons and your daughters shall prophesy, your old men shall dream dreams, and your young men shall see visions" (Joel 2:28). These passages from Numbers, Joel, and Acts also bring to mind the promise concerning a new covenant in Jeremiah: "But this is the covenant that I will make with the house of Israel after those days, says the LORD: I will put my law within them, and I will write it on their hearts; and I will be their God, and they shall be my people. No longer shall they teach one another, or say to each other, 'Know the LORD,' for they shall all know me, from the least of them to the greatest, says the LORD" (Jer. 31:33-34a). Moses' wish—"Would that all the LORD's people were prophets, and that the LORD would put his spirit on them!"—seems to be fulfilled on the day of Pentecost in fulfillment also of the promises in Jeremiah and Joel.

As we share in the events of the day of Pentecost even now in our own day in our own assemblies, we, too, share in the fulfillments of the Scriptures concerning the new covenant written on hearts, the Spirit resting on us for divine power to prophesy. And when all members of Christian liturgical assembly share in Spirit-led holy conversation, we fulfill Moses' wish, in a new sense, that it is not just a singular leader, nor a group of leaders, but the whole assembly that fully participates in the Spirit-laden prophetic activity of the liturgy—"Would that all the LORD's people were prophets, and that the LORD would put his spirit on them!" So it is in our assemblies when the people of God attend to the Word of God with all their heart, soul, mind, and strength.

At the conclusion of this silent and spacious dwelling with the readings, which you see is full of the living Word of God for us in our own season, the reader proclaims, "The Word of the Lord," or "Word of God, Word of life," or "Hear what the Spirit is saying to the churches." The assembly, continuing the dialogue in holy conversation, offers its acclamation, "Thanks be to God." This dialogical practice that concludes the reading is a custom that dates from medieval times. This acclamation offered *after* the silence also calls attention to the fact that the Word of God, as living Word, is not simply reduced to words on the scriptural page, but is part of the assembly's discerning appropriation of and reflection on that Word. Offering acclamation and thankful response following the silence after the readings heightens awareness of the performative nature of the Word, that in the silence the Word continues to act on us as we soak in it and dwell with it and think about what it means.

THE PSALM

Psalms are sung in liturgy in a variety of musical styles, reflecting multiple cultures and ecclesial traditions. So it is that we in our liturgies participate in an ancient tradition, using Judaism's first hymnbook. This practice of using psalms in the service on the Lord's Day dates from the fourth century. Believers throughout the centuries have felt a natural impulse to sing in response to hearing God's Word. The particular psalm appointed for the day of Pentecost, portions of Psalm 104, is itself one of the psalms in hymn style. Anciently, it was used in services of daily prayer and for occasions of sacrifice and other festivals. Its intent seems to be to draw the mind of the worshiper to the praise of God, particularly in terms of God's transcendence as Creator. So, antiphonally between choir and assembly, or cantor and assembly, the psalm is sung:

> How manifold are your works, O LORD!
>> In wisdom you have made them all;
>> the earth is full of your creatures.
> Yonder is the sea, great and wide,
> with its swarms too many to number,
>> living things both small and great.
> There go the ships to and fro,
>> and Leviathan, which you made for the sport of it.
> All of them look to you
>> to give them their food in due season.

You give it to them; they gather it;
   you open your hand,
   and they are filled with good things.
When you hide your face, they are terrified;
   when you take away their breath,
   they die and return to their dust.
You send forth your Spirit, and they are created;
   and so you renew the face of the earth.
May the glory of the LORD endure forever;
   O LORD, rejoice in all your works.
You look at the earth and it trembles;
   you touch the mountains and they smoke.
I will sing to the LORD as long as I live;
   I will praise my God while I have my being.
May these words of mine please God.
   I will rejoice in the LORD. . . .
   Bless the LORD, O my soul. Hallelujah! (Ps. 104:24-34, 35b)[1]

As the assembly shares in the singing of the psalm and in silence following, the dialogical processes of holy conversation continue.

A Living Word from the Psalm

What would God's Spirit reveal to us in this hymn of praise from Scripture? Borrowing themes from Mesopotamian and Canaanite creation myths—this psalm predates the Genesis creation narratives—the psalm focuses on the praise of God for creation, particularly the ordering and thereby taming of creation. "Yonder is the sea, great and wide, with its swarms too many to number, living things both small and great. There go the ships to and fro, and Leviathan, which you made for the sport of it" (Ps. 104:25-26). The sea in ancient times was and even now is a place of mystery, of seemingly uncontrollable natural power. Leviathan, the great sea monster, is tamed, domesticated by our God, and frolics sportingly in the waters calm enough also to support commerce of ships in shipping lanes.

   Behind this work of ordering creation is the Lord's responsibility for life itself and for its ongoing renewal: "You send forth your Spirit, and they are created; and so you renew the face of the earth" (104:30). The Hebrew word *ruach* translates variously as spirit, breath, or wind, all forces of life and of creation. On the day of Pentecost this psalm may move us in such a way as to give thanks and praise to God for the work of creation and for the Spirit's guidance in giving order to, taming creation. "In the beginning when God created the heavens and the earth, the earth was a formless void and darkness covered the face of the deep, while a wind from God swept over the face of the waters" (Gen. 1:1-2).

In another creation story from Genesis, humans share in the creative work of bringing order through giving names to the creatures (Gen. 2:19-20). Since the day of Pentecost, and our personal sharing in that day in the life-giving waters of baptism over which the Spirit again broods, we, too, share in the Spirit-led creative and ordering work of discerning the meanings of God's life-giving Word for us. The forces at work in creation are again at work in our holy conversation.

SECOND READING

The use in Christian assembly of literature from what would become the New Testament emerges from the instructions of the apostle Paul himself: "And when this letter has been read among you, have it read also in the church of the Laodiceans; and see that you read also the letter from Laodicea" (Col. 4:16). Here we have a reading from the Acts of the Apostles, recounting the events on the day of Pentecost. It is a custom in some churches on Pentecost to read portions of this passage in different languages, particularly languages spoken by members of the local congregation, calling attention to the gift of cultural diversity. These readers offer this Word from God in the power of the Spirit not unlike the Pentecost of old:

> When the day of Pentecost had come, they were all together in one place. And suddenly from heaven there came a sound like the rush of a violent wind, and it filled the entire house where they were sitting. Divided tongues, as of fire, appeared among them, and a tongue rested on each of them. All of them were filled with the Holy Spirit and began to speak in other languages, as the Spirit gave them ability.
>
> Now there were devout Jews from every nation under heaven living in Jerusalem. And at this sound the crowd gathered and was bewildered, because each one heard them speaking in the native language

of each. Amazed and astonished, they asked, "Are not all these who are speaking Galileans? And how is it that we hear, each of us, in our own native language? Parthians, Medes, Elamites, and residents of Mesopotamia, Judea and Cappadocia, Pontus and Asia, Phrygia and Pamphylia, Egypt and the parts of Libya belonging to Cyrene, and vistors from Rome, both Jews and proselytes, Cretans and Arabs— in our own languages we hear them speaking about God's deeds of power." All were amazed and perplexed, saying to one another, "What does this mean?" But others sneered and said, "They are filled with new wine."

But Peter, standing with the eleven, raised his voice and addressed them, "Men of Judea and all who live in Jerusalem, let this be known to you, and listen to what I say. Indeed, these are not drunk, as you suppose, for it is only nine o'clock in the morning. No, this is what was spoken through the prophet Joel:

'In the last days it will be, God declares,
that I will pour out my Spirit upon all flesh,
    and your sons and your daughters shall prophesy,
and your young men shall see visions,
    and your old men shall dream dreams.
Even upon my slaves, both men and women,
    in those days I will pour out my Spirit;
        and they shall prophesy.
And I will show portents in the heaven above
    and signs on the earth below,
        blood, and fire, and smoky mist.
The sun shall be turned to darkness and the moon to blood,
    before the coming of the Lord's great and glorious day.
Then everyone who calls on the name of the Lord shall be saved.' "
    (Acts 2:1-21)

Silence follows this reading to nurture openness on the part of listeners to the Spirit's quickening work in our discernment of meanings of this passage. What are the results of this deep listening for meaning?

A Living Word from the Second Reading

In the Jewish tradition the day of Pentecost had been an agricultural festival, but by the time of the event recorded in Acts it was a day to commemorate the giving of the law on Sinai. Known as the Feast of Weeks, it came fifty days after Passover. Christian Pentecost is the fiftieth and final day of Easter. The sound of the violent rush of wind calls to mind *pneuma*—spirit, breath, wind—where wind (*pnoe*) derives from *pneuma*, the word behind "Holy Spirit." The appearance of tongues as of fire is suggestive of the presence of God: "The voice of the LORD flashes forth flames of fire" (Ps. 29:7). Together, wind of the Spirit and flame bring to mind John the Baptist's prediction of the coming Messiah and perhaps its fulfillment: "He will baptize you with the Holy Spirit and fire" (Luke 3:16b). Now is that time.

Peter's sermon after the strange and compelling incident of Galileans speaking the languages of the visitors to Jerusalem suggests also that now is the fulfillment of the prophecy of Joel, that daughters and sons will prophesy, that young men will see visions and old men will have dreams, that even slaves, men and women, will have the Spirit's power to prophesy, not unlike Moses' wish in Numbers, that all the Lord's people would receive the spirit to be prophets. But now, according to Peter's proclamation, Jesus is the Lord whom Joel named and Moses invoked. Moreover, the great and glorious day is this day of the Spirit's outpouring for making known this Jesus' death and resurrection to all people, all the nations of the world as represented by the multiple languages heard and understood in the pentecostal moment.

We reflect, as did the onlookers and hearers at Pentecost—"All were amazed and perplexed, saying to one another, 'What does this mean?'" (Acts 2:12)—and we ask ourselves, What does all of this mean for us in our day? What are the nations and cultures and subcultures and who are the peoples represented in our own communities who might be attracted by the commotion of our assemblies, who might join us to discern who Jesus is and what the Holy Spirit might be up to in our proclamation? In what ways does our church's presence and mission in the community include or exclude those from other cultures, languages, and nations? Moreover, who are the ones in our assemblies prophesying and seeing visions and dreaming dreams, looking for portents and signs as we look for the "coming of the Lord's great and glorious day"? Is our welcome big enough to embrace them?

As our minds and hearts are actively engaged in varied, free-flowing reflections, a reader calls us back to the order of the day and the further holy conversation to be had: "The Word of the Lord." We respond out of the depths of our musings, appreciating that the Spirit continues to come to us and to lead us into all truth: "Thanks be to God."

THE HOLY GOSPEL, VERSE, AND ACCLAMATIONS

In this liturgy of the Word, the reading of the Holy Gospel has a special place. It is the final reading, a place of honor, a climax and culmination. We surround this proclamation with particular activities that honor this reading and call attention to the sacramental qualities of the Holy Gospels in biblical literature, recognizing that Christ is present in the Gospel narrative. Unlike the other readings, there is a custom of standing for this reading, and there may be a procession to the center of the assembly with ministers carrying a decorated, ceremonial book containing the Gospel, a sign of Christ's presence in our midst. Such enactments echo the Jewish practice of bringing the Torah into the midst of the synagogue so that the faithful may touch and kiss the sacred scroll while a cantor sings joyful songs.

The reading is preceded by the singing of *alleluias* (meaning "praise the Lord") and a special verse for the day. By the third century, it was customary to sing alleluias to welcome the Gospel. In some traditions a cantor or the whole assembly sings a hymn—the Gradual, from *gradus*, that is, the step from which it was sung. This hymn carries the voice of our rejoicing as the Gospel comes into our midst. Particular verses, often from Scripture, and thematically appropriate for the liturgical day, have been created to serve to build anticipation for the Gospel's proclamation. The verse for the day of Pentecost happens not to come from Scripture, but is derived from an eleventh-century antiphon and is sung by a choir or solo voice: "Alleluia. Come, Holy Spirit, fill the hearts of your faithful, and kindle in us the fire of your love. Alleluia." Here is the language of invitation, anticipation, and desire for sacred encounter—come, fill our hearts, kindle in us the fire of your love. The heart, the seat of human will, an expression of soul as our deepest identity in God, is best open—not hardened—and filled with the Spirit's presence, that we might indeed experience the fullness of Christ's presence carried via the Gospel narrative.

In the Orthodox Liturgy of St. John Chrysostom, the Gospel book is carried into the midst of the people from behind the holy doors. The deacon cries aloud, "Wisdom. Stand steadfast. Let us hear the Holy Gospel. Peace unto all." The priest then proclaims, "Let us give heed."[2] These dramatic practices, which employ our whole bodies and many of our senses, invite us into deep engagement with Christ in the Word. They are practical ways of suggesting that indeed we are on holy ground. Other practices surrounding the reading of the Gospel can be simpler. The reader announces the Gospel: "The Holy Gospel according to John." Many make the sign of the cross over forehead, mouth, and heart, a custom dating from the eleventh century. The assembly says or sings an acclamation before the reading: "Glory to you, O Lord." The reader continues:

> When it was evening on that day, the first day of the week, and the doors of the house where the disciples had met were locked for fear of the Jews, Jesus came and stood among them and said, "Peace be with you." After he said this, he showed them his hands and his side. Then the disciples rejoiced when they saw the Lord. Jesus said to them again, "Peace be with you. As the Father has sent me, so I send you." When he had said this, he breathed on them and said to them, "Receive the Holy Spirit. If you forgive the sins of any, they are forgiven them; if you retain the sins of any, they are retained." (John 20:19-23)

As with the other lessons, silence may follow this reading. The members of the assembly engage in holy conversation in their mind's eye, reflecting on the possible meanings of this passage, perhaps seeing themselves in the story.

A Living Word from the Gospel Reading

This story describes incidents in Jesus' first appearance to his disciples after the resurrection. Its telling is close to the events of Jesus' last days, particularly his suffering and death—"he showed them his hands and his side"—to indicate that the one who was dead is the one standing before the disciples when he appears in their midst in the locked room. In the context of John's Gospel, this passage constitutes the Pentecost event. Jesus himself—not a tongue as of fire, nor the sound of a violent wind—becomes the vessel through which the Holy Spirit is passed on to the disciples: "He breathed on them and said to them, 'Receive the Holy Spirit'" (John 20:22). This is the Spirit whom Jesus had promised them in his farewell discourse and other moments in the days preceding his Passion, the Spirit ultimately sent from the One whom Jesus called Abba, Father (John 14:15-31).

The imaginative work of holy conversation continues. Through Word and sacrament, Jesus stands in the midst of our assemblies, the houses of worship where we meet. It may be that we have our doors locked, literally or figuratively, and yet he is in our midst, doing the same things with us as with the disciples of old. Jesus shows them his hands and his side. Calling attention to those same wounds, we preach Christ crucified, Jesus dead and risen. Jesus says to them, "Peace be with you." We likewise share the peace of the Lord. His hands, his side, evoke images of his body, his blood, in, with, and under the gifts of bread and wine at our sacramental table. "The disciples rejoiced when they saw the Lord." We likewise rejoice when we recognize Jesus in the breaking of the bread—*chairo* in the Greek, "rejoice," and related to *eucharistia*, "gratitude, thanksgiving, Eucharist." Jesus breathes on the disciples. In some liturgical traditions the priest breathes on the sacramental elements in the *epiclesis*, invoking the Holy Spirit. Jesus says to the disciples, "As the Father has sent me, so I send you." Christ likewise sends us from our liturgy. He gives the disciples the ministry of reconciliation, the same ministry entrusted to us: "If you forgive the sins of any, they are forgiven them; if you retain the sins of any, they are retained." In the power of the Spirit imparted during our assembly, we leave to do the work of reconciliation in the world to which we are sent.

Through our imaginative musings rooted in our careful listening to the Word, the realization is striking: we stand in continuity through the centuries with Jesus' first disciples and with Jesus himself, who still comes to be with us through the Spirit. This realization provokes our worship, our *proskynesis*, our bowing in awe of this wonder of ongoing presence. We give voice to this worship in dialogue with the reader who announces, "The gospel of the Lord," and we respond with deep sincerity, "Praise to you, O Christ." Praise to you, indeed.

At this point in the service, God's Word in the form of the various readings has been offered to the assembly. The Word has made its claim on us, even as we have begun to engage it in our own meditations. This meditative work continues now in earnest in the sermon.

Chapter 6

MEDITATION

Meditation as a movement in *lectio divina* builds on and goes beyond the basic proclamation laid out in the readings. During the reading of passages from Scripture, God's voice in holy conversation is primary. We have the secondary role as obedient listeners seeking insight into the more objective meanings of the readings. In meditation, our role in the dialogue becomes more prominent as we intentionally further explore our initial musings concerning that which the readings evoked in us based on our attentive listening. In meditation we discern different levels of meaning beyond the more objective, intended historical meanings, particularly aspects of meaning that have to do with us in our own day, *pro me*, for me, *pro nobis*, for us. In meditation we seek the ongoing revelation that builds on the once-and-for-all Revelation of the Scriptures as the Spirit leads us into all truth.

THE SERMON AND HOLY CONVERSATION

Meditation proper, in terms of the movements of *lectio divina* applied to the liturgy, is formalized in the sermon as an expository, interpretive act of commentary that seeks specific implications of scriptural passages for faith and mission in our own day, in our own particular contexts, but based on and emerging from the givenness of the Revelation. It is typically in the sermon that we seek meanings *pro me*, for me, and *pro nobis*, for us.

What is a sermon? And what is it to preach? As with worship, there may be as many definitions as there are traditions and devotional styles. Additionally, there are layers of connotations that distract from a faithful appropriation or reappropriation of this proclamatory activity. Curiously and revealingly, in fact, the second-option definitions of the words *sermon* and *preach* in the *Concise Oxford English Dictionary* are negative in tone. Acknowledging it as an informal understanding, a sermon is "a long or tedious admonition or reproof," and to preach, colloquially understood in terms of preaching *at* someone, is "to give moral advice . . . in a self-righteous way."[1] *Sermon*'s closely related synonym, *homily*, also suffers from negative understanding in the second-option dictionary definition: "a tedious moralizing lecture." Clearly, these alternative understandings have resulted from people's conclusions about their experiences, and these experiences have been common enough to be included in a major dictionary.

Exploring word origins can aid in redeeming important theological words and also spiritual practices from their negative connotations. *Sermon* comes from the Latin *sermo*, meaning "discourse, discussion, talk, speech, conversation," even "common talk" or "everyday language—all categories of relational experience far from negative connotations of sermons as tedious lectures. *Sermo* also relates to *sero*, from which is derived the word *series*, and means "to link together, connect, join, entwine." In terms of an understanding constructed in part from word origins, a sermon is common conversation that links together, entwines God's Word and our lives and builds us up as the body of Christ in the church, in community. The word *homily* in its relatedness to Greek word origins emphasizes the communal aspect of this discourse: *homilia* is conversation addressed to the crowd, the assembly, *homilos*, with whom the speaker consorts, *homilein*.

The practice of offering reflection on Scripture in the form of a public speech is an inheritance from Judaism and has been centrally featured in Christian faith practice and worship since the earliest days of the church. Peter's address to the crowd in Jerusalem that follows on the heels of the Spirit's coming at Pentecost, discourse that results from the Spirit's empowerment, is itself reflective of sermonic style. That address, recorded in Acts 2:14-36, focuses in large measure on Peter's use of Scripture to interpret present events. He sees the Spirit's appearing and the unleashing of tongues, allowing the followers to speak intelligibly in foreign languages, as evidence of the fulfillment of promises recorded by the prophet Joel: "In the last days it will be, God declares, that I will pour out my Spirit upon all flesh, and your sons and your daughters shall prophesy" (Acts 2:17a). Peter also alludes to and/or directly quotes from Psalms 16, 110, and 132, and from 2 Samuel, all in an effort to reinforce his proclamation of Jesus' resurrection, suggesting, for example, that David the psalmist predicted that resurrection: "Foreseeing this, David spoke of the resurrection of the Messiah, saying, 'He was not abandoned to Hades, nor did his flesh experience corruption'" (Acts 2:31, paraphrasing Ps. 16:10). Peter's homiletical method featuring the interpretation of current events and experiences in light of Scripture has been a time-honored—but also abused—method throughout the Christian centuries.

In terms of the Word spoken by preachers and its performative nature, effective sermons can have a rather sacramental quality in conveying the experience of the living and resurrected Christ. The sermon occasions sacred encounter. At its best, it is not just a monologue crafted by a religious professional. In the sermon we trust that the Spirit of Christ speaks a living word to us capable of creating and nurturing and sustaining faith. The sermon contributes to our formation, our conformation to the mind of Christ, our reformation, and our transformation as new creations in Christ.[2] Sermons thus carry a lot of weight in the liturgy. In an hour-long service, a fifteen-minute sermon constitutes a full quarter of the entire time spent in assembly. Beyond that, the sermon as phenomenon carries the weight of high expectation. So often, it is the sermon that evokes the assembly's anticipation that they will be fed, formed, inspired, challenged, and comforted on any particular day for assembly. Anticipating the assembly's expectations, the preacher then may spend a significant percentage of her or his work week in preparation for the big homiletical event.

But it is crucial to recognize, especially in this work that emphasizes the dialogical quality of the entire liturgical experience, that the sermon as interpretive proclamation is not just the domain of the preacher. Each member of the assembly has the divine privilege and responsibility to be in dialogue with the Scriptures and with the preacher. Proclamation thus is the work of the whole assembly, the preacher and congregation in conversation with each other. Those entrusted with the ministry of preaching cannot take it for granted that members of the assembly know how to listen to sermons in such a way as to engage in meditative dialogue, holy conversation. Likewise, the whole people of God cannot take it for granted that preachers know how best to offer sermons in a dialogical way. Reflections on the respective roles of preacher and listeners in holy conversation are thus illuminating.

The Role of the Preacher

Preachers who seek to nurture holy conversation in liturgy will preach in such a way as to invite dialogue and attentive listening. They may leave rhetorical open spaces that invite hearers to wonder and to fill in the blanks in their own meditative imaginations. They view proclamation as an act that has sacramental qualities in conveying God's grace concretely and addressing the multiple dimensions of human experience; they understand that a sermon should as much as possible evoke imagination in relation to all of the senses. An effective sermon might, as it were, be tasted, touched, even smelled in the mind's eye in addition to being heard and seen.

Preaching that nurtures the holy conversation between preacher and listeners is well served by an approach to sermon preparation that views this preparation as a spiritual discipline rather than a professional task to accomplish. *Lectio divina* itself can serve as a method for sermon preparation. The multiple dimensions and movements of sacred reading comprise a framework for undertaking sermon preparation as a spiritual exercise:

- *Preparation* involves the preacher's nurturing prayerfully a presence that is not task oriented.
- *Reading* requires the preacher's rigorous exegetical study of scriptural passages, but this inquiry is motivated by awe-filled curiosity.
- In *meditation*, the preacher discerns meanings of texts for the faith community in its current mission context.
- In the movement of *prayer*, the preacher prays that which emerges from meditative study, including prayers for anticipated listeners.
- The preacher takes time for *contemplative prayer* so that she or he may experience God's presence, being silent in relation to her or his prayer, meditations, and readings. The preacher brings this contemplative experience to the pulpit.
- *Incarnation for mission* involves the further processes of birthing a sermon: manuscript or notes preparation, attention to matters of style and delivery in terms of embodying the Word, continued dwelling with Christ as the living Word, then the actual preaching event.

Bringing this full range of holy conversation to the act of preaching nurtures the holy conversation of those who will listen, as the people of God witness a preacher who is experientially available to the presence of God.

The Role of Listeners

Preaching is not a spectator sport. Listeners, therefore, offer to preachers an active presence that seeks engagement beyond entertainment, though good sermons can be quite entertaining. You might come to the sermon as an event having done some homework, having engaged in prior individual or group reading and study of the lectionary Bible passages for a given day. You might come to the assembly having practiced *lectio divina* with the texts for the day.

During the sermon, engage in mental dialogue with the preacher, seeking to translate the preacher's observations in relation to your own particular circumstances: What does this mean for me in my own faith journey and in my own ministry in daily life? Engage the sermon to such an extent that when greeting the preacher on the way out of the liturgy, you might be in a position to offer a more substantive comment than the common phrase, "Nice sermon today, Pastor."

Pray for the preacher and nurture a hermeneutics of affection for the one whose task it is to proclaim the gospel. See the sermon in the broader contexts of the whole liturgy and indeed of the whole of pastoral and congregational ministry. Proclamation cannot be reduced to a single sermon. Rather, one sermon relates to another and to many others over the long haul in the years of pastoral ministry and pastoral relationships in a congregation. Nurture a healthy and engaged relationship with pastors and others who bear the privileged responsibility of proclamation. Such relationships serve well the possibility of deep holy conversation taking place in the homiletical exchange.

You may feel moved to embrace the tradition common in African American settings of responding to preachers with your own affirmative acclamations, providing dialogical and exclamatory feedback that can have the effect of buoying up a preacher. A bold assembly might even embrace a southern evangelical tradition of "singing the preacher down," spontaneously erupting in singing a hymn when a sermon is not well received or goes on for too long!

A GUIDED HOMILETICAL MEDITATION FOR THE DAY OF PENTECOST

There may be alternatives to the traditional monologue sermon in some liturgical settings. Dialogue sermons, which literally involve more people than the singular preacher, can be effective in provoking the assembly's very active participation. Likewise, in smaller gatherings, it can be effective to engage in the group practice of *lectio divina* in place of a traditional sermon in the context of which actual conversation takes place between leaders and members of the assembly toward the end that the entire body discerns together the meanings of biblical passages for our day. Many homiletical styles and methods can nurture the discerning, meditative work of holy conversation—it is not so much the *what* of a particular preaching method, but *how* it is undertaken, in what spirit and with which attitudes, that makes the difference for holy conversation.

Using the appointed passage from John's Gospel as a focus, I envision a sermon for the day of Pentecost as a kind of guided meditation that invites hearers' imaginative participation in the story. The exercise of imagining yourself in biblical narrative emerges out of the spiritual traditions and practices associated with St. Ignatius of Loyola, the founder of the Society of Jesus, the Jesuits. Through a retelling of the story and a series of open-ended questions that relate closely to the language of the biblical narrative and that encourage listeners to imagine what they see, hear, feel, smell, and perhaps even taste, the preacher invites listeners to wonder and to place themselves in the biblical time and setting in their mind's eye, thus nurturing their palpably imaginative participation and contributing to the sacramental qualities of preaching. Spacious silence can be incorporated into the exercise to allow time for the imagination of the assembly to work in response to the evocative questions asked. The following gives a sense of the flavor of this guided-meditation type of homiletical exercise:

> It is evening on the first day of the week. Jesus' disciples are in a room with the doors locked. They are fearful of the authorities. Might they be next in line for arrest, trial, and ultimately execution? As you imagine yourself there, are you one of the disciples? A curious onlooker? A seeker? What is the room like? Is the room spacious or cramped? Are there windows? Are they shuttered? What is the evening light like in the room? Or is it dark? Does a lamp give some light? Take a moment to feel the fearfulness that the story reports. Suddenly, inexplicably, someone else is in the room with you. Who is it? Does this person's presence add to the fear? He says, "Peace be with you," and calls attention to his hands and his side, his wounds from having been crucified. Is it the sound of a familiar voice, and that in connection with the sight of wounded hands and side, that causes you to recognize this person as Jesus? Your companions rejoice at this recognition. What is it like for you to recognize your teacher, friend, and Lord? Take a moment to experience the rejoicing, if indeed you can share in that rejoicing. Are embraces exchanged? Do you or the others touch Jesus'

hands and side as Thomas later will? Jesus says it again, "Peace be with you," but then continues: "As the Father has sent me, so I send you." What does this mean? Are you baffled? Do you recall words like this that Jesus has used before? Then Jesus breathes on the disciples and you in their company. How close is Jesus? Do you feel the breath? Is it warm? Is it cool? Dare I ask, do you smell the breath? Jesus speaks again: "Receive the Holy Spirit. If you forgive the sins of any, they are forgiven them; if you retain the sins of any, they are retained." What does this mean? Has Jesus said anything like this before? Or will you think about it later because these moments are just too filled with wonderment?

Such invitations to reflect can serve as the first half of an imaginative homiletical exercise of meditative holy conversation, locating imagination in the ancient story. The second half brings this narrative into the present, into our very assembly:

We have gathered in this room on the first day of the week, the day of resurrection, the fiftieth day of Easter, the day of Pentecost, the day celebrating the coming of the Holy Spirit. We have heard the story about Jesus' resurrection-day appearance to his disciples when he imparted to them the promised Spirit. You have imagined yourself in that place and at that time. But *here* we are. What is the mood here and now? Many fears seize people in our day, fears about the economy, about war, about the environment, fears about the viability of our churches. In what ways do you know fear? Yet something other than fear is in our midst, centered on someone else, that same one who said, "Peace be with you." Think of the parallels between what Jesus did generations ago with his followers and what he does now with us in this very assembly. The parallel pattern between Jesus' appearance with his disciples and his presence in this worshipful place is striking. Anticipate in your mind's eye what we are about to do, connecting it with what Jesus did. We will share the peace of the Lord, peace in the power of the Holy Spirit on this day of festival even as Jesus shared that peace with his disciples. Relish the embraces, the handshakes, even the kisses. Pay attention to the breath that carries the word of peace, the voice of God's en-Spirited life in us as we share that peace. Imagine this to be Jesus himself appearing to you in the familiar faces of your neighbors here. As Jesus showed himself to his disciples, imagine the hands and the side in our proclamation of Jesus who was crucified and then was raised by God. See, touch, taste, and even smell the hands and the side in the bread, the wine, the body and blood. Rejoice—*chairete*—in our Eucharist—*eucharistia*—our thanksgiving, our holy meal, our further and deep embrace with our Lord in quiet contemplation of the holy mysteries. Hear the exhortation again as if for you now in this place: "As the Father has sent me, so I send you. . . . Receive the Holy Spirit. If you forgive the sins of any, they are forgiven them; if you retain the sins of any, they are retained." Let these words echo in your ears as you leave this place to mull over again and again: What does this work of reconciliation mean for you in your ministry in daily life, for us in our life together? But know this: the Holy Spirit gives us the power, the courage to be about God's work of reconciliation. And the Spirit may unleash your tongue, giving you a reconciling word to speak in languages understood by all of our diverse neighbors.

The meditative, imaginative reflections of deep listeners may contribute to continued formation, reformation, transformation in Christ as a feature of the fruit of the Spirit leading us into deeper truth through our holy conversation. The reverberations of meditation do not end with the sermon's concluding *Amen.* When our engagement with the biblical stories in connection with our lives plumbs the depths of study and experience, holy conversation continues.

This further holy conversation can formally be part of a congregation's program. Congregations actively seeking to promote more extensive dialogical engagement could schedule times for sermon discussions. Such discussions could take place in the context of or after a fellowship hour. Sermon conversations give hearers a chance to speak directly with the preacher, offering occasion to rebut what was said in the sermon, as well as a time to seek clarification and to offer their own insights and reflections. During these occasions, members of the assembly could explore together, for example, the sermon's implications for mission and ministry in the local setting. They could tackle together more controversial points that may have to do with politics, thus avoiding a common complaint of preachers being too political in the sermon itself. Save the explicit politics for face-to-face conversational exchange where there is a more level playing field and members of the assembly can speak their piece.

THE HYMN OF THE DAY

Hymn singing often accompanies preaching in Christian liturgical practice and can serve to deepen the work of proclamation and meditation in this movement of the service. Hymn texts—often paraphrases of Scripture—serve as further reiterations of the readings joined by memorable and meaningful tunes that can deeply resonate with members of the singing assembly. In some traditions, a hymn may precede or follow the reading of the Gospel. The Hymn of the Day has a special place in Lutheran liturgy, due in part to the prominence of music in general and hymnody specifically in the Lutheran tradition and in its spirituality. But linking preaching with hymn singing is by no means limited to Lutheran practice. Many Christian traditions employ hymns in the service of proclaiming the gospel. A hymn may also follow the sermon. In a current worship book, *Evangelical Lutheran Worship*, the instruction that describes the singing of a hymn after the sermon notes that "the assembly stands to proclaim the word of God in song."[3] Quite importantly, congregational song makes possible the whole assembly's participation in holy conversation that is proclamation.

As is the case with the sermon itself, hymns are meditations on the Word of God, the scriptural passages for the day. Worship planners typically choose hymns that complement, reinforce, or expand upon the themes for the day. This is an expression of an understanding of meditation consistent with *lectio divina*, seeking to restate by way of elaboration the meaningfulness of God's Word for our particular circumstances through the gift of music and beloved tunes.

The Hymn of the Day also serves as a bridge that moves the assembly from meditation to prayer, again following the movements of *lectio divina*. Lyric, poetic language can provoke the imagination; it can communicate desire, the expression of our deepest yearnings and aspirations. The language of hymnody is often exalted and heightened, expressing the best human ideals. The singing of hymns is thus consonant with prayer, understood in *lectio divina* as the expression of our deepest yearnings, especially to know the closer presence of God. As prayer moves us in *lectio divina*, so the singing of hymns can move us literally to get up out of our seats, offering more fully our physical selves in the act of singing.

Setting of the hymnic text to music thus also contributes to the increasing embodiedness of liturgy as we move closer to the gift of the Lord's Supper, when we meet Christ in, with, and under the gifts of bread and wine, knowing there Christ as embodied, enfleshed Word. We know a deepening of the divine encounter in holy conversation. Now we begin to have some greater sense that even in our singing the "Spirit intercedes with sighs too deep for words" (Rom. 8:26).

The following hymn illustrates how the poetic language of a hymn can serve holy conversation by being proclamation, a meditation on scriptural themes, and itself an expression of prayer. Herman G. Stuempfle Jr. was a pastor, professor of homiletics, seminary chaplain, academic dean, and seminary president who died in 2007. In addition to his scholarly writings, he also authored some 550 hymn texts, including this one appropriate for the day of Pentecost:

> God of tempest, God of whirlwind, as on Pentecost descend!
> Drive us out from sheltered comfort! Past these walls your people send!
> Sweep us into costly service, there with Christ to bear the cross,
> There with Christ to bear the cross!
>
> God of blazing, God of burning, all that blocks your purpose, purge!
> Through your church, Christ's living Body, let your flaming Spirit
>   surge!
> Where deceit conceals injustice, kindle us to speak your truth,
> Kindle us to speak your truth!
>
> God of earthquake, God of thunder, shake us loose from lethargy!
> Break the chains of sin asunder; for earth's healing set us free!
> Crumble walls that still divide us; make us one in Christ our Lord,
> Make us one in Christ our Lord!
>
> God of passion, God unsleeping, stir in us love's restlessness!
> Where the people cry in anguish, may we share your heart's distress.
> Rouse us from content with evil; claim us for your kingdom's work,
> Claim us for your kingdom's work![4]

In, with, and under the lines of this text, the language of Scripture is apparent, and thus the poetry itself proclaims the Word. Stuempfle's first and second stanzas evoke thoughts of the events of Pentecost recorded in Acts 2 when the Spirit descended in tongues as of flame accompanied by the sound of wind: "God of whirlwind, as on Pentecost descend! . . . Let your flaming Spirit surge!" Likewise, the hymn evokes a recollection of the story in the day's Gospel from John 20 when the disciples gather in the room with locked doors only to be encountered by the risen Lord who imparts to them the gift of the Spirit: "Drive us out from sheltered comfort; past these walls your people send!" The story of Paul and Silas's release from the chains of imprisonment, recorded later in Acts 16:25ff., is implied in the third stanza: "Break the chains of sin asunder, for earth's healing set us free! Crumble walls that still divide us; make us one in Christ our Lord." The attribute of God addressed in Psalm 121:4—"He who keeps Israel will neither slumber nor sleep"—is echoed in the fourth stanza: "God of passion, God unsleeping, stir in us love's restlessness!"

The words used to describe God in this hymn text—God of tempest, whirlwind, blazing, burning, earthquake, and thunder—are taken directly from the prophet Isaiah: "And in an instant, suddenly, you will be visited by the LORD of hosts with thunder and earthquake and great noise, with whirlwind and tempest, and the flame of a devouring fire" (Isa. 29:5c-6), prophetic words addressed to the people of Jerusalem under siege, speaking to the hope that God would deliver them from their foes. In complete contrast, the reference to the manner of God's appearing in Isaiah 29 and in the hymn also evokes thoughts of the God who appears to Elijah at Horeb, not in wind, earthquake, and fire, but in the "sound of sheer silence" (1 Kgs. 19:11-12). The point of these explorations is this: four brief stanzas of hymnic poetry contain a lot of Scripture and reinforce its proclamation through reiteration.

Hymns do not simply repeat the Word, but also serve as vehicles of praise through which we elaborate on that Word in meditative exercise in terms of what God would have us be about today. Through writing, authors of hymn texts engage in this work of meditation. We who sing the hymns also participate in this meditation, as we allow the poetic language to evoke our own meditative reflections. In terms of illustrating the poet's meditations, Stuempfle uses the language of Scripture to advance thoughts about how God propels the often lethargic church into mission. The forceful tone of his language echoes that of the prophets—for example, Hosea, Amos, Nahum, Zechariah, and Jeremiah, in addition to Isaiah—and suggests the prophetic nature of the church's mission in costly service, cross bearing, speaking the truth in settings where conceit and injustice reign, being about the earth's healing, unity among God's people, kingdom work amid people's anguished cries.

As we sing, we add our voices and reflecting minds to meditation, as we in holy conversation imagine the ways in which we can be the prophetic church that we sing about. Coming in the order of service in close proximity both to the Gospel from John 20, where Jesus sends his disciples to do the work of reconciliation, and to the homiletical invitation to reflect on what this ministry might look like for us, the singing of this hymn suggests to us aspects of the content of this forgiving ministry in the church's prophetic witness in the world and what this might look like in our particular settings.

Hymns can likewise give expression to prayer, thus anticipating the next movement in *lectio divina*. Indeed, Stuempfle's text is itself a prayer addressed to the God of the aforementioned forceful attributes, petitioning the God who comes in Spirit at Pentecost to free the church and energize it for mission. Note how the active verbs convey the prayerful petitions: "Drive us out from sheltered comfort. . . . Sweep us into costly service. . . . All that blocks your purpose, purge. . . . Kindle us to speak your truth. . . . For earth's healing set us free. . . . Make us one in Christ our Lord. . . . Stir in us love's restlessness. . . . Claim us for your kingdom's work!" The prayerful winds and energies of the Spirit are carried on such active verbs, motivating our resolve to act.

THE CREED IN HOLY CONVERSATION

Reciting the Apostles' or Nicene Creed is a liturgical practice many take for granted and pass over without much thought or deeper engagement. Yet once again, conceiving liturgy as holy conversation invites a revisiting and reclaiming of the practice of using the creeds for worship. In the very earliest centuries of the church, creeds were not used liturgically. Rather, the eucharistic prayer functioned as a statement of faith, declaring the basic content of what Christians believe. The use of actual creeds in liturgy began during the theological controversies in the fifth century when the creeds we know first came to be formalized. The location of the creed in the Western church's order of service, following the Gospel and sermon and preceding the intercessions, dates from the tenth century.

In terms of the logic of the movements of *lectio divina*, the creeds serve holy conversation as proclamation, interpretation, and praise as a form of prayer. As proclamation, they are distillations of basic Christian teaching and echo many scriptural themes. As interpretation, they are the church's meditation, the fruit of deep engagement with the scriptural revelation about God, and means through which the Spirit has been leading us into all truth. They are expressions of orthodoxy, the trustworthy and true conclusions about the divine nature of the trinitarian God based on, we confess, Spirit-led discussion, deliberation, and debate in the ancient church councils.

The creeds are also expressions of prayer, especially in their location in the liturgy conceived in light of *lectio divina* as the assembly moves from meditation into prayer. In the case of the prayerful recitation of the creed, it is prayer understood not in terms of petition, but in terms of praise. Orthodoxy of teaching leads to doxology, the praise of God in prayerful recitation. This is suggested by the varied meanings of the Greek word *doxos*, which can mean "opinion" (as in orthodoxy as straight or right opinion) and "appearance" and "glory," related to doxology as giving praise to God. We in current Christian assemblies do well, then, to think in terms of meditating with and praying the creeds, not just reciting them as proclamation of Christian truth. As we recite, reflect, and pray, we join our voices with others through the centuries in the communion of saints and in the power of the Spirit in giving utterance to Christian theological truth as well as worshipful praise of God in three persons.

On a liturgical festival such as the day of Pentecost, it is appropriate for the assembly to recite the Nicene Creed:

> We believe in one God, the Father, the Almighty, maker of heaven and earth, of all that is, seen and unseen.
>
> We believe in one Lord, Jesus Christ, the only Son of God, eternally begotten of the Father, God from God, Light from Light, true God from true God, begotten, not made, of one Being with the Father; through him all things were made. For us and for our salvation he came down from heaven, was incarnate of the Holy Spirit and the virgin Mary and became truly human. For our sake he was crucified under Pontius Pilate; he suffered death and was buried. On the third day he rose again in accordance with the scriptures; he ascended into heaven and is seated at the right hand of the Father. He will come again in glory to judge the living and the dead, and his kingdom will have no end.
>
> We believe in the Holy Spirit, the Lord, the giver of life, who proceeds from the Father, who with the Father and the Son is worshiped and glorified, who has spoken through the prophets. We believe in one holy catholic and apostolic church. We acknowledge one baptism for the forgiveness of sin. We look for the resurrection of the dead, and the life of the world to come. Amen.

Holy conversation with the creeds can be enriched by knowing the history of their origins and how they have been used throughout the centuries. This knowledge can deepen our awareness of our unity with Christians throughout the centuries and also in our current age as we share with each other in the prayerful and worshipful use of the ecumenical creeds. The Nicene Creed, like all creeds, emerged from traditions of early affirmations of faith. It found its first articulation at the Council of Nicea in 325. The Nicene Creed was expanded at the Council of Constantinople in 381 and was adopted at Chalcedon in 451. Arguably this evolutionary development is an example of the Spirit's leading the people of God into all truth through the avenue of doctrinal development in the historic church councils.

The Nicene Creed's own conversation with Scripture is evident in its language and sensibilities. Belief in "one God . . . maker of heaven and earth" resonates with affirmations of the creation stories in Genesis. The Nicene Creed shares some of the theological language of the prologue to John's Gospel: "In the beginning was the Word, and the Word was with God, and the Word was God. He was in the beginning with God. All things came into being through him, and without him not one thing came into being. What has come into being in him was life, and the life was the light of all people. The light shines in the darkness, and the darkness did not overcome it" (John 1:1-5). The nativity stories in both Matthew and Luke are behind the affirmations of Jesus' incarnation through the Spirit's work in Mary. The creed shares with all the Gospels the stories of crucifixion and resurrection. The ascension, affirmed by the creed, is found in Luke and in a longer version of the ending of Mark. The promise to return again appears variously in the Gospels. The third article concerning the Holy Spirit, particularly the relationship among Father, Son, and Spirit, has its moorings in thought consistent with John's Gospel: "But the Advocate, the Holy Spirit, whom the Father will send in my name, will teach you everything, and remind you of all that I have said to you" (John 14:26). The Nicene Creed is thus a distillation of central teachings of Scripture.

As meditation, the seeking of the additional deeper meanings of the scriptural Word, the Nicene Creed represents many of the doctrinal affirmations of the early church, particularly the doctrine of the Holy Trinity and belief in the humanity and divinity of Jesus. This theological meditation is not static and reduced to the church's earliest years, though. We continue to chew on the meanings of Christian teachings in our own day and perpetuate the work of meditation.

Many struggle with the meanings of the creed's affirmations. What does it mean, for example, to confess that "on the third day he rose again"? How does this belief square with current scientific understandings? Rather than engaging in disputations in one's mind while reciting the creed during the liturgy, taking up the creed in terms of the movements of *lectio divina* may take the edge off the argument for the moment. Theological debate and deliberation have their important places, but perhaps not during worship. In the course of years, the belief in Christ's resurrection may even grow on the doubter through meditative, prayerful liturgical recitation. I have heard that Eastern Orthodox Christians are fond of saying that if the creeds do not at first make sense, keep saying them and praying them, and your mind will follow your practice, leading you to deeper faith, deeper trust in Christian affirmations.

Getting Personal with the Creeds

Calling to mind your own experience of having recited the creeds in various settings and on different occasions may deepen your meditative holy conversation with the creeds and their affirmations. For example, I had occasion on an ecumenical pilgrimage to recite the Nicene Creed with companions in the ruins of the basilica in the current city of Iznik in Turkey, formerly known as Nicea, where the ecumenical council that gave birth to the Nicene Creed was held centuries ago. Because of that experience, reciting the Nicene Creed will never be the same for me again, as each recitation can be enriched by the memory of that occasion. Also by way of example, I witnessed the recitation of the Apostles' Creed by young confirmands in a village in Tanzania, whose recitation was precise, energetic, and offered in a unified voice that conveyed passionate belief in the God understood in the words of that creed. Likewise, my own recitation of the Apostles' Creed is enriched by the memory of that experience. You, too, no doubt, have had such experiences. Perhaps you have memories of saying the creed at family baptisms or at your own confirmation. Recollection of such occasions can make the creed more personally meaningful. Your reminiscence can deepen your holy conversation while you recite the creed with the whole assembly, thus making your confession of faith more prayerful and worshipful.

Another way of engaging the creeds more meaningfully is to follow Martin Luther's example of praying in relation to the articles of the creed, in the context of which he made out of each article a "fourfold interwoven wreath," considering each article a teaching, an occasion for giving thanks, an opportunity for confession, and a stimulus to prayer. In this way, Luther meditatively considered the meanings of each article, gave thanks to God for what each aspect of the creed teaches, confessed his shortcomings in failing to live up to the fullness of the confession of faith, and then, finally, prayed for the guidance and wisdom and so on to live a more devoted life in relation to the themes and teachings of the creed.[5] Such an exercise is most effectively undertaken as an individual devotional practice. However, there may be particular liturgical contexts in which observing silence between the recitations of the articles of the creed could make the space for our meditations and reflections along the lines of the fourfold interwoven wreath.

The day of Pentecost may occasion particular reflections on the third article of the Nicene Creed and the relationship of belief in the Holy Spirit—"who has spoken through the prophets"—to prophetic witness and ministry, a reflection that emerges out of the day's sermon and Hymn of the Day. Likewise, the relationship between the Holy Spirit and the development of the church, recorded in Acts 2 and the subsequent chapters of Acts, comes to mind. Believing in the Holy Spirit who proceeds from the Father leads naturally to an affirmation of the church, and the Spirit's role in the holiness, catholicity, and apostolicity of the church. Confessing the Spirit connects with our belief in the efficacy of baptism in imparting the gift of the Spirit and offering forgiveness of sin. Confessing the Spirit gives us the hope to anticipate the day of our resurrection and the promise of eternal life.

The Nicene Creed, finally, in the recitation by the whole assembly is a prayerful expression of praise, another hymn of praise, if you will, to the trinitarian God whom we worship and adore. As proclamation, as occasion for interpretive meditation, and as a vehicle for praise, the Nicene Creed expresses its multivalence, its varied meaningfulness for us in holy conversation. Our worshipful recitation leads us more deeply into the next movement of liturgy: prayers of intercession.

Chapter 7

PRAYER

The act of praying is a feature of liturgical worship from the beginning of the liturgy to its conclusion. Hymns can be prayers of petition. Recitation of the Nicene Creed as an expression of praise is a form of prayer. And so on. But there is a special place for praying in the Western Rite in the form of the prayers of intercession that occur at the conclusion of the proclamations of and meditations on the Word. This is a point in the liturgy where the pattern of worship advances the movements of *lectio divina*, where meditation on the reading of the Word leads to prayer.

Prayer is variously conceived as praise and thanksgiving, confession, petition, and intercession. Prayer in terms of the movements of *lectio divina* is the expression of our deepest aspirations that emerge from meditation in response to the reading of Scripture. Through reading and meditation, we are inspired as the Spirit breathes into us—*inspirare*—the living Word of God. In prayer, we exhale, breathing out our deepest yearnings and desires, that to which we aspire—*ad spirare*—informed by the Word. Most deeply conceived, our prayer is the Spirit praying in us with sighs too deep for words (Rom. 8:26), God's very Spirit breathing into and breathing out of our bodies as temples of that Spirit. Prayer in this sense is an active experience in which we experience the effects of the Spirit's quickening work in us. Prayer moves us into activity.

In this movement of the liturgy, our aspirations are expressed in varied ways: through the prayers of intercession, but also in the sharing of the peace and in the prayerful activities surrounding the gathering and presentation of gifts as symbols of our self-offering, our prayerful oblation, our sacrifice of praise and thanksgiving. The segment of the liturgy that includes these activities serves as a fulcrum for and bridge to our more direct, contemplative participation in Christ in the Eucharist. To aspire to something is to direct attention toward its fulfillment. In fact, sharing the peace is itself an embodied act of participation as reconciled community, a leaning into an answer to our prayers for peace when we participate in Christ's peace. The gathering and presentation of gifts as a prayer of aspiration is a living into an answer to our yearnings that the world would be fed through our gift giving. Our gifts and their use in mission are signs of and contributions to our prayers' fulfillment.

Prayers of Intercession

Praying has been central to Christian practice since the very beginning, attested to by Jesus' own prayer life and the devotion of the earliest assemblies to the prayers (Acts 2:42). The call to pray for the needs of the world is an early one in our tradition: "First of all, then, I urge that supplications, prayers, intercessions, and thanksgivings be made for everyone, for kings and all who are in high positions, so that we may lead a quiet and peaceable life in all godliness and dignity" (1 Tim. 2:1-2). Intercessions were included in the liturgy as early as the second century. By the fourth century, these prayers were often bid in the style of a litany. Prayers of intercession in the style where a deacon or assisting minister invites the assembly's particular petitions, followed then by the priest or presiding minister's offering of a collect, dates from the fifth century in Rome. The pattern of our prayer, then, occurs in a way consistent with that of the company of the saints through the centuries.

The prayers of intercession can follow a general form, but the particulars emerge from specific concerns in local communities of faith. We are called upon to pray

- for the church universal, its ministry, and the mission of the gospel;
- for the well-being of creation;

- for peace and justice in the world, the nations and those in authority, the community;
- for the poor, oppressed, sick, bereaved, lonely;
- for all who suffer in body, mind, or spirit; and
- for the congregation and special concerns.[1]

Additional petitions may be offered, and the petitions conclude with thanksgiving for the faithful departed. Following this basic pattern, the local assembly crafts and prepares the prayers of intercession appropriate for its own context and emerging from its own concerns and aspirations.

An ideal is to make the most of both scripted and nonscripted language in giving voice to prayers of intercession. The general pattern and/or written prayers form a skeleton for the particular prayers to become flesh and sinews that can be offered extemporaneously, prayers that emerge from the particular meditations relating to the scriptural passages appointed for the day. Such a practice calls for deep and careful listening to the readings for the day and the interpretation of those readings in sermon and in song. It may even be that particular words or phrases from the day's biblical readings will form the basic language for the prayers of intercession. Praying closely with the Scriptures and the living Word of God that emerges from our meditation on that Word is the key to deeply engaged prayer that advances holy conversation. Such praying also suggests deep listening to our own desires and yearnings, the ones identified when the assembly gathered and prepared for the liturgy. Again, what is on our hearts and minds today, and how might this inspire our prayers? When individually and communally we pray close to these aspirations in connection with the readings and our meditation on those readings, we take holy conversation to a yet deeper level, inviting the whole assembly's fully felt participation in heart, mind, soul, and strength. Corporate prayer involves corporate responsibility for prayer.

In addition to building on the preceding movements of the liturgy in gathering to prepare to hear the Word and to respond with our meditative reflections, the particular prayers offered by the assembly relate importantly to and anticipate the sending rite, the conclusion of the liturgy when the people are dismissed to do God's work in the world. There is a significant sense in which the prayers of intercession set the agenda for and establish the content of the church's specific ministry and mission in the coming week. If we pray for the well-being of creation, we endeavor to do in ministry that which seeks that well-being. If we pray for peace and justice, we are called to work for peace and justice. If we pray for the poor, oppressed, sick, bereaved, and lonely, we pledge to undertake ministries with the same. It may be that the various meditations on the scriptural passages for the day illuminate and call attention to very specific ministry opportunities in the coming week, nurturing in us an awareness of what we aspire to in mission and ministry. Prayers of intercession do not simply address God, seeking God's direct intervention in human affairs. These prayers seek God's guidance and power in helping us to do the work God has called us to do in and for the world, thus contributing to the fulfillment of our aspirations.

In your experience, how often do the typical prayers of intercession in liturgy convey this sense of passion and deep connectedness to Scripture in their actual enactments? Sometimes these prayers can seem rote, mechanical, *pro forma*, or reduced to scripted prayers on a printed leaflet. The goal here is to both deepen and heighten the experience of praying in liturgy in the spirit of holy conversation. It is important to give greater attention to how we pray in liturgy and not just call attention to the fact that we pray.

In order to deepen prayerful holy conversation, it is crucial to create a sense of spaciousness while praying the prayers of intercession. A period of silence or at least a pregnant pause between petitions allows people the time to engage in prayer more deeply. The assisting minister asking for the prayers, often through slowing down the pace of praying and observing silence, opens up the space for people from the assembly to offer their own prayers aloud or silently.

The practice of praying in the assembly calls for effective catechesis, education about prayer, and formation by modeling the kind of prayer that is faithful and appropriate. Members of the assembly are called to understand, for example, that the offering of extemporaneous petitions is not a time to make overt political statements or to engage in an act of rebuttal in response to a petition offered by someone else in the assembly. Small prayer groups meeting during the week could undertake this educational and formational task, modeling and calling forth the kind of engagement that makes for praying deeply in response to the Word. Worship planners could employ these groups to craft the prayers for the upcoming Sunday. Small groups practicing *lectio divina* with the lectionary texts for the coming Sunday may be an ideal "committee" for writing prayers that emerge from the Scriptures.

Praying Closely with the Readings and Our Meditations

When I think of prayers of intercession on the day of Pentecost, offered in the manner described above, prayed with a sense of closeness to the readings and meditations on the themes of the day, I imagine the following exchanges between an assisting minister and the assembly in prayerful holy conversation—notice how the language employs words, images, and ideas from the day's readings, hymn texts, and other Pentecost themes:

Assisting minister: "With the whole people of God in Christ Jesus, let us pray for the church, those in need, and all of God's creation."

Silence is kept as members of the assembly anticipate the prayers they may offer.

Assisting minister: "Let us pray for the church universal, its ministry, and the mission of the gospel."

Time is observed for silent prayer and/or for members of the assembly to offer their own spoken prayers.

Petitioner: "Gracious God, the disciples of old were full of fear and remained in a locked room. We, too, live in an age of fear when we are tempted to lock ourselves in and away from others, even in our churches. May the winds of your Spirit rush in to our closed-off places that we may be released from the fears that bind us and keep us silent. In your Spirit's power, give us the courage to proclaim your deeds of power as on the day of Pentecost."

After a pregnant pause—

Another petitioner: "God of tempest, of whirlwind, of blazing and burning, of earthquake and thunder, of passion unsleeping, drive us out from sheltered comfort into costly service, to bear the cross, speak the truth. We beseech you to break our chains of sin so that in our oneness in Christ we may be agents of the earth's healing, as you claim us for your kingdom's work."

After another period of silence, when it seems clear that no further audible petitions will be offered, this segment of petitioning concludes.

Assisting minister: "Hear us, O God."

The whole assembly: "Your mercy is great."

Again, the assisting minister invites our prayers: "Let us pray for the well-being of creation."

Petitioner, after a silent pause: "Our dear Mother Earth is feverish and we, your people, may be contributors to her malaise. As your Spirit brooded over the face of the deep at creation, so send forth your Spirit now to renew the face of the earth. Use us to bring healing to the environment during this global warming crisis."

Another petitioner: "O God, we know your majesty in creation even in earthquakes and volcanoes. Thank you, God, for your extreme wonders that provoke our worshipful awe of you, even as we pray for victims of natural disaster. Like the psalmist, 'I will sing to you, O LORD, as long as I live; I will praise my God while I have my being.' May our praise deepen our resolve to aid those in the way of nature's fury."

Assisting minister: "Hear us, O God."

The assembly: "Your mercy is great."

Assisting minister: "Let us pray for peace and justice in the nations of the world."

Petitioner: "As Jesus offered peace to his disciples in the locked room after his resurrection, so may we enter the forbidden and foreboding places to make for that same peace of God."

Another petitioner: "You send us to forgive and so entrust us with the ministry of reconciliation; give us the power and courage of your Spirit to do this reconciling work in such a way as to bring about your justice."

Still another petitioner: "May our peacemaking and our preaching be living proclamations intelligible in the languages and cultures of all the nations of the earth, that more and more may know of your righteousness and mercy. May our proclamation be more in the spirit of Pentecost than Babel, drawing all people to yourself."

Assisting minister: "Hear us, O God."

The assembly: "Your mercy is great."

Once again, the assisting minister: "Let us pray for those in authority in our communities."

Petitioner: "May our leaders not be judged to be filled with new wine; rather, may they lead with all wisdom and truth."

Another petitioner: "There is so much partisan bickering in the public arena that seeks to silence voices of the other. Give us the generosity of Moses to proclaim an inclusive vision: 'Would that all the LORD's people were prophets, and that the LORD would put his spirit on them.'"

Assisting minister: "Hear us, O God."

The whole assembly: "Your mercy is great."

Assisting minister: "Let us pray for the poor, the oppressed, those bereaved, the lonely and those who are sick, and for all who suffer in body, mind, or spirit . . ."

Here, engaging a familiar custom in our churches, the assembly gives voice to the names of those on their hearts and in their minds . . .

The assisting minister concludes this time for bidding: "Hear us, O God."

With some heaviness of heart, the assembly: "Your mercy is great."

Assisting minister: "Let us pray for the special needs and concerns of this congregation."

Members of the assembly add their varied prayers that name specific circumstances, ministries, and initiatives of the local congregation: "That on this day of Pentecost and always we would offer an incarnate Word in the power of the Spirit in all that we do as a congregation." "That the Spirit would continue to speak through our prophetic ministries." "That we may rejoice in the presence of the risen Lord always even in the changes and chances of our lives—Holy Spirit, let it be so." "That we would feel the Spirit's breath as that of Jesus even now in our celebrations in these latter days, that our ministries would be full of the living God . . ."

Sensing that the prayers for the local assembly, for its life and witness, could continue for some time, the assisting minister gently draws this bidding to a close: "Hear us, O God."

Once again, the assembly replies: "Your mercy is great."

The assisting minister finally invites prayerful remembrance of the blessed dead: "We commend to your mercy all who have died, praying in thanksgiving for their lives and witness, especially . . ."

Here the assembly adds names of those near and dear, also including those commemorated in the church's calendar of saints.

After names are offered, the assisting minister concludes: "We pray that we may share with all your saints in your eternal kingdom. Hear us, O God."

The assembly once again: "Your mercy is great."

The presiding minister then draws to a close the prayers of intercession, expressing the deep aspirations on behalf of the whole assembly: "Into your hands, gracious God, we commend all for whom we pray, trusting in your mercy; through Jesus Christ, our Savior."

Accompanied by sighs too deep for words, carried on the breath of the Spirit, the assembly says to let it be so: "Amen."

During this time of intercession, individual members have both prayed aloud and offered silently the prayers of their hearts in an intimacy with God we can never fully know. Hearing the audible prayers offered by members of the assembly further deepens the individual prayer and gives courage to others to give voice to the prayers of their hearts. In this prayerful way, the Spirit builds us up as the body of Christ in community together, taking us to new levels of intimacy as a congregation. During the prayers, when names are named and particular circumstances are brought to our attention, members of the assembly make mental notes—"I will send a card to the one for whom we have prayed"; "I will pay a visit"; "I am moved to join the commission for social justice." And so on. In these ways, the Spirit moves us to take action, to become in mission and ministry answers to our own aspirations, all the while quickened by the Spirit's movement in our midst.

In some liturgical traditions, the prayers of intercession are followed by prayers of confession and forgiveness. Deep prayer can lead to compunction, a cutting to the quick, a breaking through defenses that reveals our shortcomings and inspires our repentance. When confession is made, the presiding minister offers absolution, creating by God's grace in the power of the Spirit the conditions for reconciliation and knowing God's peace.

The Peace

As suggested previously, sharing the peace is a fulcrum moment in the liturgy, a transition from focusing on the Word to that segment of the service that focuses on the meal as visible Word. In terms of the movements of *lectio divina* applied to liturgical participation, the peace marks the progression from the prayers to contemplation, that which emphasizes our communion, if not to say union, with God in Christ and with others in the assembly and throughout the world. Itself an enacted prayer, the sharing of the peace moves the assembly into more physical activity as we literally get up from our seats to greet others with handshakes and hugs and perhaps even kisses.

This moment in the liturgy evokes recollections of various biblical instructions that often conclude New Testament epistles. Here is Paul's instruction at the end of his second letter to the Corinthians: "Finally, brothers and sisters, farewell. Put things in order, listen to my appeal, agree with one another, live in peace; and the God of love and peace will be with you. Greet one another with a holy kiss. All the saints greet you. The grace of the Lord Jesus Christ, the love of God, and the communion of the Holy Spirit be with all of you" (2 Cor. 13:11-13). In addition to instruction about the holy kiss, this passage contains the language of greeting that begins the liturgy for the day of Pentecost that we have been exploring. As that greeting marks the gathering, the sharing of the peace is an additional greeting that demarcates the beginning of another segment of the liturgy in this fulcrum moment. These verses from 2 Corinthians also suggest elaborations on what the peace means, that it involves order and agreement, living in peace in community, buoyed up by the very love of God and accompanied by the greetings of all the saints. The holy kiss contains and conveys these divine and human communal realities.

The final verse of the first letter of Peter contains the instruction and the language that inform our liturgical practice: "Greet one another with a kiss of love. Peace to all of you who are in Christ" (1 Peter 5:14). The actual practice of sharing the peace in the liturgy dates from the second century. It was the custom then for communing members of the assembly to greet each other after having dismissed the catechumens, those not yet baptized and thus who were not communicants.

Sharing the peace may itself be an answer to our prayers for peace, begun in the singing of the *Kyrie* during the gathering rite: "In peace, let us pray to the Lord; Lord, have mercy." Sharing the peace is in part God's reply to our pleas in holy conversation, nurturing a space for peace in our very midst, as we don't just talk about peace, but participate in its very enactment. Guigo describes this turn from prayerful pleas to the more direct experience of the God of peace in this way:

> So the soul by such burning words [in prayer] inflames its own desire, makes known its state, and by such spells it seeks to call its spouse. But the Lord, whose eyes are upon the just and whose ears can catch not only the words, but the very meaning of their prayers, does not wait until the longing soul has said all its say, but breaks in upon the middle of its prayer, runs to meet it in all haste, sprinkled with sweet heavenly dew, anointed with the most precious perfumes, and He restores the weary soul, He slakes its thirst, He feeds its hunger . . .[2]

For Guigo, such a meeting, such an embrace between lovers, is the beginning of contemplation. In the liturgy, sharing the peace also marks contemplation's beginning, the time for communion, even as it follows on the heels of prayer, is itself prayer, and is a fulfillment of our prayer. The lines between the movements of *lectio divina* and also those of the liturgy are not always easily demarcated. Our spiritual movements flow naturally into each other.

The presiding minister announces, "The peace of Christ be with you always." The assembly replies in dialogue, "And also with you." Here it is as though Christ himself meets us in assembly in these words of greeting and in the embraces that accompany them. With these words evoking images of Jesus appearing to his disciples on the day of resurrection in the room with locked doors, it is as if Jesus himself suddenly appears in our midst as we are Christ to each other. The assembly erupts into mini holy conversations, one-on-one, as we embrace each other, voicing Jesus' own words to each other: "Peace be with you." When we approach each other it is as though the Lord himself is rushing to greet us, having broken in on our prayers just offered, as Guigo suggests. We may even feel the breath of our partners in assembly, in the body of Christ, as if Jesus is breathing on us, imparting once again to us the Holy Spirit. Our prayer in the sharing of the peace thus takes on increasingly embodied expression in our actions that point to union with each other and with God. In these enactments the liturgy also turns from texts to signs and symbols in our behavior, so that we become the Word of peace as we are doers of that Word (James 1:22).

Sharing the Peace in Your Context

Think of how the peace is enacted in your assembly and reflect on the meaningfulness of the signs of peace you share with each other. On a continuum, is this a time of greater formality or informality? On a continuum, would you describe the qualities of peace sharing as more sacred or profane? Do people offer hugs, handshakes, or kisses? What does a hug convey in contrast to a handshake or a kiss? Consider why it is that sharing the peace is a practice resisted in some communities. What is behind that resistance? Embraces and kisses have been sources of abuse in Christian communities. Pray that a practice that has such sacred potential would not be cause for further sin and brokenness in community. These considerations call for meditative attention, since how we share the peace has a great deal to do with what in fact is conveyed, what word is proclaimed through our actions, our behavior, our attitudes in sharing the peace.

If an order for confession and forgiveness began the liturgy or if such an order immediately preceded this moment, the peace becomes the occasion to enact and model the work of reconciliation with those perhaps estranged from us. In this, the sharing of the peace relates intimately to what comes next in the liturgy, namely, the gathering and presenting of gifts, activity only to be undertaken in the conditions of peaceful reconciliation as suggested by Jesus in the Sermon on the Mount: "So when you are offering your gift at the altar, if you remember that your brother or sister has something against you, leave your gift there before the altar and go; first be reconciled to your brother or sister, and then come and offer your gift" (Matt. 5:23-24). The precondition for moving on in the liturgy to the offering of gifts is making peace within the assembly.

Furthermore, the peace also anticipates the sending rite in that our embrace of each other in the liturgical assembly leads to our embrace of others in the world in doing the work of reconciliation. The peace is a time to experience and share the peace we know in the gospel having been proclaimed. Sharing the peace expresses Christian unity and prefigures the communion we will know at the table in the Eucharist. It is the work Jesus has given us to do: " 'Peace be with you. As the Father has sent me, so I send you.' When he had said this, he breathed on them and said to them, 'Receive the Holy Spirit. If you forgive the sins of any, they are forgiven them; if you retain the sins of any, they are retained' " (John 20:21-23).

The peace, then, is a crucial dimension of liturgy as holy conversation. In other words, sharing the peace is far more than mere glad-handing and saying "Good morning." It is far more than a prefiguring of the social hour. Rather, the social hour best emerges from the peace known in liturgical settings. Moreover, sharing the peace is not a seventh-inning stretch. Know the gravitas of this encounter. It is Christ's peace we share, God's *shalom*, the holistic well-being for all that is the mark of the very reign of God. It is a peace that passes understanding, that contains and proclaims the gospel, our peace with God, our salvation made possible through justifying grace. Our peace with God makes possible peace with each other. It is the peace of the Lord, of Christ, taken up in the power of the Spirit and that Spirit's breath, not mere human efforts at hospitality. Inspired by Benedictine spirituality, we see in each other and perhaps especially our guests, the strangers in our midst, the very face of Christ. The focus is Christ, and then seeing Christ in each other.

GATHERING AND PRESENTING GIFTS, AND TABLE PREPARATION

Following the peace, the gathering and presentation of gifts and preparation of the table accompanied by musical offerings continue our prayer, building on the previous movements of the liturgy and propelling the assembly on the liturgical continuum toward the contemplative sacramental meal. The liturgical practice of gift gathering dates from the second century when people offered varieties of gifts, often common foods, their first fruits, an affirmation of the goodness of creation, and materials useful for ministry to the poor. In common current practice, ushers pass plates or other receptacles to collect monetary gifts from members of the assembly. Here a choir may sing an anthem specially prepared for the day, or other music is offered. The assembly may sing a hymn. Gifts—money, bread, wine, and sometimes other in-kind donations designated for ministries of the church—are brought forward in a procession, thus anticipating the sending rite, the liturgy's conclusion when we are propelled into the world to do the work God has given us to do in the power of the Spirit. Following custom that also dates from the second century, deacons or assisting ministers during this time also prepare the table for the eucharistic meal. This segment of the liturgy may conclude with an offertory prayer.

Like the peace, the experience surrounding the gathering and presentation of gifts is active and embodied, and also full of sights—signs and symbols—and sounds. It is a busy time, with seemingly competing activities, a choir singing an anthem while ushers collect money and assisting ministers occupy themselves preparing the table. The busyness of this movement evokes thoughts of Jesus' visit to the house of Mary and Martha (Luke 10:38-42). Martha busied herself about the house with preparations that she might be hospitable to Jesus, while Mary, in contrast, sat at Jesus' feet to attend carefully to what he was saying. Now in the liturgy is our time to be Martha. In a few moments, when the table is ready, we return to a state of deeper prayerfulness, a more contemplative mode of presence in the spirit of Mary, as we gather around Jesus' feet, as it were, during the meal.

All of this activity—the gathering and presentation of gifts, the musical offering, the table preparation—together constitutes a singular offering in keeping with the apostle Paul's exhortation: "I appeal to you therefore, brothers and sisters, by the mercies of God, to present your bodies as a living sacrifice, holy and acceptable to God, which is your spiritual worship" (Rom. 12:1). Recalling Guigo's image, as Christ broke in on the middle of our prayers to offer his peace to us, we reply with appreciation, having offered ourselves to each other in the peace of Christ, and now run to greet him, offering ourselves via material gifts as an enacted and embodied prayer of praise and thanksgiving. Recall that *body—soma* in the Greek—includes all that we are, in terms of our physicality, yes, but also in the totality of our thoughts, words, and deeds, symbolized in the materiality of bread, wine, and monetary gifts.

As ushers take up the collection, members of the assembly understand that the notion of offering is not reduced to collecting cash, so often an idolatrous symbol in our society. Nor is this action reduced simply to the mechanics of collection. This activity speaks; it proclaims in meaningful ways at symbolic levels. Money is a sign in our society of wider resources, blessings, and gifts, but it is a sign fraught with difficult associations, representing greed and injustice, for example, alongside the many blessings related to vocation and livelihood.

Visual Meditations on the Gifts and the Table

What associations do you have with money—represented in the form of bills, coins, and checks—signs that point beyond themselves to other meanings? Likewise, picture the bread and the wine commonly used where you worship. What kinds of bread are employed? Individual wafer-like hosts? Loaves? What kinds of wine? Varied styles of classic liturgical symbols convey different connotations, nuances of meaning. In brief, they speak in different ways, pointing to the rich meaningfulness of symbolism. Reflection on the particularities of the symbols and their meaningfulness to you can be a rich aspect of holy conversation during this movement of the liturgy.

In similar imaginative exercise, consider the table and how it is set. Does it bespeak the manner of a formal dinner with elaborate appointments? Or is it suggestive of common family meals? What vessels are used to contain and deliver the consecrated gifts? Are they made of precious metals, glass, or stoneware? Reflect on the manner of gathering at the table. Will communicants gather around the table? Will they stand? Kneel? How do these considerations speak to you? Again, your reflections can serve to deepen your prayerful holy conversation, enriching a time that may otherwise seem routine and simply pragmatic.

OFFERTORY MUSIC

It is an ancient custom to join music, for example, the singing of psalm texts, with the gathering of gifts and the setting of the table. In contemporary practice, it is common for a choir to sing an anthem during this time or for other musicians to offer musical selections. In order to deepen holy conversation, musicians offer music in a manner that conveys a prayerful presence that avoids performance and overtones of entertainment. This music is an offering on behalf of the whole assembly, giving expression to the offering of our bodies, the living sacrifice that is our spiritual worship. Prayerful listening to this musical offering (*audio divina* or sacred listening), appreciating the weddedness of text to tune, deepens the assembly's holy conversation. This music serves not simply to cover the mechanics of receiving gifts and setting the table, thus marking time. Rather, the musical offering heightens both our prayerfulness and our experience of the spiritual encounter taking place.

Appropriate for the day of Pentecost, a choir sings an anthem setting of this text by Bianco da Siena, translated from the Italian by Richard Frederick Littledale:

> Come down, O Love divine;
> seek thou this soul of mine
> and visit it with thine own ardor glowing;
> O Comforter, draw near;
> within my heart appear
> and kindle it, thy holy flame bestowing.
>
> Oh, let it freely burn,
> till worldly passions turn
> to dust and ashes in its heat consuming;
> and let thy glorious light
> shine ever on my sight,
> and clothe me round, the while my path illuming.
>
> Let holy charity
> mine outward vesture be,
> and lowliness become mine inner clothing—
> true lowliness of heart,
> which takes the humbler part,
> and o'er its own shortcomings weeps with loathing.
>
> And so the yearning strong,
> with which the soul will long,
> shall far out-pass the pow'r of human telling;
> no soul can guess Love's grace
> till it become the place
> wherein the Holy Spirit makes a dwelling.[3]

Bianco da Siena, who died in 1434, wrote this text, part of a longer poem, in the tradition of *Laudi*, Italian vernacular devotional songs dating from the days of St. Francis of Assisi.[4] The poetry makes reference to the flames associated with the coming of the Spirit at Pentecost by way of pointing to the spiritual theme of purgation or the burning away of sinful chaff that leads to greater purity of faith and devotion. It likewise calls attention to the theological virtues of charity (love) and lowliness (humility), emerging from compunction, each virtue being the fruit of the Spirit's burning and illumination in our lives. The poetry likewise speaks to our aspirations, the yearning, the longing that accompanies the prayerful self-offering of the assembly at this point in the liturgy as we eagerly anticipate the communion, when Word and bread and wine are joined with us via the power of the Holy Spirit, making for our speechless, contemplative dwelling with Christ.

At the conclusion of the choir's musical offering, the whole assembly stands to make its own music. Many assemblies sing a familiar doxology at this point: "Praise God from whom all blessings flow . . ." Or a hymn may be sung that expresses thanks for God's abundant gifts in our lives and calls for our thankful self-offering. A canticle text by John Arthur that alludes to various biblical passages gives lovely expression to the prayerful offering of ourselves, including our deepest aspirations, and can be sung by the whole assembly as the gifts are brought forward:

> Let the vineyards be fruitful, Lord [cf. Isa. 5:1; Hos. 10:1; Ezek. 19:10], and fill to the brim our cup of blessing [cf. Ps. 23:5]. Gather a harvest from the seeds that were sown [cf. Rev. 14:15], that we may be fed with the bread of life [cf. John 6:48]. Gather the hopes and dreams of all; unite them with the prayers we offer now. Grace our table with your presence, and give us a foretaste of the feast to come.[5]

In the prayerful singing, petitioning God to "gather the hopes and dreams of all," we call attention to our deepest aspirations, offering those alongside the material gifts, signs of all that we are, our living sacrifice, our spiritual worship. We likewise anticipate the contemplative encounter soon to be before us.

OFFERTORY PRAYER

An assisting minister next may pray on behalf of the whole assembly in a manner that parallels a tradition of the priest praying over the gifts and echoing themes of Jewish table prayers: "Blessed are you, O Lord our God, maker of all things. Through your goodness you have blessed us with these gifts. With them we offer ourselves to your service and dedicate our lives to the care and redemption of all that you have made, for the sake of him who gave himself for us, Jesus Christ our Lord."[6] While the actions of this portion of the liturgy may speak for themselves, this brief collect summarizes the sense of this time of prayerful self-offering of our bodies as living sacrifices. This offering does not intend to curry favor with God in the sense of earning grace through our own merit or through the giving of material gifts. Rather, the sense is of thankful response with wide-open hands and arms, knowing that all of what we offer comes first from God. So it is that our prayerful offering is a sacrifice of praise and thanksgiving. In this Spirit, the assembly responds, "Amen."

The table preparations for the banquet have been completed. Busy hands, like Martha's, may now rest. In the spirit of Mary who sat at Jesus' feet, members of the assembly can lift their hearts in prayer, anticipating meeting Christ himself in the breaking of the bread.

Chapter 8

CONTEMPLATION

In contrast to meditation, which involves very active mental processes, contemplation in *lectio divina* emphasizes receptive, directly participatory, and experiential modes of awareness. Contemplation also features a reintegration with our sense of being embodied, an appreciation for how God in Christ through the Spirit is present in our bodies as temples of that Spirit. It is natural, then, to link contemplation with that movement of the liturgy focused on the meal, the Eucharist, the Holy Communion, the context in which the liturgy is most embodied. Direct, experiential contact is the essence of what contemplation means in *lectio divina*, and this is very much what is experienced in the Eucharist. Here is occasion for embodied participation. We confess Christ's real presence as visible Word in, with, and under the gifts of bread and wine. We take these physical gifts into our own bodies through eating and drinking. The characteristics of contemplation—incarnate uniting, reconnection, remembering, communion—are the experiential gifts of Holy Communion.

In terms of the modalities of holy conversation, this is the time for deep, wordless communication—communion—with the beloved other who is Christ, and also doing so in companionship—*com* + *panis* in Latin, those who share bread—with other members of the assembly. How very appropriate for this communication to occur around the table while sharing a meal.

THE GREAT THANKSGIVING

Leading up to this deep participation in Christ is further proclamation, meditation, and prayer. The language of the Great Thanksgiving, the prayer preceding the communion, having creedal overtones and consistent with Jewish table blessings, proclaims again God's mighty deeds throughout history and particularly in Christ as a culmination of God's work for humanity. Our attentive listening to that language invites our meditation: What does this mean for us in our day? The lengthy discourse that leads to the communion is carried in the language of prayer as praise and thanksgiving, thus providing continuity with the prayers of intercession and other prayers that have preceded this moment in the liturgy. Furthermore, Christ meets us in the condition in which we gathered, hearkening back to the preparatory activity at the service's beginning. And this movement in the liturgy anticipates worship's final movement, the sending—we are here fed that we may be empowered to go and feed the world. The Great Thanksgiving, then, links us with all of the movements of the liturgy and those of *lectio divina*.

The Eucharist also has a special place in connection with the day of Pentecost. Our communion with Christ in the Eucharist is another resurrection appearance, a celebration of Easter. The day of Pentecost is the fiftieth day of Easter, the culmination of these days of celebration of the resurrection. Thus, Pentecost cannot be separated from Easter, as Easter cannot be separated from the Eucharist. In Acts 2, it is the resurrection that Peter proclaims in the power of the Spirit. In John's Gospel appointed for the day of Pentecost, Jesus in the flesh—"he showed them his hands and his side" (John 20:20a)—appears where the disciples gathered. It is Jesus' breath emerging from his resurrected, physical body that carries and imparts the gift of the Holy Spirit to the disciples. It is this same body that we participate in through a simple meal of bread and wine in the power of the Spirit.

Christian spirituality, understood in light of the events associated with the celebration of Pentecost as Easter's culmination, is an earthy, embodied spirituality that does not separate flesh from spirit, but joins them in enduring unity. Spirituality's connection with the Eucharist is thus also an intimate one. During the Great Thanksgiving, the presiding minister invokes the presence of the Holy Spirit—*epiclesis* in the Greek—and it is the Spirit's power speaking in the Word in connection with the gifts of bread and wine that makes it possible for us to know, recognize, and experience Christ in the breaking of the bread.

CONTEMPLATION AND THE MEANINGS OF EUCHARIST

As a phenomenon, the Eucharist carries an extraordinary multivalence. That is to say, its meaningfulness extends far beyond singular themes. The names for this meal point to its variety of meanings: Last Supper, Lord's Supper, Holy Communion, Holy Eucharist, Mass, Blessed Sacrament, and so on. Each term highlights different features of the meaning of the sacrament.

At the level of operational theology—the theological affirmations enacted in common piety and the way our practices proclaim theological meaning—there may be tendencies to reduce the meaning of the Eucharist to a primary theme, for example, the forgiveness of sins. Sometimes this dimension becomes routinized, as if the act of giving bread and wine mechanically dispenses forgiveness. Taking seriously the multiple meanings of the Eucharist in connection with contemplation and the rhythms of *lectio divina* offers us an opportunity to explore the riches of the meanings of this sacrament. Forgiveness is indeed one of the profound gifts of the Eucharist. But we cannot reduce the significance of the sacrament to this one aspect. Following are meditations on the rich meanings of the meal.

In the Eucharist, the past, present, and future blend in a moment of remembrance and hopeful anticipation. Through deep remembrance, the kind of remembrance that re-presents past activity—suggested by the Greek word for remembrance, *anamnesis*—the event of the Last Supper, indeed the whole Passion of Christ's death and resurrection, is made real to us in the present time. As we enjoy a foretaste of the feast to come, the future of promise breaks in upon us and we enjoy a taste of heaven. Thus, we experience even now the inbreaking of the reign of God, the fullness or consummation of which we await with eager anticipation.

The Eucharist is a fellowship meal, an embodiment of the church's *koinonia*, its communal life. As we enjoy communion with Christ, we also commune with our neighbors in assembly. Our fellowship extends, likewise, to the communion of saints from every time and place, every nation, ethnicity, and culture that has known believers. The sacramental table is surrounded by the presence of the saints of blessed memory who have gone before us as we share, as a popular hymn suggests, "mystic sweet communion with those whose rest is won."[1]

Furthermore, the meaningfulness of the Eucharist relates to the church's mission among all nations. In the sacrament we manifest Christian unity. When Christians can share the meal together, we know some fulfillment of Jesus' prayer in John's Gospel that all of his followers might be one—and here is the missiological purpose of our unity—"so that the world may believe" (John 17:21). Moreover, in this holy meal we are fed that we might feed, giving bread to a hungry world, becoming the body of Christ as church to be broken for that world in ministries of serving. Thus, the Eucharist also relates thematically to the justice-seeking mission of the church to work to eradicate the injustices that keep so many hungry.

In that the gifts of creation in bread and wine, grain and grapes are utilized in the sacrament, the Eucharist's meaningfulness relates importantly to the earth and our call to be stewards of creation. Even as human hands have exercised stewardship in the production and distribution of the bread and wine, so, too, we exercise this stewardship in our participation in economic activities. In this sense, the Eucharist connects with themes of natural theology and social ethics, our concerns for the earth reflected in our socioeconomic lives.

Quite importantly for purposes here, but not in any way disconnected from the preceding explorations of meanings, the Eucharist as communion points to its contemplative features. Like friends silently enjoying each other's presence, in the moments of communion speech is minimized and we enjoy the intimacy of receiving Christ's presence in visible expressions of grace in bread and wine, not unlike good friends who end their talking, but who nonetheless enact deeper, wordless conversation by just being in each other's company—company as it relates etymologically to companions, again, those who share bread together. But the meaningfulness of Eucharist in connection with contemplation goes beyond friendship. The contemplative aspects of the Eucharist can evoke a sense of deeper intimacies, like the child at the mother's breast and the embrace of lovers. There is a long and venerable history in Christian spiritual writings to employ both sexual and mother-child imagery to describe the contemplative encounter. Of the experience of contemplation, Guigo includes both images in a single sentence: "O my soul, recognize your spouse, embrace Him whom you long for, make yourself drunk with this torrent of delight, and suck the honey and milk of consolation from the breast."[2]

In communion we are united with Christ in parallel fashion to the union between lovers, two becoming one flesh in the nuptial embrace. In this sense, the chancel becomes a bedchamber and the sacramental table the marital bed. Voices in the Christian tradition have viewed the whole church as the bride of Christ, who is our bridegroom. So it is that the embrace known in Eucharist cannot be reduced to an individualistic experience. We, as church, are communally united to Christ also. At the same time, we lay alongside these adult experiences recollections of our earliest experiences of receiving sustenance from our mother's breast; in this case, as Julian of Norwich suggested in her writings, it is Christ who is our mother. "The mother can give her child to suck of her milk, but our precious Mother Jesus can feed us with Himself, and does, most courteously and most tenderly, with the blessed sacrament, which is the precious food of true life"[3]

Furthermore, as we are united with Christ in the sacramental meal, we in a real sense become Christ, his body to be offered for the world. The Eucharist is the occasion for our becoming partakers of the divine nature in faith, enacted sacramentally. You are what you eat. As we consume the visible, sacramental Word that conveys Christ's real presence, so, too, do we become that Word to be offered up in our incarnate mission and ministry in the world.[4]

In the Eucharist we can know experientially what Jesus describes as the divine reality of his relationship with the God whom he calls *Abba*. "I will not leave you orphaned; I am coming to you. In a little while the world will no longer see me, but you will see me; because I live, you also will live. On that day you will know that I am in my Father, and you in me, and I in you" (John 14:18-20). As we abide with Christ in eucharistic presence in the meal, we share in the trinitarian life of God.

In short, with Christ's presence known in the breaking of bread comes everything that is Christ: forgiveness, life, salvation, his whole life and ministry, his death and resurrection, and all of the blessings that come to us thereby. Bread and wine as signs contain the fullness of this proclamation. Meditation on the holy mysteries nurtures the possibility of our seeing this proclamation more fully, and then also the possibility that we would experience its transformative benefits more deeply.

These meditations on the Eucharist as a meal, replete with significations that convey a multiplicity of meanings, may provoke and evoke your own particular imaginative reflection on the meanings of Eucharist for you that are likewise consonant with the traditions handed down to us through the centuries.

Longing to Be Home at the Table

During my early childhood—and this was before the days when noncommuning children were brought forward for a blessing—I recall longing to be present at the table. My mother, father, and older brother would go forward to receive communion. I stayed in my place. Perhaps it was simply a childhood sensitivity to being left behind. But I did sense that something extremely important and profound was happening at the chancel rail, and I wanted to be part of it. Was this longing an incipient cue indicating the central role the Eucharist would play in my emerging faith journey and spirituality? Was my desire to be at the table the beginning of the Spirit's nudging me, calling me to ordained ministry where I could find my true home and life's vocation? Who knows? I do affirm the Spirit's working through ordinary longings and desires. I do know that the eucharistic banquet table is a place where we are not left behind, but fully included and radically embraced.

Our experience of the meaningfulness of the Eucharist will vary with circumstances and the seasons of our lives, even as it may vary according to liturgical season. During Advent, we may experience the Eucharist as a foretaste of the feast to come. During Christmas it may be the embodied, incarnational dimensions of the Eucharist on which we focus. Epiphany may evoke the revelatory aspects, as in the showing forth of Jesus at the wedding feast in Cana of Galilee. Forgiveness may be the experiential focus during penitential seasons such as Lent. The Eucharist as a resurrection feast is a highlight of Easter. Pentecost may focus on the Spirit's power in making Christ known in the breaking of bread. Celebration of the Eucharist on All Saints' Day may help us be aware of the many saints who have gone before who are also present with us at the sacramental table.

It is this kind of meditative work that deepens holy conversation and nurtures greater openness to contemplative experience. In the Eucharist, Revelation and ongoing revelation coexist, a blending of once-and-for-all Revelation with the particularities of our own subjective experience. The cosmic and particular, the transcendent and immanent become blessedly mixed together when the body of Christ is given *for you*, and the blood of Christ is shed *for you*. Eucharistic experience also includes the paradoxical mixing of intense, intimate, and individual personal experience with experience that is simultaneously communal, even as *you* in English is simultaneously both singular and plural.

The experience of the Holy Communion can accommodate a wide array of feelings, ranging from joy to sorrow. To be sure, the Eucharist is an occasion for profound joy that the risen Christ is known in the breaking of bread. But this joyful embrace also paradoxically may create the sense of freedom to express deep grief and other feelings long repressed.[5] Guigo himself links tears with the experience of contemplation:

> Can it be that the heralds and witnesses of this consolation and joy are sighs and tears? . . . The wonderful reward and comforts which your spouse has brought and awarded you are sobbings and tears. . . . O Lord Jesus, if these tears, provoked by thinking of you and longing for you, are so sweet, how sweet will be the joy which we shall have to see you face to face? If it is so sweet to weep for you, how sweet will it be to rejoice in you?[6]

St. Ignatius of Loyola, the founder of the Society of Jesus, frequently experienced tears and sobbing when he celebrated the Eucharist as a priest. Writing in his diary, he says:

> As I finished vesting the name of Jesus imprinted itself so intensely within me and I was so fortified or seemingly confirmed for the future that tears and sobs came upon me with a new force. As I began Mass, overwhelming motions of copious grace and devotion continued to help me, along with peaceful, continual tears. Even when Mass was finished, a great devotion and impulses to tears lasted until I had unvested.[7]

The Word which is Christ in the Eucharist can reach us at our deepest levels. In these deep places our authentic conversion and transformation can occur beyond superficialities and very much at the core of that which needs to be healed, changed, forgiven, renarrated in our lives. Hence the catharsis of healing tears. The Eucharist is no simple memorial exercise or rite. Rather, it is Christ himself present as visible and performative and effective Word to give us all his gifts in our deepest, speechless conversation with him. Christ comes to us in bread and wine as visible Word that we literally assimilate into ourselves, flesh upon flesh. Christ enters our bodies as temples of the Holy Spirit (1 Cor. 6:19). In this temple—as in *templum*, anciently the place set apart for the examination of the entrails of sacrificed animals in a search for signs and omens—we meditatively look for signs in our viscera, in our gut. What in Christ's sacramentally embodied Word touches our embodiment? We carry meaning and metaphor in our bodies. A stiff neck, for example, points beyond itself to the stories of stress in our lives, to the meanings we attach to challenging circumstances. In a word of peace conveyed in the act of eating and drinking of the Prince of Peace, we may know some reduction in anxiety, some peacefulness and greater equanimity. This Word proclaimed in the act of eating and drinking may have a physiological effect in reducing the physical symptoms of stress. Imagine the Word of Christ touching you in healing ways in those parts of your body crying out for such healing.

A crucial question for sacramental practice is this: If the Eucharist is such an intimate participation in Christ and contains the profound meanings here explored, and furthermore, if the Word known in eating and drinking of the sacramental meal in fact can begin to enact our transformation, with what devotional activity do we surround this encounter? Current popular devotional practice related to the Eucharist can be very casual, if not perfunctory, and lacking in the sort of gravitas that may lead to the kind of deeper experiences that make for transformation.

The attitude that we would do well to cultivate in eucharistic devotional practice is worshipfulness as in *proskynesis*, the awe and wonder that inspire a sense of falling on our faces in light of the presence of Christ. So it is that some kneel during portions of the eucharistic liturgy. Observing significant silence during eucharistic celebration also creates the spaciousness for sustained reflection on what occurs in the sacrament. Liturgical leadership that is steeped in deep awareness and experience of the sacrament conveys the attitude of prayer and worshipfulness that invites the assembly's own sense of worship.

Preface Dialogue

The presiding minister begins a conversation with the assembly, a back-and-forth exchange that sets the stage for the further discourse of the Great Thanksgiving:

The Lord be with you.
And also with you.
Lift up your hearts.
We lift them to the Lord.
Let us give thanks to the Lord our God.
It is right to give our thanks and praise.

In this exchange between the presiding minister and the assembly, we see holy conversation, members of the assembly mirroring and echoing back to the presiding minister divine greetings, a heightened sense of expectation, and the invitation to share in thanksgiving, which is what *eucharist* means after all. This opening dialogue of the Great Thanksgiving begins among mortals, extends in the *Sanctus* ("Holy, Holy, Holy") to the choirs of angels, and culminates with the voice of Christ in our midst: "Take and eat; this is my body, given for you. Do this for the remembrance of me. . . . This cup is the new covenant in my blood, shed for you and for all people for the forgiveness of sin. Do this for the remembrance of me."

There is a sacred intimacy in the first exchange: "The Lord be with you"— or "The Lord is with you," according to another faithful translation of the original Latin. The statement is a recognition of the holy in our midst, the holiness of this encounter. Implied in this exchange, in the back-and-forth between presiding minister and assembly, is an important ecclesiological statement, an affirmation that it is the nature of the church that it takes the whole assembly to celebrate the Eucharist. The presiding minister has authority because of the assembly's presence; the assembly, as it were, "concelebrates" with the presiding minister. There is no private mass. Our Great Thanksgiving involves the whole assembly.

This simple exchange likewise evokes recollections of encounters recorded in the Bible. In the book of Ruth, Boaz greets his reapers: "The LORD be with you." They reply, "The LORD bless you" (Ruth 2:4). This moment of dialogue is set in the context of a story about hospitality and generosity, an attempt to address at least in part poverty endured by Ruth. Boaz gives permission for Ruth to glean from the fields what the reapers left behind, thus providing some food for herself and her people. Boaz extends his generosity to mealtime with this invitation: "Come here, and eat some of this bread, and dip your morsel in the sour wine" (Ruth 2:14a). Ruth happily accepts this invitation: "So she sat beside the reapers, and he heaped up for her some parched grain. She ate until she was satisfied, and she had some left over" (Ruth 2:14b). Such hospitality and generosity that seek to alleviate want are anticipated in our meal encounter when soon we will eat bread and drink or perhaps dip bread in wine. So shall we be satisfied. There promises to be enough left over to go and feed those who could not join us at the table.

"Lift up your hearts"—a curious instruction that has been present in the liturgy since at least the third century—literally, perhaps, "stand up," a practical instruction. But it is more than a literal directive. The heart is the seat of the human will. The invitation evokes a sense that the fullness of human willingness be turned to the divine, the fullness of who we are at the level of soul, of human identity, standing on tiptoes in expectation that Christ will be known in the breaking of bread. As the author of Colossians suggests, "So if you have been raised with Christ, seek the things that are above, where Christ is, seated at the right hand of God. Set your minds on things that are above, not on things that are on earth" (Col. 3:1-2). So we lift our hearts, our souls, all that we are, to the Lord in keeping with the words of the psalmist: "Gladden the soul of your servant, for to you, O LORD, I lift up my soul" (Ps. 86:4).

"Let us give thanks to the Lord our God. *It is right to give our thanks and praise.*" This exchange has origins in Jewish prayers. Giving thanks: in the Greek, *eucharisteo*, from which is derived *eucharist*. But contained in the Greek root word is the fullness of the gospel and related dispositions in response to good news:

- *charis* is grace;
- *chara*, joy;
- *chairo*, to rejoice;
- *synchairo*, to rejoice with;
- *charizomai*, to give freely;
- *charitoo*, to bestow favor or to bless;
- *charisma*, gift; and
- *eucharistia*, gratitude and thanksgiving.

What makes our thanksgiving possible in the first place is Jesus' cross and resurrection, of which the Eucharist is a celebration. The women had visited the tomb and found it empty. Angelic witnesses indicated to them that he had been raised. "Suddenly Jesus met them and said, 'Greetings'" (Matt. 28:9a)—*chairete*, in the Greek, translated variously but essentially an exhortation to rejoice, and in a single word in its root in connection to the above string of words, again, a proclamation of the whole gospel. Indeed, "it is right to give our thanks and praise" along with and in the manner of the women who, filled with both fear and joy, "came to him, took hold of his feet, and worshiped him" (Matt. 28:9b). In our ever-deepening holy conversation, this is what we are up to in exploring the contemplative dimensions of the sacred banquet.

PROPER PREFACE

The presiding minister continues with the Proper Preface, focusing our praise and thanksgiving according to the particularities of the seasonal themes of the day, a tradition common in Western Christianity since early days. The following

Proper Preface, portions of which are adapted from a preface in Thomas Cranmer's 1549 Prayer Book, is one appointed for the day of Pentecost:

> It is indeed right, our duty and our joy, that we should at all times and in all places give thanks and praise to you, almighty and merciful God, through our Savior Jesus Christ. Fulfilling the promise of the resurrection, you pour out the fire of your Spirit, uniting in one body people of every nation and tongue. And so, with Mary Magdalene and Peter and all the witnesses of the resurrection, with earth and sea and all their creatures, and with angels and archangels, cherubim and seraphim, we praise your name and join their unending hymn.[8]

Giving thanks and praise at all times and in all places, we heed Paul's exhortation to the church at Philippi: "Rejoice in the Lord always; again I will say, Rejoice" (Phil. 4:4a). In the liturgy, the Proper Preface corresponds with the particular season of the church year—Advent through the season after Pentecost. This preface echoes themes of the readings appointed for the day of Pentecost: the outpouring of the Spirit in connection with Jesus' resurrection, the tongues as of fire, and the unity known in the intelligibility of the proclamation of God's mighty deeds of power despite the diversity of languages through which proclamation was offered. But we add to this the seasons of our own lives individually and communally. Think of those times and places in the specific circumstances and seasons of our lives that give rise to our thanks and praise or challenge our ability to do so.

The presiding minister concludes the preface: "And so, with Mary Magdalene and Peter and all the witnesses of the resurrection, with earth and sea and all their creatures, and with angels and archangels, cherubim and seraphim, we praise your name and join their unending hymn." Holy conversation here extends to the cosmic and angelic realms and to the wideness of the communion of saints throughout the world and throughout history. There is a sense of crescendo as our song is lifted to the highest heights, emanating from the deepest depths, the specifics of our lives blending with the whole universe.

SANCTUS—HOLY, HOLY, HOLY

Paralleling the singing of the *Gloria*, the song of praise when we gathered, the whole assembly again erupts into an exuberant hymn sung by Christians in liturgy since at least the fourth century:

Holy, holy, holy Lord, God of power and might, heaven and earth are full of your glory. Hosanna in the highest. Blessed is he who comes in the name of the Lord. Hosanna in the highest.[9]

We join our voices with all the others, the witnesses of the resurrection, all creation, and the celestial hierarchies as we sing, "Holy, holy, holy . . ." We typically sing the *Sanctus* each time we celebrate the Eucharist. But it is so familiar that we might not think too much about it. Yet this is a high point of the liturgy, a deep expression of worship as *proskynesis*, of bowing down. Indeed, some liturgical ministers do make profound bows at the singing of the first half of the *Sanctus*. But what does this hymn mean? Here it is compelling again to turn meditatively to the scriptural passages from which this text comes to deepen our encounter with the language of worship as another expression of our holy conversation. The prophet Isaiah had a vision:

> In the year that King Uzziah died, I saw the Lord sitting on a throne, high and lofty; and the hem of his robe filled the temple. Seraphs were in attendance above him; each had six wings: with two they covered their faces, and with two they covered their feet, and with two they flew. And one called to another and said: "Holy, holy, holy is the LORD of hosts; the whole earth is full of his glory." The pivots on the thresholds shook at the voices of those who called, and the house was filled with smoke. (Isa. 6:1-4)

Joining our voices with the seraphs in singing "Holy, holy, holy" takes us to the place of the vision in our mind's eye if we allow ourselves to go there imaginatively. What would our liturgical experience be like if we had a sense of the thresholds of our worship spaces shaking and smoke, perhaps of incense, filling the room? How often does our singing of the *Sanctus* have this flavor, this sense? Deepening the holy conversation in meditation can take us to that imaginative but palpable place. The use of incense during the liturgy and evocative musical settings of the *Sanctus* may take us to the experience of the holy place as well.

In the presence of such holiness, Isaiah was filled with compunction: "Woe is me! I am lost, for I am a man of unclean lips" (Isa. 6:5a). But this does not stop the angelic figures from ministering to Isaiah: "Then one of the seraphs flew to me, holding a live coal that had been taken from the altar with a pair of tongs. The seraph touched my mouth with it and said: 'Now that this has touched your lips, your guilt has departed and your sin is blotted out'" (Isa. 6:6-7). This encounter ultimately ends in Isaiah's being called and commissioned to speak the word of the Lord: "Then I heard the voice of the Lord saying, 'Whom shall I send, and who will go for us?' And I said, 'Here am I; send me!'" (Isa. 6:8). Visiting the holy place, encountering the very power and majesty of God, propelled the prophet to speak. Isaiah so responded, as did Jesus' followers and Peter at Pentecost. So do we when holiness claims us. "Here am I; send me!"

The second half of the text of the canticle—"Hosanna in the highest. Blessed is he who comes in the name of the Lord"—comes from Psalm 118:25-26. Note this phrase in the larger context of the psalm, which is a hymn of victory:

> O give thanks to the LORD, for he is good;
>   his steadfast love endures forever! . . .
> Open to me the gates of righteousness,
>   that I may enter through them
>   and give thanks to the LORD.
> This is the gate of the LORD;
>   the righteous shall enter through it.
> I thank you that you have answered me
>   and have become my salvation.
> The stone that the builders rejected
>   has become the chief cornerstone.
> This is the LORD's doing;
>   it is marvelous in our eyes.
> This is the day that the LORD has made;
>   let us rejoice and be glad in it.
> Save us, we beseech you [in Hebrew, *Hosanna*], O LORD!
>   O LORD, we beseech you, give us success!
> Blessed is the one who comes in the name of the LORD.
>   We bless you from the house of the LORD.
> The LORD is God,
>   and he has given us light.
> Bind the festal procession with branches,
>   up to the horns of the altar.
> You are my God, and I will give thanks to you;
>   you are my God, and I will extol you.
> O give thanks to the LORD, for he is good,
>   for his steadfast love endures forever. (Ps. 118:1; 19-29)

These verses of the psalm serve as elaboration on the *Benedictus*, and exploring them thus deepens our participation in this language of praise.

Jesus himself invokes the words of the *Benedictus* emerging from Psalm 118:26 in his lament over Jerusalem in Matthew's Gospel. Speaking of his longing to nurture the children of Jerusalem as a mother hen "gathers her brood under her wings," he concludes by noting the troubled and apocalyptic times and the people's unwillingness to be nurtured: "For I tell you, you will not see me again until you say, 'Blessed is the one who comes in the name of the Lord'" (Matt. 23:39). Our praise in our own day is mixed with lament and passionate concern about our troubling time in history as we look for the one who comes in the name of the Lord.

This context of the second half of the *Sanctus* extends the meaningfulness of the single phrase we sing. Though not intended by the psalmist, we may meditatively and imaginatively read Psalm 118 with a christocentric view, seeing Jesus as the gate of righteousness, the stone having been rejected by the builders, who is the chief cornerstone. This psalm is filled with the language of thanksgiving, which, again, is what *eucharist* means. The "festal procession with branches" evokes Passion or Palm Sunday themes as we "proclaim Christ's death until he comes," anticipating our own procession to the altar to receive Christ's body and blood in the gifts of bread and wine. Indeed, "Blessed is the one who comes in the name of the Lord" was also the cry of the people in Jerusalem as Jesus entered the city: "Many people spread their cloaks on the road, and others spread leafy branches that they had cut in the fields. Then those who went ahead and those who followed were shouting, 'Hosanna! Blessed is the one who comes in the name of the Lord! Blessed is the coming kingdom of our ancestor David! Hosanna in the highest heaven!'" (Mark 11:8-10).

EUCHARISTIC PRAYER

After the assembly sings the *Sanctus*, the presiding minister continues with the Eucharistic Prayer, a prayer of thanksgiving at the table inspired in part by Jewish table blessings that included, for example, prayers over a cup. This prayer traditionally follows a particular pattern that includes the following:

- a thankful recollection of aspects of salvation history;
- the words of institution, that is, Jesus' own words at the Last Supper;
- remembrance (*anamnesis*) of Jesus' life, death, resurrection, and promise to come again;

- an invocation of the Holy Spirit (*epiclesis*);
- sometimes intercessions; and
- a final word of praise (doxology) and amen.

This prayer begins with human words and culminates with the divine voice, Jesus' own words, his presence in our midst in deep remembrance. In the meditative movements in *lectio divina*, memory deepens from reminiscence or recollection to *anamnesis*, when we more directly experience and participate in that which we remember, in this case, Christ's real presence in, with, and under the bread and the wine and in connection with the particularities of our own lives, experiences, and deep memories. The prayer of thanksgiving at the table, in its classic pattern, follows this movement. Our prayer turns into contemplative participation, and yearning and desire become fulfillment.

While early Christian eucharistic prayers were not scripted—it was the mark of a good bishop to be able to pray extemporaneously according to the traditional pattern—many classic prayers have been set to the page through the centuries. In addition to biblical material from the Gospels and a New Testament epistle, the following prayer of thanksgiving, constituent parts of which I will explore in turn, draws from ancient, Reformation-era, and modern sources, including the ancient liturgies of St. James of Jerusalem and St. John Chrysostom, the *Apostolic Constitutions*, *Apostolic Tradition*, the 1549 *Book of Common Prayer*, the Scottish Presbyterian *Book of Common Order* 1940, and the Roman canon in translation[10]—voices of the faithful speaking through the ages in ecumenical diversity. The presiding minister begins, maintaining a focus on the holy that lets the *Sanctus* just sung continue to echo:

> You are indeed holy, almighty and merciful God. You are most holy, and great is the majesty of your glory. You so loved the world that you gave your only Son, so that everyone who believes in him may not perish but have eternal life. We give you thanks for his coming into the world to fulfill for us your holy will and to accomplish all things for our salvation.

This segment of the prayer also serves as proclamation in that it offers up the beloved and well-known words of John 3:16 and calls attention to Jesus' last moments on the cross also in John's Gospel: "When Jesus knew that all was now finished, he said (in order to fulfill the scripture), 'I am thirsty'" (John 19:28). The bystanders offered him a wine-soaked sponge attached to a branch. "When Jesus had received the wine, he said, 'It is finished.' Then he bowed his head and gave up his spirit" (John 19:30). This scriptural voice contained in the thanksgiving invites the assembly's recollection and affirmation of Jesus' saving death that makes for our life.

The presiding minister continues with the words of institution, following closely the scriptural accounts of Jesus' words at the Last Supper (cf. Matt. 26:26-28; Mark 14:22-24; Luke 22:17-20; 1 Cor. 11:23-25):

> In the night in which he was betrayed, our Lord Jesus took bread, and gave thanks; broke it, and gave it to his disciples, saying: Take and eat; this is my body, given for you. Do this for the remembrance of me.
>
> Again, after supper, he took the cup, gave thanks, and gave it for all to drink, saying: This cup is the new covenant in my blood, shed for you and for all people for the forgiveness of sin. Do this for the remembrance of me.

In some liturgical traditions, the presiding minister's repetition of these words is the extent of the consecratory prayer. But for the sake of nurturing a sense of the sacred drama of these moments toward deepening holy conversation, we do well to use these words of Jesus in the context of the whole pattern of table blessing with which Jesus himself would have been very familiar given his Jewish faith and which he would have practiced. The Holy Spirit speaks through the language and action of the whole Great Thanksgiving, that Christ's presence may be made known in the gifts of bread and wine.

Quoting the apostle Paul in 1 Corinthians 11:26, the presiding minister continues: "For as often as we eat of this bread and drink from this cup, we proclaim the Lord's death until he comes." The assembly in unison proclaims the mystery of faith by way of assent and affirmation: "Christ has died. Christ is risen. Christ will come again."

With humility—acknowledging that "we do not know how to pray as we ought, but [the] Spirit intercedes with sighs too deep for words" (Rom. 8:26) and realizing that the deepest expression of holy conversation is the divine voice speaking in us—the presiding minister proceeds with the *anamnesis*, the remembrance of the salvific events of Christ's life, and the *epiclesis*, the invocation of the Holy Spirit:

> Remembering, therefore, his salutary command, his life-giving passion and death, his glorious resurrection and ascension, and the promise of his coming again, we give thanks to you, O Lord God Almighty, not as we ought but as we are able; we ask you mercifully to accept our praise and thanksgiving and with your Word and Holy Spirit to

bless us, your servants, and these your own gifts of bread and wine, so that we and all who share in the body and blood of Christ may be filled with heavenly blessing and grace, and, receiving the forgiveness of sin, may be formed to live as your holy people and be given our inheritance with all your saints.

The Spirit is invoked not just over the gifts of bread and wine, but over the whole assembly, in recognition that sacred presence is not reduced simplistically to the gifts, but that the wind of the Spirit blows through the whole room and on all participants. Again recalling Jesus' resurrection appearance in the Gospel for the day of Pentecost, we may imagine Jesus' very breath, Jesus present now via Word and bread and wine, imparting the Spirit anew to us as at the peace, that we may receive the spiritual gifts that empower us to lead and serve as holy people, forgiven, heirs of eternity, full of blessing and grace, in company with all the saints.

The presiding minister concludes with a doxology, a final expression of praise: "To you, O God, Father, Son, and Holy Spirit, be all honor and glory in your holy church, now and forever." The assembly replies with its threefold affirmation, "Amen. Amen. Amen." The Eucharistic Prayer ends as it began: with words of praise and thanksgiving and the assembly's agreement that, yes, it is most certainly true that Christ is in our midst.

The Lord's Prayer

The presiding minister next invites the assembly to pray the Lord's Prayer. Locating this prayer at the conclusion of the Eucharistic Prayer dates from the time of Gregory the Great in the sixth century. Here we share the desire of Jesus' first disciples, "Lord, teach us to pray" (Luke 11:1b), as we find fulfillment of that desire in Jesus' own words:

Our Father in heaven, hallowed be your name, your kingdom come, your will be done, on earth as in heaven. Give us today our daily bread. Forgive us our sins as we forgive those who sin against us. Save us from the time of trial and deliver us from evil. (cf. Matt. 6:9-13; Luke 11:2-4)

The doxology that commonly concludes the Lord's Prayer in many traditions dates from the time of the *Didache*, a document describing life and practice in the church of the second century: "For the kingdom, the power, and the glory are yours, now and forever. Amen."

Think of this not so much as our prayer, but Jesus' own prayer, his own words, in the power of his presence in our midst. Our giving utterance to the words of the "Our Father" is really Christ speaking through us in the power of the Spirit. In holy conversation, we began this segment of the liturgy with our own words. Now Jesus is present, speaking to us and praying his own word in us and through us—and perhaps in spite of us when we pray this well-known prayer by rote, inattentive to its significance, sidetracked by the routine of giving voice to such familiar words. This praying shares in the contemplative movement, our participation with Christ, directly and experientially, as we are linked to him through his words.

BREAKING THE BREAD

The presiding minister now breaks the bread, observing a custom dating from about the fourth century. This is both symbolic action and a practical matter. At the level of symbol and visible Word, breaking bread signifies the body of Christ broken for us and for the world. This broken bread is also a sign through which we recognize the resurrected Christ, even as the disciples on the road to Emmaus recognized Jesus in the breaking of the bread (Luke 24:28-35). As a practical matter, the bread needs to be divided into pieces for distribution. Some is reserved for later use in bringing the consecrated gifts to those who are sick, infirm, or otherwise cannot be present at the assembly. When a bishop celebrates the Eucharist, there has been a custom of the bishop taking some of the consecrated gifts to other churches visited by the bishop as a sign of church unity. Likewise, sometimes bits of bread from one particular service will be saved to be dropped in a vessel at the next liturgy, a sign of unity and continuity in Christ, ever present, the one who was, and is, and is to come.

Perhaps this moment in the liturgy, when the gifts are elevated during the final doxology of the Eucharistic Prayer, is the time for "adoration of the blessed sacrament," a reclaiming and redirecting of the medieval practice of the Benediction of the Blessed Sacrament, when worshipers would adore a consecrated host contained behind glass in a monstrance. Rather than adoration of the host, or bread, as object, here is a call for time, for spaciousness, that worshipers in fact may worship, may bow in the presence of the mystery that Christ is known to us in the breaking of bread. We may turn our gaze to the table and its surroundings in contemplative wonder that Christ is in our midst through Word and earthy gifts in the power of the Spirit. This is not a time for rushed activity, and this movement in the liturgy may call for the sound of sheer silence, or at least a pregnant pause, that we may have the time and mental space for wonder, awe, adoration, worship, anticipating the reception of the holy gifts into our very selves.

AGNUS DEI—LAMB OF GOD

After the breaking of the bread, the assembly may join in song, often singing the *Agnus Dei*, a classic text of the ordinary of the Mass at least since the early eighth century when this hymn, originally embedded within the *Gloria in Excelsis*, was made its own independent song. Custom had been to sing the phrases for as long as it took to break the bread for distribution—there is great spiritual power in repetition as the words of the text soak deeper into our consciousness, ever deepening holy conversation:

> Lamb of God, you take away the sin of the world; have mercy on us.
> Lamb of God, you take away the sin of the world; have mercy on us.
> Lamb of God, you take away the sin of the world; grant us peace.[11]

In this song is the implied language of sacrifice—the lamb who was slain for our forgiveness and for our peace. When we sing, we echo the words of John the Baptist, who upon seeing Jesus draw near exclaimed: "Here is the Lamb of God who takes away the sin of the world!" (John 1:29). The language about the lamb slain links us importantly to themes of contemplative experience, again as in *templum*, the space cordoned off for examination of the entrails of sacrificed animals. We are about to take into our flesh, into our bodies as temples of the Holy Spirit, the very body of Christ, the flesh of the lamb, the bread that comes down from heaven. We look for signs of how this bread of life will feed us anew for our journey of faith and of ministry. We sing the plaintive song—have mercy, have mercy, grant us peace—in relation to the particularities of our own lives, those in our circumstances crying out for mercy, for peace, one more prayer of deep yearning before the fulfillment in communion.

In addition to sacrificial language, there is also the language of victory in connection with the banquet about to be enjoyed. The lamb sacrificed is also the one at the throne of victory in the vision in the book of Revelation, when thousands and thousands sing in heavenly worship: " 'Worthy is the Lamb that was slaughtered to receive power and wealth and wisdom and might. . . . To the one seated on the throne and to the Lamb be blessing and honor and glory and might forever and ever!' And the four living creatures said, 'Amen!' And the elders fell down and worshiped" (Rev. 5:12-14). Linking our imaginative reflections with visions of heavenly worship helps in our own worship and preparation to receive the food of the Paschal Lamb. With the heavenly multitude in our mind's eye, we may also cry out: "Hallelujah! For the Lord our God the Almighty reigns. Let us rejoice and exult and give him the glory, for the marriage of the Lamb has come, and his bride has made herself ready; to her it has been granted to be clothed with fine linen, bright and pure" (Rev. 19:6-8). We likewise hear the message of the angel to the author of Revelation: "Blessed are those who are invited to the marriage supper of the Lamb" (Rev. 19:9a). We are among those invited, and adorned with fine linen by virtue of our baptism, and so we are bold to come. It is to this more embodied and most intimate contemplative experience of the Christian life that we now turn: the communion, our receiving the visible Word which is Christ himself into our own flesh through the gifts of bread and wine.

THE COMMUNION: OUR INTIMATE PARTICIPATION IN CHRIST

The presiding minister may invite the people to the table: "Taste and see that the Lord is good." "Come to the banquet, for all is now ready." "The gifts of God for the people of God." Participants in the assembly move to the table to receive the gifts. It is the tradition of the early church to receive communion while standing. Some in the Western church observe a custom of kneeling to receive. Either way, we move to present our bodies, the fullness of who we are, as Christ presents himself fully to us. The ministers offering the gifts to us may use these words of administration: "The body of Christ, given for you. The blood of Christ, shed for you." We hear this in the delightful ambiguity of the English second-person pronoun. It is singular and plural simultaneously. The body and blood of Christ are for you, in your particularity and individuality, and for you, that is, all of us in our communities. In either case, we know the intimacy of the gift of Christ's presence—*for you*. Those receiving this gift offer assent, affirmation, confirmation: "Amen," let it be so, this is most certainly true.

This exchange, when the assembly eats and drinks, is holy conversation at the deepest level. Now is the contemplative moment, as explored previously. Here is holy conversation that needs few words, when friends and lovers simply enjoy the deep communication of being in each other's presence. Contemplation as a mode of experience that is of the more direct experience of God calls for simplicity, spaciousness, less activity. Perhaps this is a time in the liturgy for extended silence, the absence of speech. When there is direct experience, we do not need words. Speech, in part, is a phenomenon of response to absence, calling out for the one missing. That is how language emerges early in life. The child calls out for the mother. There is no need for such calling out at the time of communion when we enjoy the embrace of our beloved Christ.

"For You"—Making Communion More Intimate

In addition to simply being in the presence of Christ in our communities of faith, we can view communion as a time to give more meditative attention to what we actually experience when we receive the bread and wine, the body and blood of Christ.

- What are you thinking?
- What are you feeling?
- What are you aware of in your experience of your body?
- Who and what do you remember?
- How are you responding to your neighbors?
- Who are your neighbors in this assembly, and what are their hopes and dreams?
- In what ways do you in fact experience Christ's presence?

Response to these kinds of questions in the quiet of your own thoughts can take you to deeper levels of holy conversation. Offering prayers that emerge from your reflections likewise takes converse further, perhaps even to that silent resting place with your beloved, sacred Other.

MUSIC DURING COMMUNION

The discerning use of music can invite deeper awareness and experience of this holy time. It is a long tradition, dating from at least the fourth century, to sing psalms and hymns during the communion. Choirs and others may offer musical selections to nurture the experience of contemplation. Any additional music and activity would do well to serve the sense of intimate participation in Christ that is characteristic of this high point in the liturgy. Fewer hymns and an economy of words may best nurture this contemplative time. Less is more. Perhaps a singular hymn during communion is appropriate, such as this one following, a text written in the seventeenth century by Johann Franck, who was known for cultivating a mystical sense in his poetry. This hymn calls attention to themes of bridal mysticism appropriate to nurture meditation on the meanings of communion, our being joyfully united with Christ in the sacrament, our awe that this takes place in a simple meal:

> Soul, adorn yourself with gladness,
> leave the gloomy haunts of sadness,
> come into the daylight's splendor,
> there with joy your praises render.
> Bless the one whose grace unbounded
> this amazing banquet founded;
> Christ, though heav'nly, high, and holy,
> deigns to dwell with you most lowly.
>
> Hasten as a bride to meet him,
> eagerly and gladly greet him.
> There he stands already knocking;
> quickly, now, your gate unlocking,
> open wide the fast-closed portal,
> saying to the Lord immortal:
> "Come, and leave your loved one never;
> dwell within my heart forever."
>
> Now in faith I humbly ponder
> over this surpassing wonder
> that the bread of life is boundless
> though the souls it feeds are countless;
> with the choicest wine of heaven
> Christ's own blood to us is given.
> Oh, most glorious consolation,
> pledge and seal of my salvation.
>
> Jesus, source of lasting pleasure,
> truest friend, and dearest treasure,
> peace beyond all understanding,
> joy into all life expanding:
> humbly now, I bow before you,
> love incarnate I adore you;
> worthily let me receive you,
> and, so favored, never leave you.[12]

Singing this hymn as part of our holy conversation in this contemplative move-ment of the liturgy deepens our awareness of what is now transpiring in our union with Christ, in our lovers' embrace, in the awareness that in the seal of the communion in the context of which we are given life and salvation, noth-ing "will be able to separate us from the love of God in Christ Jesus our Lord" (Rom. 8:39b). So it is that we bow our hearts in loving adoration, our worship, our *proskynesis*.

Nunc Dimittis—Now, Lord, You Let Your Servant Go

Beginning to bring the communion to a close, the assembly may sing the *Nunc Dimittis*, a canticle long associated with liturgical prayer, a centerpiece of Compline, or Night Prayer, and Evensong, and also linked with the Eucharist as part of the priest's devotion in the liturgy of St. John Chrysostom and sung by the assembly in the Mozarabic rite and in many Lutheran liturgies:

> Now, Lord, you let your servant go in peace: your word has been ful-filled. My own eyes have seen the salvation which you have prepared in the sight of every people: a light to reveal you to the nations and the glory of your people Israel. Glory to the Father, and to the Son, and to the Holy Spirit. As it was in the beginning, is now, and will be forever. Amen.[13]

This Song of Simeon is taken from Luke's Gospel when the devoted and righteous watcher Simeon, led by the Spirit, took the child Jesus in his arms and said, "Master, now you are dismissing your servant in peace, according to your word, for my eyes have seen your salvation, which you have prepared in the presence of all peoples, a light for revelation to the Gentiles and for glory to your people Israel" (Luke 2:29-32). In the Lukan account, Mary and Joseph were amazed at what Simeon proclaimed about their child. So Simeon elabo-rated, "This child is destined for the falling and the rising of many in Israel, and to be a sign that will be opposed so that the inner thoughts of many will be revealed—and a sword will pierce your own soul too" (Luke 2:34). Perhaps Simeon's enigmatic words added to Mary and Joseph's marveling.

There is a sense in which each worshiper who sings the Song of Simeon as a postcommunion canticle lives anew Simeon's revelatory experience. Hav-ing taken the bread into our hands, it is as if we have taken the child into our arms. We also can confess, echoing the ancient insight of the righteous watcher, "My own eyes have seen the salvation which [God has] prepared in the sight of every people." The bread of life as sign may be opposed in our own lives of faith and in our ministries in the world. It may well reveal our own inner thoughts, and a sword may pierce our souls too (cf. Heb. 4:12). Going deeply with the Word of God is like this. Taking this Word into our bodies and lives also propels us into mission, martyrdom, as we are witnesses to the salvation we have seen. Yet we seek to go in peace as Simeon. Peace has been a major feature of the liturgy from beginning to end, from the *Kyrie*—"In peace, let us pray to the Lord"—to the Gospel story where Jesus says to his disciples, "Peace be with you," to our own sharing of Christ's peace in assembly, to our prayer for peace while singing the *Agnus Dei*, to now, singing prayerfully, "Let us go in peace," that we may be peacemakers. Yet we must acknowledge that there is a long history of those promoting peace often getting into trouble with those who embrace agendas other than peace. Simeon's prescient, prophetic witness to Mary and Joseph speaks to us as well. Still peace beckons, even as we are haunted by other words of Jesus: "Do not think that I have come to bring peace to the earth; I have not come to bring peace, but a sword" (Matt. 10:34).

PRAYER AFTER COMMUNION

In keeping with a common practice through the centuries, an assisting minister concludes the communion with a brief prayer, summarizing the meaningfulness of what has taken place in the sacrament and anticipating our being sent back into the world to do the work God has called us to do:

> God of abundance, with this bread of life and cup of salvation you have united us with Christ, making us one with all your people. Now send us forth in the power of your Spirit, that we may proclaim your redeeming love to the world and continue forever in the risen life of Jesus Christ, our Lord. Amen.[14]

This prayer brings us to the brink of the final movement of the liturgy: the sending rite. We have basked in Christ's presence in the banquet, having ascended in our mind's eye the holy mount of transfiguration, knowing our own transformation in sharing in Christ's real presence. We have been fed in order that we might now be propelled out by the winds of the Spirit to feed a hungry world.

Chapter 9

SENDING

The concluding movement of *lectio divina* takes up the theme of incarnation for mission, particularly how encounter with the Word will be embodied in our lives and ministries. This follows on the heels of the contemplative dwelling, which itself emerged in relation to prayers and meditation in response to the Word. The focus of this movement involves the question, "Now what?" Having shared in the movements of holy encounter and holy conversation, what now will we birth in our lives and practice of ministry? What words and meanings and experiences will continue to reverberate beyond this time, now that we are buzzing with the Spirit's activity, contributing to our ongoing formation and transformation in Christ? How will this experience contribute to what in fact we are called to do in our lives? Those are the questions addressed at the conclusion of *lectio divina*. This final movement of *lectio divina* gives it an outward focus, connected to mission and to ethics. Who will we be, having had holy conversation, and what will we do in the Spirit as we are sent forth to lead and to serve?

THE SENDING RITE

Worshiping God is an end in itself to be sure, and it is more than that. Liturgical worship sets the stage for the "liturgy after the liturgy," as the Greek

Orthodox are fond of saying, that is, the work of the people in our ministries in daily life, the work of the church in mission to the world. Mission relates intimately to sending, since *mission* derives from the Latin words *missio* and *mittere*, meaning "to send," but also quite proactively and instructively, "to fly, throw, hurl, launch"—appropriate action verbs for what can happen in the power of the Spirit. The sending helps to set the agenda for the church's specific mission that emerges from the movements of *lectio divina* applied to liturgical participation. Specific directives concerning mission may emerge from the holy conversation consisting of the reading, meditation, prayer, and contemplation that occur during the liturgy.

Generally the sending rite is very brief. Before the fourth century, when the people had communed, the liturgy simply ended. There was no specified concluding rite. In the fourth century and beyond, the conclusion of the liturgy began to take on more activity. Additional prayers were affixed to the conclusion. The deacon officially dismissed the congregation. A priest or bishop gave a blessing. This all became more elaborate over the centuries until recent liturgical practice has suggested a return to the comparative simplicity of the earliest centuries' customs.

The sending rite in current practice may consist of the following activities:

- the sending of eucharistic ministers;
- the commissioning of others who will serve the church's mission;
- conversation and announcements related to the church's mission;
- a blessing;
- a sending hymn; and
- a dismissal.

The point is to get people out the door and into the world for ministry and mission. Still, in keeping with the contemporary church's rediscovery of the centrality of mission to its understanding of what it is to be church, more can be made of the sending rite and its role in bringing to conclusion the discernment and articulation of the church's particular ministries that emerge specifically from the day's liturgical worship.

SENDING OF EUCHARISTIC MINISTERS

Formally sending persons bearing the consecrated gifts of bread and wine to those unable to be part of the assembly is a fairly recent practice in contemporary liturgy, but it recovers a particularly ancient custom. The intent is for the ones absent to know presence—the presence of Christ in, with, and under the bread and wine, and the presence of those bearing the gifts, that those not in assembly may share indirectly by extension in the gathered community. This practice has the effect of building the relationships in the body of Christ beyond the particular confines of the walls of the church. The assembly gathered around Word and sacraments is the hub of the wheel of the church from which extend various missional spokes, such as the pastoral care of members unable to attend the assembly through sending people to visit them in homes and hospitals and other settings. A simple prayer sends forth these communion ministers for their visits:

> Gracious God, loving all your family with a mother's tender care: As you sent the angel to feed Elijah with heavenly bread [cf. 1 Kgs. 19:4-8], assist those who set forth to share your word and sacrament with those who are sick, homebound, and imprisoned. In your love and care, nourish and strengthen those who will receive this sacrament, and give us all the comfort of your abiding presence through the body and blood of your Son, Jesus Christ, our Lord. Amen.[1]

A mother's tender care is a gift embodied in the presence of those who visit, evoking thoughts of Jesus' own care for us: "How often have I desired to gather your children together as a hen gathers her brood under her wings" (Luke 13:34b). Visiting has this effect of gathering vulnerable members of the community under the care of God's mothering wings. It is the Spirit's work of re-membering the body, knitting us together as a community of faith.

The eucharistic ministers journey forth as Jesus sent the Twelve and then also the seventy, two-by-two. "He said to them, 'The harvest is plentiful, but the laborers are few; therefore ask the Lord of the harvest to send out laborers into his harvest. Go on your way'" (Luke 10:2-3a). With the healing gifts of life in bread and wine, we proclaim, "The kingdom of God has come near to you" (Luke 10:9b). Offering the sacramental gifts and also attending to the material needs of those whom they visit, the communion ministers relive the parable of the sheep and goats (Matt. 25:31-46). In feeding the hungry, giving drink to the thirsty, welcoming the stranger, clothing the naked, taking care of the sick, and visiting those in prison, they encounter Christ. As Jesus said, "Truly I tell you, just as you did it to one of the least of these who are members of my family, you did it to me" (Matt. 25:40). In such eucharistic visitation we extend holy conversation, proclaiming the Word of God in deed. In our assembly we were fed in order to be equipped to feed. The comfort of God's abiding presence through the body and blood of Jesus Christ is known in assembly and in the world through this ministry, thus breaking down walls between church and world. All the baptized can share in this ministry, which itself emanates from the Eucharist, our thanksgiving, the center of our life together.

Affirmation of the Vocation of the Baptized in the World

In addition to sending eucharistic ministers, it is appropriate to include in the liturgy's sending rite additional rites related to Christian mission and ministries, such as affirmation of Christian vocation, recognition of ministries in the congregation, perhaps the installation of elected parish officers and other leaders, installation or commissioning of lay professional leaders, farewell and Godspeed for those leaving the congregation for new vistas of service, and perhaps various other dedications. Rites related to the church's ministry and mission make sense at this point in the liturgy in terms of the logic of the flow of the service as the church is being sent in the power of the Spirit into the world. Each of these exercises relates to specific ministries that the people of God undertake in one way or another during the times between liturgical assemblies. They are integral to what the church is called to do in the liturgy after the liturgy, taking holy conversation to the world in our actions.

Especially appropriate for the day of Pentecost is Affirmation of the Vocation of the Baptized in the World. At the beginning of the liturgy, we gave thanks for the gift of baptism in general. Now we turn attention to what baptism means in terms of the mission of the church. Those adults who were baptized or who affirmed their baptism at the Easter Vigil may now affirm their baptismal vocation for work in the world. It is an ancient tradition of the church to baptize at the Easter Vigil. It also has been the custom of the church to appoint the period before Easter as a time for instruction and formation in the Christian faith, known traditionally as the *catechumenate*. These students— *catechumens*—participate in programs of education—*catechesis*. Historically, Eastertide has been a time for additional instruction, namely, mystagogy, that is, literally, "opening the mysteries," or being led into deeper understandings of what baptism and the Eucharist mean in relation to the Christian life. The fifty days of Easter can also be a time for the newly baptized or those who have affirmed baptism to discern their spiritual gifts that they may offer in service to the church's mission. During this season, the newly baptized share in directed conversations and further educational events in the context of which they explore their gifts and skills in connection with the church's and world's needs. Perhaps a dimension of mystagogy involves being led by the Spirit through a process of discernment—a special kind of holy conversation—toward deepening understandings of the mystery of God at work in our own lives, identifying what our spiritual gifts are and how they might be employed for the sake of the church's mission. After we have come to some conclusion about this work, the day of Pentecost is a time to go public with commitments to the church's mission.

The presiding minister begins this rite of vocational affirmation:

Dear Christian friends: Baptized into the priesthood of Christ, we are all called by the Holy Spirit to offer ourselves to the Lord of all creation in thanksgiving for all that God has done and continues to do for us. It is our privilege to affirm those who are endeavoring to carry out their vocation as Christians in the world.[2]

Another member of the assembly reminds us of what baptism means for the life of discipleship:

Through Holy Baptism our heavenly Father set us free from sin and made us members of the priesthood we share in Christ Jesus. Through word and sacrament we have been nurtured in faith, that we may proclaim the praise of the Lord and bear God's creative and redeeming word to all the world.[3]

A sponsor, who has shared in the journey toward baptism through the whole catechumenate process including this particular affirmation, may present those affirming vocation to the assembly, describing the nature of the Christian service and witness to which they are committing, whether it be proclaiming the good news in word and deed, sharing in ministries of service to all people, or striving for justice and peace throughout the world, all echoing the themes of the baptismal covenant.

Supporting each in their commitment, the whole assembly may say or sing: "May the God of all grace who has called you to glory support you and make you strong."[4] The presiding minister continues with this address to those affirming baptismal vocation:

Sisters and brothers, both your work and your rest are in God. Will you endeavor to pattern your life on the Lord Jesus Christ, in gratitude to God and in service to others, at morning and evening, at work and at play, all the days of your life?[5]

Acknowledging the holiness of all of life in the rhythms of the day, at work and at leisure, and the sacredness of their particular area of service giving expression to God's call to us, each one affirming responds in turn: "I will, and I ask God to help me." The presiding minister then offers this prayer:

> Almighty God, by the power of the Spirit you have knit these your servants into the one body of your Son, Jesus Christ. Look with favor upon them in their commitment to serve in Christ's name. Give them courage, patience, and vision; and strengthen us all in our Christian vocation of witness to the world and of service to others; through Jesus Christ our Lord. Amen.[6]

Thus seeking the gifts and fruit of the Spirit for persons committing to share more fully in the life and mission of the church, we all endeavor to be doers of the word and not hearers only (cf. James 1:22), knowing that actions can speak louder than words. We join our prayers with those who have made new commitments this day, that all of us who are the baptized may birth in our lives and ministries the Word that we have heard and tasted in this assembly. We pray that through our varied vocations, we may be faithful witnesses, martyrs—for that troubling word simply means "witness"—in all that we do once we are sent from this place in the power of the Spirit.

CONVERSATION CONCERNING THE CHURCH'S MISSION

For the benefit of the whole assembly in calling attention to opportunities for all to give expression to their vocation to serve, announcements may be made concerning the church's work in the coming week. In some contexts, these announcements might be made after the liturgy during a time for fellowship. In settings with smaller numbers in attendance, this movement in the liturgy can take the form of free-flowing conversation among those assembled concerning the mission of the church, particularly as it relates to what we have heard and learned and discerned in the day's liturgy.

Giving announcements extends holy conversation in a more practical direction: What shall we as church do to be in mission according to the gospel proclaimed this day? Each program announcement points to deeper signification, relating specific activities to incarnate expressions of the church's ministry and mission. Each program announcement is a sign of ministry that plays its own unique role in extending holy conversation and bringing the Word of God into the world. Each program announcement serves as glue binding the work of the people in worship to the work of the people in the world. At their best, such announcements help people see the connections between the church's scheduled activities and what has been proclaimed, interpreted, and prayed about in the liturgy. Effective announcements echo the concerns indicated in the prayers of intercession offered previously in the liturgy, such that those assembled know that what we pray for is also what we will do. Furthermore, faithful announcements are offered according to the categories expressed in Acts 2:42—devotion "to the apostles' teaching and fellowship, to the breaking of bread and the prayers"—and relate to the themes of the baptismal covenant: "to live among God's faithful people, to hear the word of God and share in the Lord's supper, to proclaim the good news of God in Christ through word and deed, to serve all people, following the example of Jesus, and to strive for justice and peace in all the earth"[7] In these ways, announcements go beyond utilitarian function and are themselves proclamation of God's work in the world through our efforts in the Spirit. Rather than simply listing activities, the person given the task of making announcements is called to claim the teaching moment and gently draw attention to how the church's work emerges out of its liturgical worship and how it relates to all that we have encountered in the liturgy and in the gospel.

BLESSING

At the conclusion of mission-related announcements, an unscripted time of holy conversation, a final blessing may be given. With hands raised, the presiding minister offers a blessing over the whole assembly following custom that dates from the fourth century. The words of blessing are commonly given in the trinitarian name of God, accompanied by the sign of the cross, echoing by way of *inclusio* the baptismal beginnings of the liturgy—ending where we began. Or the presiding minister may bless the whole assembly using words contained in the Lord's instruction to Moses concerning Aaron and his sons, and describing the manner of blessing the Israelites: "Thus you shall bless the Israelites: You shall say to them, The LORD bless you and keep you; the LORD make his face to shine upon you, and be gracious to you; the LORD lift up his countenance upon you, and give you peace" (Num. 6:23-26). This blessing of Aaron hearkens to Jewish temple and synagogue traditions and to practice in Christian liturgies through the centuries. These words carry the weight of further proclamation of the gospel, reiterating in a few words all that we have experienced in liturgical worship—our being blessed and kept, the very face of God shining graciously on us, giving us, yet again, peace. This is no simple good-bye.

This concluding action by the presiding minister also evokes thoughts of culminating moments in Jesus' earthly ministry, for example, at the end of Luke's Gospel, Jesus' final exchange with his disciples: "Then he led them out as far as Bethany, and, lifting up his hands, he blessed them. While he was blessing them, he withdrew from them and was carried up into heaven. And they worshiped him, and returned to Jerusalem with great joy" (Luke 24:50-52). So it is that Christ known in Word and sacraments disappears from our sight and direct experience. But the lingering effect of his presence reverberates in our lives as we prepare to go on our way in the power of the Spirit, joyful, worshipful.

By way of reminiscence in *lectio divina*, when musing on scriptural passages draws the mind's eye to additional passages, other culminating moments in the Gospels come to mind in connection with this moment in the liturgy. The resurrected Jesus directs his disciples to the mountain, meets them there, and commissions them: "All authority in heaven and on earth has been given to me. Go therefore and make disciples of all nations, baptizing them in the name of the Father and of the Son and of the Holy Spirit, and teaching them to obey everything that I have commanded you. And remember, I am with you always, to the end of the age" (Matt. 28:18-20). This Great Commission gives further elaboration on what we are called to do when we depart. The instruction comes with the promise of blessing, that Christ is always with us in the power of the Spirit.

Concluding moments of John's Gospel likewise give a sense of the broader understandings of the blessing for sending. Three times Jesus asks Peter, "Do you love me?" Three times Peter affirms his love for Jesus. Three times Jesus instructs him: "Feed my lambs. . . . Tend my sheep. . . . Feed my sheep" (cf. John 21:15-17). Feeding the flock is another dimension of the work we have been called to undertake. And then the ominous words: " 'Very truly, I tell you, when you were younger, you used to fasten your own belt and to go wherever you wished. But when you grow old, you will stretch out your hands, and someone else will fasten a belt around you and take you where you do not wish to go.' (He said this to indicate the kind of death by which he would glorify God.) After this he said to him, 'Follow me' " (John 21:18-19). Our discipleship can be like this, too.

> ## A Final Blessing to Conclude a Pastorate
>
> I had given the Aaronic blessing nearly every Sunday for twelve years. The day I have in mind was my last Sunday at Bethlehem Lutheran Church in Pittsburgh's inner city. I had accepted a call to teach at a theological seminary in New York City. Now it was time to say good-bye. I looked out at the assembly, people I had baptized, confirmed, married, people whose spouses I had buried, people with whom I had shared countless sad and joyous times. It was poignant, it was wrenching. But what better words with which to conclude a ministry? "The Lord bless you and keep you. The Lord make his face shine on you and be gracious to you. The Lord look upon you with favor and give you peace." What more could I say? What else would need to be said? Words of God's servants echoing through the centuries were enough to carry the weight of the moment.

SENDING HYMN

The assembly may sing a hymn of sending, at a practical level covering the activity of the departure of liturgical ministers and perhaps others from their places, but also reinforcing the missional meanings of this concluding movement in the liturgy. This text by a contemporary hymnwriter, Sister Delores Dufner, Order of St. Benedict, is appropriate for the day of Pentecost:

> The Spirit sends us forth to serve;
> we go in Jesus' name
> to bring glad tidings to the poor,
> God's favor to proclaim.
>
> We go to comfort those who mourn
> and set the burdened free;
> where hope is dim, to share a dream
> and help the blind to see.
>
> We go to be the hands of Christ,
> to scatter joy like seed
> and, all our days, to cherish life,
> to do the loving deed.

Then let us go to serve in peace,
the gospel to proclaim.
God's Spirit has empowered us;
we go in Jesus' name.[8]

The first two stanzas of this hymn invoke themes recorded in Luke's Gospel, which itself quotes from the prophet Isaiah: "The Spirit of the Lord is upon me, because he has anointed me to bring good news to the poor. He has sent me to proclaim release to the captives and recovery of sight to the blind, to let the oppressed go free, to proclaim the year of the Lord's favor" (Luke 4:18-19; cf. Isa. 61:1-2). The setting is the synagogue where Jesus was in the habit of attending. He read from the prophet and concluded, concerning the focus of his own ministry, "Today this scripture has been fulfilled in your hearing" (Luke 4:21). In Jesus' name, we go now to similar ministries propelled as we are by the winds blowing from God's Spirit. The third stanza of the sending hymn makes clear the incarnational manner of our mission, being the hands of Christ in loving, joyful service, having been fed in the Eucharist to be Christ's body for the world. The final stanza—"let us go to serve in peace"—anticipates the dismissal to which we now turn. At the conclusion of singing this hymn, a procession of liturgical ministers and others may have found their way to the threshold of the church entrance, on the very brink of being back in the world to continue God's work.

DISMISSAL

In another tradition from the fourth century, an assisting minister or deacon, who stands in a special place between church and world as a gateway between the two, dismisses the congregation with dispatch: "Go in peace; serve the Lord." This instruction is practical as it intends to get people moving, now that our time here is complete and the time is ripe for our ministerial work. The words of dismissal are likewise full of theological meaning. Here is *peace* yet again, a consistent theme throughout this liturgy, a theological word signifying our reconciliation with God and each other—accomplished in this liturgical celebration—and the content and quality of our mission to the world. We are called to promote peace through our own peacefulness nurtured by our worshipful holy conversation. In terms of the meaningfulness of the second half of the dismissal—"serve the Lord"—experts from Paul's exhortations in his letter to the church at Rome illuminate what it means to serve: "Let love be genuine; hate what is evil, hold fast to what is good; love one another with mutual affection; outdo one another in showing honor. Do not lag in zeal, be ardent in spirit, serve the Lord. Rejoice in hope, be patient in suffering, persevere in prayer. Contribute to the needs of the saints; extend hospitality to strangers" (Rom. 12:9-14). Paul goes on with this list of exhortations indicating the qualities of Christian living, but you get the point. Serving the Lord calls for the response of our whole lives, even as we have offered the fullness of who we are in our bodies as living sacrifice, our spiritual worship (cf. Rom. 12:1).

The people respond with what has been the customary reply historically—"Thanks be to God"—fitting words for liturgical worship as our sacrifice of praise and thanksgiving. This brief dialogue concludes liturgy's holy conversation. Off the people go to begin the work God has given us to do, carried by celebratory music reflecting the many cultures of the world into which we are sent.

The Liturgy after the Liturgy

The people of God depart to do their work in the world, the liturgy after the liturgy, the worship service leading to specific service and servanthood. Again, the principal Sunday assembly is the hub of the wheel from which emanate the spokes of varied ministries, congregational life lived in response to liturgical worship. The echoes of holy conversation are heard throughout the week beyond the walls of the church. The world hears these echoes as it benefits from the church's ministry.

The sending is its own preparation for the next gathering. There is no definitive end to the liturgy and the worship of the people of God. We live and serve in spiraling fashion toward God's promised end, the completion of all things in the consummated reign of God. Just as the gathering begins long before the appointed liturgical hour, so, too, the sending flows into the following hours and days until we gather again.

Liturgical worship as holy conversation following the movements of *lectio divina* in relation to the patterns of the rite—that we move more deeply into participation in Christ—constitutes us as the body of Christ for mission in the world. Through holy conversation, we become that body to be broken again for the world's healing and salvation. The Spirit—working in Word and sacraments—forms, conforms us to Christ, reforms, and transforms us to give expression to that Spirit's work as we live out the disciplines of Christian spirituality focused in the themes of Acts 2 and the baptismal covenant.

After the dismissal—"Go in peace; serve the Lord. Thanks be to God"—the people who had assembled now disassemble, leaving their places to begin the movement out. Yet we do not leave as body parts, fragmented and disjointed. Rather, we go separate ways with a palpable sense of being the body of Christ together, each with different gifts for different callings and ministries in varied contexts. We leave in boisterous conversation, itself holy, reflecting the joyous thanksgiving we have known in the Eucharist. On our way out, we again shake hands with each other and embrace, further cementing the bonds of affection in Christian community. The people of God greet the ministers at the door, continuing the replies of holy conversation, perhaps commenting on the meaningfulness of something in the sermon or in song, in word or in the ceremonies, the Spirit giving us the gift of appreciative utterance.

In many settings, activities of Christian community building (*koinonia*) continue—coffee hour, brunch, a potluck meal. These occasions extend the eucharistic table to the tables of fellowship, a linking of the spiritual meal with the hearty food that sustains us more practically in body, strengthening us for our work. But the conversation in community nourishes as well, especially when it invites further reflection on the meanings of the day's worship. Where was God for us in the liturgy today? What were the evidences of the Spirit's quickening activity in us? This aspect of holy conversation is most compelling when it simply describes experience, when it refrains from analyzing or critiquing the liturgy. Such conversation can happen informally, and it can be part of the church's program when those who wish to do so remain after the service, gather chairs in a circle, and explore together their actual spiritual experiences of the liturgy, led by one who gently guides the conversation, keeping it focused on the experience of the holy.

The experiential data of the whole liturgy—the gathering to hear God's Word, meditate on that Word, pray in relation to it, and eat and drink the visible Word in the sacrament that unites us to Christ in contemplative experience, ending with the Spirit's sending us into mission—all of this also becomes food for discernment of mission. What particular word do we take with us as a result of the day's encounter? How might we give birth to this word in our activities during the coming weeks? These questions parallel by way of conclusion a similar conversational encounter at the liturgy's beginning. When we gathered, we considered what we brought to the assembly. In the context of the sending rite, the conversation is the complementary mirror opposite of the dynamics of gathering conversation: What word do we take with us as we return to our ministries in the world?

In terms of discerning mission, there is a sense in which the liturgical assembly functions as a kind of congregational meeting. In holy conversation, the people of God listen for missional directives in the proclamation of and commentary on the Word. The prayers of intercession as expressions of our deep desires for the healing of God's world also evoke directives for ministry and mission. Again, if we pray for the well-being of the church, we are called to work for that well-being. If we pray for the sick and those who suffer, we are called to work for those same people. If we pray for peace, we are called to work for peace. In the eucharistic meal, Christ feeds us that we may go and feed, being bread for and bringing bread literally to the world. Conversations after the sending rite can pull all of these themes together. What have we experienced in liturgical worship today that gives focus and content to our particular mission this week and in the coming weeks? Our encounter with Christ in Word and sacraments sets an agenda for mission. We as the people of God are called to discern what the Spirit is saying through these means to the churches.

Imagine a group of elected congregational leaders who meet together following the liturgy to explore in an explicit, disciplined way the potential directives for mission, seeking to hear the Spirit's word that emerges from worship. The gathering of such a group of leaders can nurture spiritual brainstorming and holy daydreaming that contribute to a vision for the particular opportunities for a community of faith to exercise leadership and service.

On this festival celebrating the day of Pentecost, several themes might emerge from the particular lessons for the day, reinforced by the hymns and other liturgical texts and by the sermon that invited reflection on those themes. These themes and questions arising from them could well be the fodder for mission discernment as congregational leaders share in prayerful conversation. Meditations on these themes began in the context of the sermon, which explicitly invited reflections. Singing the Hymn of the Day elaborated on and continued the meditations. The prayers of intercession quickened our prayerful hearts and minds, giving a sense of our desire to serve and to meet needs. Now, as congregational leaders gather after the liturgy, they can give more focused attention in discerning conversation to the Spirit's possible directives for mission.

Worship on Pentecost Sets the Agenda for the Meeting

The Pentecost story recorded in Acts implies a call to make Christ known in various cultures, represented by the diversity of languages reflected in the disciples' utterances in the power of the Spirit. This raises the question of our calling to proclaim Christ intelligibly amid the cultural diversity we find ourselves in now. Peter's proclamation in the Acts lesson, which includes invocation of the prophet Joel, raises questions concerning our own prophetic ministry and missional dreams and visions—"Your sons and your daughters shall prophesy, and your young men shall see visions, and your old men shall dream dreams" (Acts 2:17b). How can our dreaming and visioning be more inclusive, multigenerational, and welcoming of the perspectives of both men and women, and of persons from varied ethnicities and cultures?

In the lesson from Numbers, Moses concludes, "Would that all the LORD's people were prophets, and that the LORD would put his spirit on them!" (Num. 11:29b). In many congregations leadership structures are closed to new people and new voices. How do we go about making room for new leaders in our communities?

Psalm 104 offers directives concerning the care of the earth. How might the Spirit use us and our stewardship locally enacted to renew the face of the earth (Ps. 104:30), even in our own places of service?

In the Gospel appointed for this day of Pentecost, Jesus appears amid the disciples who were behind locked doors due to fear. What are the fears that keep us from our mission? How might we nurture the experience of the Spirit of Jesus for more boldness in our work in the world? John's Gospel also focuses on the work of forgiveness to which we are called. What is the work of reconciliation in the particularities of our own mission contexts? Who, specifically, needs to be reconciled with whom?

Addressing the questions that emerge from the day's liturgical and thematic focus continues the liturgy after the liturgy, the kind of holy conversation that can birth through the guidance of the Spirit the specific activities that congregations feel called to undertake as the work that God has directed them to do.

The announcements that concluded the day's liturgy serve as so many spokes of the wheel of ecclesial life that emanate from the hub of Word and sacrament. Those announcements set a busy agenda for further participation in the mission of the church, further holy conversation, a continued offering of our bodies as living sacrifices, our spiritual worship. Imagine the possibilities:

- Some will attend the meeting of the Christian Education and Formation Commission, seeking ways to deepen the formation of disciples of all ages beyond merely imparting information about the faith.
- Others will attend a public rally for peace and justice in a world torn by war and strife.
- Still others will meet in an ad hoc group to figure out how the congregation can have a smaller carbon footprint, thus contributing to the renewal of the face of the earth.
- Another will meet with Christians of other traditions to plan an ecumenical vacation Bible school for the summer.
- Encouraged and inspired by the festival of Pentecost, some will join the Evangelism Commission to discern how we might proclaim the mighty deeds of God in raising Jesus from the dead in our own community.
- A prayer group will meet to continue and build on the prayers of intercession—we also will send cards to those for whom the assembly has prayed, linking our praying with a pastoral act of caring in sending the cards.
- Others will engage in work with expressions of the church broader than the local congregation, in judicatories, synods, dioceses, embracing in palpable ways the interdependence of the church regionally and globally, recognizing that we are the body of Christ together as we share in the one Word and in common worship.
- Several others will gather for two hours one evening in the week to engage in *lectio divina* with the scriptural lessons appointed for the next Sunday, that their experience of the liturgy may be deepened by prayerful attention to the texts prior to the Sunday assembly. They will also have the task of formulating some of the petitions for the prayers of the people for the Sunday liturgy, especially as those petitions emerge from our prayerful engagement with the scriptural texts.
- Many will attend a "How to Worship" workshop, exploring practical ways for all of God's people to deepen holy conversation in liturgical worship.[9]
- Those assigned to be public leaders of worship will attend a training session on how to lead liturgy more prayerfully and how to consider

such leadership as itself a spiritual discipline and a form of spiritual direction.[10]

- Likewise, the Worship and Music Commission will meet to plan liturgical experiences that make for deep holy conversation.[11]

The reverberations of holy conversation may not have such specific programmatic focus. Each person leaves the liturgy affected or changed in some way. The Spirit has been active in Word and sacrament, in the holy conversation that has occurred through all the movements of the liturgy. The Spirit's quickening work continues to reverberate in us as our stories intersect with God's story revealed in the day's proceedings. We are aware of this work's formative effect when the holy conversation has been deep and engaged. Some may take a new idea concerning the meaning of a biblical passage—"I've never thought about it that way before." Others may leave inspired, encouraged, more hopeful about meeting the challenges of the coming week. Still others may have more specific ideas about what to do and whom to serve in ministry in daily life.

These reverberations are part of the Spirit's work of formation, conformation, reformation, and transformation in our lives. Not everyone will leave each liturgy with new inspiration, a living word. Yet over the course of weeks, months, and years, there may be many occasions of such inspiration. Ongoing thoughtful participation in the liturgy is what contributes to our formation in faith for discipleship. As the narrative of the gospel meets the stories of our lives, we are gradually conformed to the mind of Christ through the Spirit's quickening work. Moreover, each liturgical holy conversation is the occasion for our reformation, as we remember who we are and whose we are in Christ, having been forgiven and renewed by Christ in Word and sacraments. Given our brokenness and sin, our rebellious ways, so much of the Christian life involves forgetting our callings and deepest identities in God, a kind of spiritual amnesia. Liturgical holy conversation is the antidote to such amnesia, being always occasion for *anamnesis*, our deep, participatory, directly experiential remembering that we are beloved children of God, called to be witnesses to God's reign known in Christ. Through these forming, conforming, and reforming processes, and through the gifts of the means of grace, we are over the course of our lifetimes transformed in Christ by the power of the Spirit, becoming that Word for the world.

The Spirit's work in liturgical holy conversation happens individually, but it also occurs collectively, as our practice is taken up together in community. In these ways, the Spirit also forms, conforms to Christ, reforms, and transforms the whole church. The dialogical dimension of our spiritual worship is a kind of Christian bodybuilding that we undertake together for the Spirit's work in building up the body of Christ. When the whole church approaches liturgical holy conversation with depth and maturity and earnestness, this effort holds promise not just in renewing the church's worship life, but in transforming the church for its mission to be a vital and courageous body of Christ for the sake of the world and God's work of salvation for that world. Applying the spirit and movements of *lectio divina* to liturgical participation as holy conversation contributes significantly to this transformation for effective and faithful mission.

GLOSSARY

Anamnesis—Greek word for remembrance, but a remembering that is directly participatory, bringing the past to present experience as real presence. The word many Christians use to describe the nature of Christ's presence in the Eucharist—"Do this for the remembrance of me." The word Sigmund Freud used to describe the experience of repressed memory finding its way to the present and to presence. Holy conversation, especially in its contemplative movement, can be full of directly experiential remembering.

Aspiration—from the Latin *ad* + *spirare*, loosely, to breathe toward, and connected to the movement of prayer in *lectio divina*, when prayer is conceived of as the expression of our deepest yearnings and desires, giving evidence of the Spirit's quickening power in us to move us toward action. Prayer thus conceived is full breath, the Spirit breathing in us and through us, full of our desires in connection with the desires of God.

Catechumenate—the context and process of Christian formation; catechumens—the people who are being formed; catechesis—the pedagogical, educational style of activities that contribute to the Spirit's formative work. Connections to liturgical holy conversation by way of the stories of the day of Pentecost, baptism, mystagogy (see below), and the Spirit's sending us forth into the world in mission.

Compunction—from the Latin *com* + *punctare*, to puncture, to be cut to the quick, a surgically precise wound that makes for healing. An important term in monastic spirituality, and going beyond preoccupations with guilt to bespeak the kind of nondefensive, authentic presence that makes us more fully aware of our desire for God. The experience of compunction is often accompanied by tears. Liturgical holy conversation can cut us to the quick in healing ways—this is an important work of the Spirit in worshipful liturgy.

Contemplatio—Latin word for contemplation, and the movement in *lectio divina* characterized by the experience of union with God, self, others, world, and cosmos. A receptive, directly experiential mode of presence that is a gift, as when lovers, friends, or family members communicatively dwell in silence with each other (in contrast to meditation in *lectio divina*, which is a much more mental and active dialogical mode). Contemplation in liturgical holy conversation links with the Eucharist, Christ known to us in the breaking of bread.

Epiclesis—related to the Greek *epikaleo*, to call out, to appeal to. That moment in the eucharistic prayer when the presiding minister invokes, or calls out for, the presence of the Holy Spirit, trusting that it is the Spirit working through God's Word and via ordinary signs of bread and wine that makes Christ known to us in real presence in the sacred banquet. This same Spirit's quickening work is evident throughout liturgical holy conversation.

Gottesdienst—a German word for worship, conveying a double sense of God's service to us and our service before God. This double meaning is compelling for purposes of this book, which emphasizes the two-way, dialogical street that liturgical holy conversation is as a divine-human phenomenon.

Kairos—Greek for time, understood popularly as high time or a decisive point. In a complementary contrast to the chronological (*chronos*) passing of time, *kairos*, moments of divine inbreaking, can occur in *chronos*, as when liturgical holy conversation erupts with sacred meaningfulness for us in our assemblies. In the spirals of time moving forward, our liturgical encounters are punctuated by these decisive moments full of God's presence and meaning for us.

Lectio—Latin for reading, and that movement in *lectio divina* focused on the initial reading and/or hearing of God's Word in the context of which we listen for the more objective meanings associated with once-and-for-all

Revelation. In liturgical holy conversation, *lectio* as a movement focuses on that part of the liturgy when the lessons are read to the assembly and participants listen attentively, obediently, and reverently to the Spirit's voice speaking through the words of Scripture.

Lectio divina—Latin for divine, or sacred, or spiritual reading of Scripture. An ancient monastic practice associated with the Rule of St. Benedict and later elaborated on by the twelfth-century Carthusian monk Guigo II, who identified four basic movements in the spiritual life: reading, meditation, prayer, and contemplation. These same movements—in addition to an initial time of preparation and a concluding time to consider incarnate mission—applied to the pattern for liturgical worship provide trajectory for and narrative structure to liturgical holy conversation.

Liturgy—from the Greek *leitourgia*, meaning service or ministry, or more popularly in our current day, the work of the people. Liturgy is in complementary contrast to worship: liturgy is the agenda of activities taken up worshipfully that may lead to worship, an attitude of bowing in awe in the presence of God's holiness (see *Proskynesis* and Worship, below). Liturgy makes worship possible. Thus, we may speak of liturgical worship and worshipful liturgy.

Mass—one name, often associated with the Roman Catholic tradition, for the principal gathering of Christians typically on or proximate to the Lord's Day (Sunday) when liturgy is celebrated in Word and sacrament. A compelling term for purposes of this book with its connotations of musical *masses* as works of art. Here we explore the artistry of the Spirit speaking in liturgical language for holy conversation that forms, conforms us to the will of God and mind of Christ, and reforms and transforms us. *Mass* is compelling also in its etymological underpinnings, from the Latin *missio* (release, liberation, sending off, dispatching) and *mitto* (to send, let fly, throw, hurl, launch, let out, free, release, dismiss)—all evocatively rich associations with liturgy, connecting liturgical holy conversation to the mission of the church and the Spirit's energy propelling us into that mission.

Meditatio—Latin for meditation, a second movement in *lectio divina* undertaken in response to reading and/or hearing the scriptural Word of God, here discerning more subjective meanings in the spirit of ongoing revelation, a living word for us in our own day. In contrast to contemplation in *lectio divina*, which is characterized by a more restful presence, meditation is a playful, active process that employs all of our mental faculties for discerning meanings for us, especially focusing on how certain words, images, and ideas evoke and provoke our thoughts, feelings, memories, and imagination. In liturgical holy conversation, meditation centers on the sermon and/or other forms of interpretive proclamation, such as music, drama, artistic portrayals, and others ways of responding to the Word.

Metanoia—Greek for repentance and conversion, related to *metanoeo*, to change one's mind. In liturgical holy conversation, *metanoia* is the fruit of the Spirit's quickening work in us associated with that same Spirit's work in us of formation in faith, conformation to the will of God and mind of Christ, reformation when we forget and are led astray, and transformation into new creations in Christ. *Metanoia* along with its corollary gifts is the result of the Spirit working in our ongoing, lifelong liturgical participation, our worshipful holy conversation.

Missio—Latin for sending off, dispatching (see Mass), and associated with the final movement of liturgical holy conversation seen through the lenses of the movements associated with *lectio divina*. In this final movement of the liturgy, the assembly engages in activities related to the discernment of and preparedness for undertaking the church's mission in and for the sake of the world. We are dismissed, dispatched, sent, hurled out, freed, released, launched in the Spirit's power to do the work God has given us to do.

Mystagogy—associated with the catechumenate, a period of discernment of the deeper meanings of the holy mysteries of Word and sacraments—and in terms of the catechumenal process, a time also to discern what we are called to do in living out these mysteries in our lives of faith and our varied ministries in support of the church's mission. In short: a time for further and deeper formation as baptized children of God. Liturgical holy conversation can occasion mystagogy, our growth in the deeper meanings of Word and sacraments and how we live in accordance with them.

Oratio—Latin for speech, language, and related to *orata*, meaning prayer or request. The third movement in *lectio divina* associated with praying, especially the prayerful aspirations, yearnings, and desires that emerge from our meditative activity in response to the reading of God's Word. The Spirit praying in us with sighs too deep for words in quickening activity that motivates our action. In liturgical holy conversation, *oratio* is associated with the prayers of intercession, but also with the prayerful activity of the sharing of the peace, the gathering and presenting of gifts for the sacred meal, musical offerings, and an offertory prayer in the context of which we offer our whole selves in thanksgiving for what God has done and is about to do for us in the Eucharist.

Ordo—emerging from Latin for line, row, series, order, methodical arrangement. In liturgical holy conversation, the *ordo* is a term for the shape or pattern of the liturgical agenda with a particular trajectory and narrative logic. In application of the movements of *lectio divina* to liturgical participation, the *ordo* involves the following ways of being present to God and to each other in holy conversation: preparation, reading, meditation, prayer, contemplation, and sending.

Pentecost—an ancient Jewish harvest festival and later an occasion to mark the giving of the law on Sinai; the fiftieth day after Passover. In the Christian tradition, the day when the Holy Spirit descended on Jesus' disciples, empowering them to be apostles, full of proclamatory energy to witness to Jesus' resurrection (cf. Acts). Liturgically, the fiftieth day of Easter and a festival likewise to commemorate the Pentecost event recorded in Acts— and an occasion to celebrate the coming of the Holy Spirit in our own lives in baptism and throughout liturgical holy conversation (see *Epiclesis*).

Praeparatio—Latin for preparation. A prelude to *lectio divina* and to liturgical holy conversation in the context of which the people of God assemble physically but also attend to what is on their hearts and minds as they grow in anticipation for holy encounter in Word and sacrament.

Proskynesis—Greek for bowing or stooping to kiss the earth. One of the Greek words for worship that especially emphasizes the attitudinal qualities of liturgical worshipfulness associated with the experience of awe, reverence, and wonder that leads us to bow before the holiness of God (see Liturgy and Worship).

Reminiscence—not just nostalgia in looking fondly back at so-called good old days. Rather, a technical term associated with monastic spirituality and the meditation movement in *lectio divina* whereby our meditative minds naturally make connections among scriptural passages, words and phrases, images, and ideas that also connect up with our own life experiences. The process of reminiscence relates significantly to the quality of evocation, of new meanings being called forth to us in a living and fresh voice from the pages of Scripture. Reminiscence drives the meditative work in liturgical holy conversation.

Sensus plenior—Latin phrase meaning fuller sense, from *sensus* (sense, self-awareness, consciousness, thought, understanding, judgment, meaning, etc.) and *plenus* (full, stout, plump, pregnant, filled, satisfied, plentiful, complete). A phrase from monastic spirituality that relates to meditation in *lectio divina* and to liturgical holy conversation in conveying how the living Word of God is pregnant with full meaning and understanding for us. This is a living word of ongoing revelation based in the once-and-for-all givenness of canonical, scriptural Revelation.

Soma—Greek for body, but not just our physical body, though it includes that. Rather, *soma* is an expansive and inclusive term embracing all that we are, heart, soul, mind, strength, our embodiment, and so on. It is all that we are in this expansive, holistic sense that we offer to God in the Spirit in liturgical holy conversation, as we present our bodies (*soma*) as living sacrifices which is our spiritual worship (cf. Rom. 12:1).

Spirituality—a much used, abused, and misunderstood popular term. Here spirituality refers to life in and according to the Holy Spirit of the Triune God who speaks through means, principally the means of grace in Word and sacraments—that is, our ordinary Christian practices related to liturgical holy conversation—in order to form us in faith, conform us to the will of God and the mind of Christ, reform us when we forget and go astray, and ultimately transform us as new creations in Christ, that we might become the very Word of God for the world in our mission and ministry.

Worship—a common word for what Christians do in liturgical assembly. Here it refers more to the attitudinal qualities of our presence in liturgical holy conversation, particularly related to the Greek *proskynesis*, the quality of bowing in reverent adoration before the holiness of God known to us in the means of grace in our holy conversation. Liturgy, in contrast, is the agenda of activities taken up worshipfully, that is, with an attitude of reverent awe, and which may bear the fruit of worship—again, our stooping to kiss the earth when we are in the very presence of God in liturgical holy conversation (see Liturgy and *Proskynesis*).

NOTES

Introduction

1. "Holy Communion: Pattern for Worship," in *Evangelical Lutheran Worship: Pew Edition* (Minneapolis: Augsburg Fortress, 2006), 92–93.

2. Austin Flannery, O.P., ed., "The Constitution on the Sacred Liturgy," *Vatican Council II: The Conciliar and Post Conciliar Documents,* (Boston: St. Paul Books & Media, 1992), 7.

Chapter 1

1. Karl Rahner, *The Practice of Faith: A Handbook of Contemporary Spirituality* (New York: Crossroad, 1984), 22.

2. Michael Downey, ed., *The New Dictionary of Catholic Spirituality* (Collegeville, Minn.: Liturgical, 1993), 931.

3. Gerhard Kittel and Gerhard Friedrich, eds., Geoffrey W. Bromiley, abr. and trans., *Theological Dictionary of the New Testament: Abridged in One Volume* (Grand Rapids: Eerdmans, 1985), 503. Background information for New Testament Greek word studies are drawn from this theological dictionary throughout this book.

Chapter 2

1. Martin Luther, *Sermons I*, vol. 51 of *Luther's Works*, ed. and trans. John W. Doberstein (Philadelphia: Muhlenberg Press, 1959), 333.

2. Peter Brunner, *Worship in the Name of Jesus*, trans. M. H. Bertram (St. Louis: Concordia, 1968), 124–25.

3. Johann Franck, "Soul, Adorn Yourself with Gladness," trans. *Lutheran Book of Worship*, in *Evangelical Lutheran Worship: Pew Edition* (Minneapolis: Augsburg Fortress, 2006), #488.

Chapter 3

1. Timothy Fry, O.S.B., ed., *The Rule of St. Benedict in English*, chap. 48.1 (Collegeville, Minn.: Liturgical, 1982), 69.

2. Guigo II, "The Ladder of Monks: A Letter on the Contemplative Life," trans. Edmund Colledge and John Walsh, Cistercian Studies 48 (Grand Rapids: Cistercian, 1981), 67–68.

3. Ibid.

4. Ibid., 68–69.

5. This book's bibliography includes several titles of works that serve as excellent introductions to *lectio divina*, its history, the theology behind it, and its practice. I commend any of these to you for your further enrichment.

6. Guigo II, "Ladder of Monks," 68.

7. Ibid.

8. Reader-response criticism and personal-voice interpretation are literary-critical foundations for affirming the crucial role of readers/hearers in the discernment of meanings of texts. For introductions to and explorations of these methods of interpretation, see Ingrid Kitzberger, ed., *The Personal Voice in Biblical Interpretation* (New York: Routledge, 1998); Jonathan Linman, *Toward a Theory of Lectio Divina: A Reader Response, Psychoanalytic and Embodied Approach* (Ann Arbor: UMI Dissertation Services, 1997); Edgar McKnight, *The Postmodern Use of the Bible: The Emergence of Reader-Oriented Criticism* (Nashville: Abingdon, 1988).

9. Jean Leclercq, *The Love of Learning and the Desire for God: A Study of Monastic Culture*, trans. Catherine Misrahi (New York: Fordham University Press, 1961), 91.

10. For further exploration of how unconscious experience can emerge in the act of reading, see Linman, *Toward a Theory of Lectio Divina*, esp. chap. 3, "Meditatio." I draw on the linguistic theory of Ferdinand de Saussure—who suggests that the relationship between a word and its meaning is arbitrary and thus words can have unintended meanings—and the linguistically based psychoanalytic work of Jacques Lacan, a theorist who posits that unconscious material appears in speech. I extend their thinking to argue that unconscious experience can reveal itself in reading/hearing particularly when, in the free-associating way the mind works, we are drawn to certain words, images, ideas from texts around which there is significant emotional energy. This affective energy can be a sign of emergent unconscious material.

11. Guigo II, "Ladder of Monks," 68.

12. For an excellent exploration of the depth psychology of prayer as it connects to human desire, see Ann Ulanov and Barry Ulanov, *Primary Speech: A Psychology of Prayer* (Atlanta: John Knox, 1982).

13. Guigo II, "Ladder of Monks," 72–73.

14. Ibid., 68.

15. William H. Shannon, "Contemplation, Contemplative Prayer," in *The New Dictionary of Catholic Spirituality*, ed. Michael Downey (Collegeville, Minn.: Liturgical, 1993), 209.

16. Ibid., 209–10.

17. Guigo II, "Ladder of Monks," 73–74.

18. Ibid., 74–75.

Chapter 4

1. An example of such gathering conversation: During an informal liturgy of Holy Communion that is the focus of a Quiet Day, participants seated in a circle around a sacramental table are asked simply to share, if they are so moved, what is on their minds, their hearts. An assisting minister notes the concerns and incorporates them into spoken petitions of a litany-style *Kyrie*, concluding each named concern with "Let us pray to the Lord," and the assembly's response, "Lord, have mercy."

2. From Martin Luther, *Liturgy and Hymns*, vol. 53 of *Luther's Works*, ed. and trans. Ulrich S. Leupold (Philadelphia: Fortress Press, 1965), 323–24.

3. Thanksgiving for Baptism, from "Holy Communion, Setting One," in *Evangelical Lutheran Worship: Pew Edition* (Minneapolis: Augsburg Fortress, 2006), 97.

4. From "Rite of Affirmation of Baptism," in ibid., 236.

5. Fred Pratt Green, "God Is Here!" in ibid., #526.

6. Philip H. Pfatteicher, *Commentary on the Lutheran Book of Worship: Lutheran Liturgy in Its Ecumenical Context* (Minneapolis: Augsburg Fortress, 1990), 115.

7. Gathering Song, from "Holy Communion, Setting One," in *Evangelical Lutheran Worship: Pew Edition*, 98–99.

8. Ibid., 99–100.

9. Proper for Day of Pentecost, Year A, in ibid., 36.

Chapter 5

1. Composite translation of Psalm 104 in *Evangelical Lutheran Worship* (Minneapolis: Augsburg Fortress, 2006).

2. *The Orthodox Liturgy* (New York: Oxford University Press, 1982), 49.

Chapter 6

1. Catherine Soanes and Angus Stevenson, eds., *Concise Oxford English Dictionary*, 11th ed. (New York: Oxford University Press, 2004), 682, 1128, 1314.

2. For an excellent portrayal of preaching as a form of spiritual direction, see Kay L. Northcutt, *Kindling Desire for God: Preaching as Spiritual Direction* (Minneapolis: Fortress Press, 2009).

3. Hymn of the Day, from "Holy Communion, Setting One," in *Evangelical Lutheran Worship: Pew Edition* (Minneapolis: Augsburg Fortress, 2006), 103.

4. Herman G. Stuempfle, "God of Tempest, God of Whirlwind," in ibid., #400.

5. Martin Luther, "A Simple Way to Pray, for Master Peter the Barber," in *Luther's Spirituality*, ed. and trans. Philip D. W. Krey and Peter D. S. Krey (New York: Paulist, 2007), 232–34.

Chapter 7

1. Prayers of Intercession, from "Holy Communion, Setting One," in *Evangelical Lutheran Worship: Pew Edition* (Minneapolis: Augsburg Fortress, 2006), 105–6.

2. Guigo II, "The Ladder of Monks: A Letter on the Contemplative Life," trans. Edmund Colledge and John Walsh, Cistercian Studies 48 (Grand Rapids: Cistercian, 1981), 73–74.

3. Bianco da Siena, "Come Down, O Love Divine," trans. Richard F. Littledale, in *Evangelical Lutheran Worship*, #804.

4. Marilyn Kay Stulken, *Hymnal Companion to the Lutheran Book of Worship* (Philadelphia: Fortress Press, 1981), 524–25.

5. The Offertory, from "Holy Communion, Setting Three," in *Lutheran Book of Worship* (Minneapolis: Augsburg; Philadelphia: Board of Publication, Lutheran Church in America, 1978), 107.

6. Prayer 240, from "Holy Communion, Setting One," in ibid., 68.

Chapter 8

1. Samuel J. Stone, "The Church's One Foundation," in *Evangelical Lutheran Worship: Pew Edition* (Minneapolis: Augsburg Fortress, 2006), #654, stanza 5.

2. Guigo II, "The Ladder of Monks: A Letter on the Contemplative Life," trans. Edmund Colledge and John Walsh, Cistercian Studies 48 (Grand Rapids: Cistercian, 1981), 75.

3. Julian of Norwich, quoted in John R. Tyson, ed., *Invitation to Christian Spirituality: An Ecumenical Anthology* (New York: Oxford University Press, 1999), 195.

4. See Jonathan Linman, "Martin Luther: 'Little Christs for the World'—Faith and Sacraments as Means to *Theosis*," in *Partakers of the Divine Nature: The History and Development of Deification in the Christian Traditions*, ed. Michael J. Christensen and Jeffrey A. Wittung (Madison, N.J.: Fairleigh Dickinson University Press, 2007), 189–99. In this chapter, I elaborate on the insights of the Finnish School of Luther Interpretation where faith is seen as the source of union between Christ and the believer, and I suggest that faith comes through hearing the Word and sharing in the sacraments. That is to say, the means of grace are crucial to understanding a Lutheran view of *theosis*/deification, and the Eucharist in particular is a locus for intimate participation in the context of which we become the Word which is Christ through eating and drinking in faith to be offered up to the world in ministry and mission.

5. Those who study the phenomenon of tears suggest that there may be no "tears of joy," but rather the release of long-held feelings of grief in the context of experiencing the relative safety and security of "happy endings." It may be that the celebration of the Holy Eucharist in the context of which we feel the radical embrace of God in Christ occasions the "aesthetic distance" that makes an opening for the release of tears associated with loss. Moreover, thematics of the Eucharist—the *Last* Supper that memorializes Jesus' death—may reinforce experiential connections to our own losses; furthermore, the thematic of "feast of victory" over death may convey the sense of safety that likewise permits release of grief-related affectivity. See Jonathan Linman, "The Eucharist as an Occasion for Mourning" (unpublished paper).

6. Guigo II, "Ladder of Monks," 74–75.

7. Ignatius of Loyola, *Spiritual Diary*, in *Light from Light: An Anthology of Christian Mysticism*, ed. Louis Dupre and James A. Wiseman, O.S.B., 2nd ed. (New York: Paulist, 2001), 301.

8. *Evangelical Lutheran Worship: Leaders Desk Edition* (Minneapolis: Augsburg Fortress, 2006), 189.

9. Ibid., 194.

10. "Eucharistic Prayer I," in ibid., 194–95.

11. Ibid., 207.

12. Johann Franck, "Soul, Adorn Yourself with Gladness," trans. *Lutheran Book of Worship*, in *Evangelical Lutheran Worship: Pew Edition*, #488.

13. "Now, Lord," in ibid., #201.

14. Ibid., 114.

Chapter 9

1. *Evangelical Lutheran Worship: Leaders Desk Edition* (Minneapolis: Augsburg Fortress, 2006), 208.

2. "Affirmation of the Vocation of the Baptized in the World," in *Welcome to Christ: Lutheran Rites for the Catechumenate* (Minneapolis: Augsburg Fortress, 1997), 59.

3. Ibid.

4. Ibid.

5. "Prayers for Affirmation of Christian Vocation," in *Evangelical Lutheran Worship: Pew Edition* (Minneapolis: Augsburg Fortress, 2006), 84.

6. Ibid.

7. From "Rite of Affirmation of Baptism," in ibid., 236.

8. Delores Dufner, "The Spirit Sends Us Forth to Serve," in ibid., #551.

9. See appendix 1, "Instruction and Formation in 'How to Worship' " at http://www .fortresspress.com/linman.

10. See appendix 2, "The Spirituality of Worship Leadership," at http://www .fortresspress.com/linman.

11. See appendix 3, "Worship Planning in Light of *Lectio Divina*," at http://www .fortresspress.com/linman.

BIBLIOGRAPHY

Abernathy, Alexis, ed. *Worship That Changes Lives: Multidisciplinary and Congregational Perspectives on Spiritual Transformation.* Grand Rapids: Baker Academic, 2008.

Atkins, Peter. *Memory and Liturgy: The Place of Memory in the Composition and Practice of Liturgy.* Burlington, Vt.: Ashgate, 2004.

Bianchi, Enzo. *Praying the Word: An Introduction to Lectio Divina.* Kalamazoo: Cistercian, 1999.

Bockelman, Karen G. *Gathered and Sent: An Introduction to Worship.* Minneapolis: Augsburg Fortress, 1999.

Bonhoeffer, Dietrich. *Meditating on the Word.* Trans. David McI. Gracie. Cambridge: Cowley, 1986.

Bowe, Barbara. *Biblical Foundations of Spirituality: Touching a Finger to the Flame.* Lanham, Md.: Rowman & Littlefield, 2003.

Braaten, Carl E., and Robert W. Jenson, eds. *Union with Christ: The New Finnish Interpretation of Luther.* Grand Rapids: Eerdmans, 1998.

Braso, Gabriel. *Liturgy and Spirituality.* Collegeville, Minn.: Liturgical, 1960.

Brown, Kathleen Hope. *Lay Leaders of Worship: A Practical and Spiritual Guide.* Collegeville, Minn.: Liturgical, 2004.

Brunner, Peter. *Worship in the Name of Jesus.* Trans. M. H. Bertram. St. Louis: Concordia, 1968.

Casey, Michael. *Sacred Reading: The Ancient Art of Lectio Divina.* St. Louis: Liguori, 1996.

Cioffi, Paul, and William Sampson. *Gospel Spirituality and Catholic Worship: Integrating Your Personal Prayer Life and Liturgical Experience.* Mahwah, N.J.: Paulist, 2000.

Cole, Donna. *Liturgical Ministry: A Practical Guide to Spirituality.* San Jose: Resource Publications, 1996.

Collins, Kenneth J., ed. *Exploring Christian Spirituality: An Ecumenical Reader.* Grand Rapids: Baker Academic, 2000.

Dahill, Lisa E. *Truly Present: Practicing Prayer in the Liturgy.* Worship Matters. Minneapolis: Augsburg Fortress, 2005.

De Wit, Han. *Contemplative Psychology.* Trans. Marie Louise Baird. Pittsburgh: Duquesne University Press, 1991.

Dix, Dom Gregory. *The Shape of the Liturgy.* Chicago: Seabury, 1983.

Downey, Michael. *Understanding Christian Spirituality.* Mahwah, N.J.: Paulist, 1996.

———. *Worship at the Margins: Spirituality and Liturgy.* Portland, Ore.: Pastoral, 1994.

———, ed. *The New Dictionary of Catholic Spirituality.* Collegeville, Minn.: Liturgical, 1993.

Dreyer, Elizabeth A., and Mark S. Burrows. *Minding the Spirit: The Study of Christian Spirituality.* Baltimore: Johns Hopkins University Press, 2005.

Erickson, Craig Douglas. *Participating in Worship: History, Theory, Practice.* Louisville: Westminster John Knox, 1991.

Fabing, Robert, S.J. *Real Food: A Spirituality of the Eucharist.* New York: Paulist, 1994.

Ferlo, Roger. *Sensing God: Reading the Scriptures with All Our Senses.* Cambridge: Cowley, 2001.

Flannery, Austin, O.P., ed. *Vatican Council II: The Conciliar and Post Conciliar Documents.* Boston: St. Paul Books & Media, 1992.

Fleming, Austin, and Victoria Tufano. *Preparing for Liturgy: A Theology and Spirituality.* Chicago: Liturgy Training Publications, 2007.

Fry, Timothy, O.S.B., ed. *The Rule of St. Benedict in English.* Collegeville, Minn.: Liturgical, 1982.

Gilbert, Marlea, Christopher Grundy, Eric Myers, and Stephanie Perdew. *The Work of the People: What We Do in Worship and Why.* Vital Worship, Healthy Congregations. Herndon, Va.: Alban Institute, 2006.

Giles, Richard. *Creating Uncommon Worship: Transforming the Liturgy of the Eucharist.* Collegeville, Minn.: Liturgical, 2005.

Guigo II. "The Ladder of Monks: A Letter on the Contemplative Life." Trans. Edmund Colledge and John Walsh. Cistercian Studies 48. Kalamazoo: Cistercian, 1981.

Hackett, Charles D., and Don E. Saliers. *The Lord Be with You: A Visual Handbook for Presiding in Christian Worship.* Cleveland: Order of St. Luke, 1990.

Hall, Thelma. *Too Deep for Words: Rediscovering Lectio Divina.* Mahwah, N.J.: Paulist, 1988.

Hoffman, Bengt R. *Luther and the Mystics: A Re-examination of Luther's Spiritual Experience and His Relationship to the Mystics.* Minneapolis: Augsburg, 1976.

Holder, Arthur, ed. *The Blackwell Companion to Christian Spirituality.* Malden, Mass.: Wiley-Blackwell, 2006.

Hotz, Kendar, and Matthew Matthews. *Shaping the Christian Life: Worship and the Religious Affections.* Louisville: Westminster John Knox, 2006.

Hovda, Robert. *Strong, Loving, and Wise: Presiding in the Liturgy.* 5th ed. Collegeville, Minn.: Liturgical, 1983.

Ignatius of Loyola. *Spiritual Diary.* In *Light from Light: An Anthology of Christian Mysticism.* 2nd ed. Ed. Louis Dupre and James A. Wiseman. New York: Paulist, 2001.

Irvine, Christopher. *The Use of Symbols in Worship.* London: SPCK, 2007.

Irwin, Kevin. *Liturgy, Prayer, and Spirituality.* Mahwah, N.J.: Paulist, 1984.

Keating, Thomas. *The Mystery of Christ: The Liturgy as Spiritual Experience.* New York: Continuum, 1994.

Kitzberger, Ingrid, ed. *The Personal Voice in Biblical Interpretation.* New York: Routledge, 1998.

Koenig, John. *Feast of the World's Redemption: Eucharistic Origins and Christian Mission.* Harrisburg, Pa.: Trinity Press International, 2000.

Kroeker, Charlotte, ed. *Music in Christian Worship: At the Service of the Liturgy.* Collegeville, Minn.: Liturgical, 2005.

Kubicki, Judith Marie. *Liturgical Music as Ritual Symbol: A Case Study of Jacques Berthier's Taizé Music.* Leuven: Peeters, 1999.

Lacan, Jacques. *Ecrits: A Selection.* Trans. Alan Sheridan. New York: Norton, 1977.

Lathrop, Gordon W. *Holy Ground: A Liturgical Cosmology.* Minneapolis: Fortress Press, 2003.

———. *Holy People: A Liturgical Ecclesiology.* Minneapolis: Fortress Press, 2006.

———. *Holy Things: A Liturgical Theology.* Minneapolis: Fortress Press, 1998.

Leclercq, Jean. *The Love of Learning and the Desire for God: A Study of Monastic Culture.* Trans. Catherine Misrahi. New York: Fordham University Press, 1961.

Linman, Jonathan. "The Eucharist as an Occasion for Mourning." Unpublished essay.

———. "Martin Luther: 'Little Christs for the World'; Faith and Sacraments as Means to *Theosis.*" In *Partakers of the Divine Nature: The History and Development of Deification in the Christian Traditions.* Ed. Michael J. Christensen and Jeffrey A. Wittung. Madison, N.J.: Fairleigh Dickinson University Press, 2007.

———. "Meditative Reading of Scripture." In *See How They Love One Another: Rebuilding Community at the Base.* Ed. Paivi Jussila. Geneva: Lutheran World Federation, 2002.

———. *Toward a Theory of Lectio Divina: A Reader Response, Psychoanalytic and Embodied Approach.* Ann Arbor: UMI Dissertation Services, 1997.

Luther, Martin. "A Simple Way to Pray." In *Luther's Spirituality.* Ed. and trans. Philip D. W. Krey and Peter D. S. Krey. New York: Paulist, 2007.

———. *Sermons I.* Ed. and trans. John W. Doberstein. *Luther's Works,* vol. 51. Philadelphia: Muhlenberg, 1959.

———. *Liturgy and Hymns.* Ed. Ulrich S. Leupold. *Luther's Works,* vol. 53. Philadelphia: Fortress Press, 1965.

Madigan, Shawn. *Spirituality Rooted in Liturgy.* Portland, Ore.: Pastoral, 1989.

Magrassi, Mariano. *Praying the Bible: An Introduction to Lectio Divina.* Collegeville, Minn.: Liturgical, 1998.

McGann, Mary. *Exploring Music as Worship and Theology: Research in Liturgical Practice.* Collegeville, Minn.: Liturgical, 2002.

McGrath, Alister E. *Christian Spirituality: An Introduction.* Malden, Mass.: Wiley-Blackwell, 1999.

McKnight, Edgar. *The Postmodern Use of the Bible: The Emergence of Reader-Oriented Criticism.* Nashville: Abingdon, 1988.

Mitchell, Nathan. *Meeting Mystery: Liturgy, Worship, Sacraments.* Maryknoll, N.Y.: Orbis, 2007.

Morrill, Bruce, ed. *Bodies of Worship: Explorations in Theory and Practice.* Collegeville, Minn.: Liturgical, 1999.

Mueller, Craig M. *Preparing the Assembly's Worship.* Minneapolis: Augsburg Fortress, 2002.

Northcutt, Kay L. *Kindling Desire for God: Preaching as Spiritual Direction.* Minneapolis: Fortress Press, 2009.

Pennington, Basil M. *Lectio Divina: Renewing the Ancient Practice of Praying the Scriptures.* New York: Crossroad, 1998.

Peterson, Eugene H. *Eat This Book: A Conversation in the Art of Spiritual Reading.* Grand Rapids: Eerdmans, 2006.

Pfatteicher, Philip H. *Commentary on the Lutheran Book of Worship: Lutheran Liturgy in Its Ecumenical Context.* Minneapolis: Augsburg Fortress, 1990.

———. *Liturgical Spirituality.* Valley Forge: Trinity Press International, 1997.

Price, Charles, and Louis Weil. *Liturgy for Living.* Harrisburg, Pa.: Morehouse, 2000.

Rahner, Karl. *The Practice of Faith: A Handbook of Contemporary Spirituality.* New York: Crossroad, 1984.

Rice, Howard. *The Pastor as Spiritual Guide.* Nashville: Upper Room, 1998.

Ricoeur, Paul. *Interpretation Theory: Discourse and the Surplus of Meaning.* Fort Worth: Texas Christian University Press, 1976.

Rimbo, Robert A. *Why Worship Matters.* Worship Matters. Minneapolis: Augsburg Fortress, 2004.

Rognlien, Bob. *Experiential Worship: Encountering God with Heart, Soul, Mind, and Strength.* Colorado Springs: NavPress, 2005.

Saliers, Don. *Worship and Spirituality.* Cleveland: Order of Saint Luke, 1996.

———. *Worship Come to Its Senses.* Nashville: Abingdon, 1996.

Salvail, Ghislaine. *At the Crossroads of Scripture: An Introduction to Lectio Divina.* Boston: Pauline Books and Media, 1996.

Satterlee, Craig A. *Presiding in the Assembly.* Minneapolis: Augsburg Fortress, 2003.

Schalk, Carl F. *Luther on Music: Paradigms of Praise.* St. Louis: Concordia, 1988.

Senn, Frank C. *The Witness of the Worshiping Community: Liturgy and the Practice of Evangelism.* New York: Paulist, 1993.

Sokolowski, Robert. *Eucharistic Presence: A Study in the Theology of Disclosure.* Washington, D.C.: Catholic University of America Press, 1994.

"The Spirituality of the Presider." *Liturgy: Journal of the Liturgical Conference* 22, no. 2 (2007).

Stevick, Daniel B. *The Crafting of Liturgy.* New York: Church, 1990.

Stulken, Marilyn Kay. *Hymnal Companion to the Lutheran Book of Worship.* Philadelphia: Fortress Press, 1981.

Torevell, David. *Liturgy and the Beauty of the Unknown.* Burlington, Vt.: Ashgate, 2007.

Torvend, Samuel. *Daily Bread, Holy Meal: Opening the Gifts of Holy Communion.* Worship Matters. Minneapolis: Augsburg Fortress, 2004.

Tovey, Phillip. *Inculturation of Christian Worship: Exploring the Eucharist.* Burlington, Vt.: Ashgate, 2004.

Tyson, John R., ed. *Invitation to Christian Spirituality: An Ecumenical Anthology.* New York: Oxford University Press, 1999.

Ulanov, Ann, and Barry Ulanov. *Primary Speech: A Psychology of Prayer.* Atlanta: John Knox, 1982.

Underhill, Evelyn. *Worship.* Guildford, Surrey, UK: Eagle, 1991.

Weil, Louis. *A Theology of Worship.* Cambridge: Cowley, 2001.

Welcome to Christ: Lutheran Rites for the Catechumenate. Minneapolis: Augsburg Fortress, 1997.

White, Susan J. *The Spirit of Worship: The Liturgical Tradition.* Maryknoll, N.Y.: Orbis, 2000.

Willimon, William. *A Guide to Preaching and Leading Worship.* Louisville: Westminster John Knox, 2008.

Wilson-Kastner, Patricia. *Sacred Drama: A Spirituality of Christian Liturgy.* Minneapolis: Fortress Press, 1999.

Wren, Brian. *Praying Twice: The Music and Words of Congregational Song.* Louisville: Westminster John Knox, 2000.

Zimmerman, Joyce Ann. *Liturgy and Hermeneutics.* Collegeville, Minn.: Liturgical, 1998.

———. *Liturgy as Living Faith: A Liturgical Spirituality.* Scranton: University of Scranton Press, 1993.

INDEX